THAT'S THE WAY THE MONEY GOES

That's the Way the Money Goes

The Financial Institutions and the Nation's Savings

JOHN PLENDER

ANDRE DEUTSCH

First published 1982 by André Deutsch Limited
105 Great Russell Street London WC1
Copyright © 1982 by John Plender
All rights reserved
Typeset by Gloucester Typesetting Services
Printed by The Blackwell Press,
Guildford, London, Oxford, Worcester

ISBN 0 233 97398 2

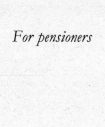

For pensioners

Contents

It is Enterprise which builds and improves the world's possessions. . . . If Enterprise is afoot, Wealth accumulates whatever may be happening to Thrift; and if Enterprise is asleep, Wealth decays, whatever Thrift may be doing.

J. M. Keynes, *Treatise on Money*

Foreword

MY ORIGINAL AIM in writing this book was to explore some of
the economic and social implications of the dramatic rise of the
financial institutions in Britain. The subject had attracted less attention than it deserved and there was clearly room for a book that set
out to make it more accessible to a wider audience. The obvious
starting point was an examination of the way in which the larger
institutions such as insurance companies and pension funds had
exercised their power and discharged their responsibilities to their
beneficiaries in the main markets in which they invested – those in
ordinary shares, government stock and property.

Before long, however, I began to realise that while there was an
enormous amount of information available, notably in the evidence
submitted to the Wilson Committee on the workings of the financial institutions, there were also huge gaps in the record. This was
particularly true of the pension funds which, as the Wilson Committee itself pointed out, were not subject to stringent disclosure
requirements. As a result I found myself turning increasingly to-
ward the investigation of these reticent institutions. The core of
the book consists of an attempt to lift the veil, a little, on some of
those areas where the activities of the pension funds of Britain's
biggest nationalised industries and private sector companies have
been least exposed to the public gaze.

Some fund managers will doubtless argue that no useful purpose
is served by examining the way the pension funds managed their
billions in the past. Yet today everyone concerned, whether politicians, trade unionists or fund managers, seems to think in billions
when it comes to the subject of savings and investment. Those
billions belong to someone else. In the absence of any serious
examination of how the pensioners' huge nest-egg has been managed in the past, it is unlikely that it will be managed very much
better (or less badly) in the future.

Given the limited time and resources available, the picture that emerges in this book is inevitably incomplete. But what stands out is that the management of these huge sums has not been as trouble-free as some of the managers would have us believe. I have, how-ever, tried to resist the temptation to take sides in some of the more contentious debates about what should be done with the institutions' money, such as the one prompted by the Trades Union Congress's proposal for a new investment bank. Although my opinions obtrude from time to time, I have also refrained from a detailed discussion of how standards of regulation of pension funds might be improved, since it seemed that there was a more useful job to be done in unearthing facts and asking questions.

The three overriding questions to which the book returns are these: From the point of view both of society and of the individual saver, how responsibly have Britain's enormously powerful finan-cial institutions invested the money under their control? Are these institutions properly accountable? Are they supplying a service that people would continue to want if they were offered more choice in the matter? I believe that savers and pensioners deserve better answers to these questions than they have received so far from politicians, institutions and pensions experts. If this book contributes to a wider debate on these questions it will have served its purpose.

A brief word on terminology. In the course of the book refer-ences to 'financial institutions' or 'institutional investors' apply principally to insurance companies or pension funds, unless other-wise stated. Any reference to 'the City' refers to the financial com-munity in general, not to those who work within the geographical confines of the Square Mile. Pension funds of individual com-panies have been referred to throughout in the singular, although there are frequently separate funds for staff and workers at the same company; while staff and workers are usually offered different pension benefits in these cases, their investments may nonetheless be jointly managed.

It would not have been possible to produce this book without the considerable support and understanding of Andrew Knight, editor of *The Economist,* to whom I am profoundly grateful. My thanks are also due to those managers in the larger insurance com-panies and pension funds who gave me interviews; the extent of their generosity with both time and assistance will be apparent to anyone who reads on. Finally, I am most grateful to my friends

Michael Brett, editor of the *Investors Chronicle* and Gordon Lee, surveys editor of *The Economist*, both of whom gave invaluable advice and unfailing encouragement while the book was being written, and to Amanda Raymer, without whose organising (and typing) abilities nothing would have reached André Deutsch. All errors, of course, are mine.

I
The rise of the financial institutions

'Fortunes . . . come tumbling into some men's laps.'
Francis Bacon, *Advancement of Learning*

AT THE START of the Second World War, private individuals owned more than 80% of the ordinary share capital of British companies listed on the stock exchange; a little over four decades later they were estimated to own between 28% and 36%. In each of those forty years a small and increasingly powerful group of collective savings institutions, such as life assurance companies and pension funds, quietly absorbed an average 1%–1½% of the share capital of quoted companies, thereby establishing a growing hold on the means of production in Britain. The resulting change, though largely imperceptible to the lay public, is as great as that brought about by nationalisation, and could prove to be no less significant to the British political economy.

In order to satisfy their voracious appetite for investments these institutions are today buying shares from private individuals at the rate of more than £20 million a week – a sum equivalent to the price of a large office block in the City of London, or to the stock market value of, say, two small-to-medium sized engineering companies. Already less than 5% of the adult population is estimated to own directly any stocks and shares. And if private individuals continue to abandon the stock market on anything like the present scale, there will be only a small core of shareholdings in non-institutional hands by the end of the century.[1]

Unlike other important post-war changes in capital ownership, such as the nationalisation of key industries or the acquisition of large segments of British industry by foreign multinational companies, the move towards institutional ownership has not been the subject of extensive debate in parliament or the press. Until a committee under the former Prime Minister Sir Harold Wilson embarked, in the late 1970s, on the first thorough review of the British financial system since the Radcliffe Committee Report in 1959, the middle class's discreet retreat from share ownership and the simultaneous rise of the financial institutions went almost unnoticed outside the City of London. Yet the gradual replacement of individual investors by collective professionally managed institutional leviathans, is having profound and sometimes disquieting political, economic and social effects, which are only now beginning to be understood.

It is not just the middle class that has been handing over its money to the financial institutions – a designation used loosely in the City to cover virtually any corporate body such as an insurance company, pension fund, investment trust, unit trust, bank, discount house or building society. Over the past twenty years a growing number of full-time workers in both the public and private sectors of British industry have come to share in the ownership of the means of production either through membership, often imposed as a condition of employment, of occupational pension schemes, or through the purchase of life assurance. Regular contractual saving of this kind accounts for more than a third of all personal saving in Britain and part of the money finds its way into the share capital of industrial and commercial companies. The result of the marked trend towards institutional saving is that capitalism has become depersonalised in Britain to an extent not seen in any other advanced Western democracy. In all, insurance companies, pension funds, investment trusts and unit trusts, the four types of institution that invest primarily in stocks and shares, are responsible for handling over £100 billion of other people's money.

The two biggest groups of institutional investors are the insurance companies and pension funds. The savings they handle have grown from £7 billion in 1957 to more than £85 billion in 1981 – about the same as Britain's total national debt. In the second half of the 1970s, they absorbed up to four-fifths of all new government stock each year. By 1980 they owned more property than all the ninety or so property companies quoted on the stock exchange. Cash was flowing in at the rate of more than £10 billion a year – enough to cover, say, the cost of developing the Concorde aircraft several times over.

The insurance companies owned marginally more investments than the pension funds at the start of the 1980s. But one of their biggest sources of new cash – perhaps as much as a third on the Wilson Committee's estimate – consisted of money earmarked for the provision of pensions. In fact, the rise of institutional investors is fast becoming synonymous with the growth of occupational pensions. And while the growth slowed down somewhat in the recession of 1980–81 as it did in the earlier recession of 1974–75, the pension funds are still expanding fast enough to ensure that they will soon become the most powerful group of proprietors in the private sector of the economy.

At the turn of the decade the biggest pension fund, that of the Post Office, had to find a home for a cash inflow of over £1½ million every working day. In a tongue-in-cheek calculation *The Economist* once pointed out that if anyone was likely to inherit the earth, it was the British postman, for:

> If the (Post Office) fund continues to grow at the rate it grew in the five years to March 1978, it will match the total equity capitalisation of today's stock market by the year 1989. A single year's cash flow would be sufficient to absorb the whole of today's equity market in one gulp by 1994. And the fund will just about match Britain's current total stock of capital assets by 1995.[2]

The Post Office fund, which invests on behalf of workers in British Telecommunications as well as in the postal service, is now growing more slowly. But by the time this book is published it will be worth around £3 billion. Only 'Shell' Transport and Trading, British Petroleum and the General Electric Company were valued at more than that figure in the stock market at the beginning of 1981.

Not far behind the Post Office was the pension scheme of the National Coal Board, with a fund valued at well over £2 billion. This was far in excess of the book value of all the assets of Britain's state-owned coal mining industry. There have been several other cases of the pension fund tail wagging the industrial dog: at various times in the recession of 1980–81 Dunlop Holdings, Reed International and Lucas Industries, among Britain's larger companies, were valued in the stock market at less than the total worth of their own pension funds' investments.

If the legal ownership of £85 billion-worth of assets is spread evenly around the population, it does not confer much power on the individuals to whom the money belongs. Their individual purchasing power will be too small to influence prices in financial markets and without highly effective collective organisation, the voting rights on their shares could not be mobilised easily against a board of directors. When, on the other hand, legal ownership of £85 billion-worth of assets is entrusted to a much smaller number of professional managers who look after those assets on behalf of the same number of beneficial owners, considerable scope does exist for the exercise of power. The greater the concentration in the hands of the few, the greater their potential influence.

There can be no doubt that legal, if not beneficial, ownership in Britain is now very heavily concentrated. A crude measure of this can be seen by looking at the amount of life assurance and pension money handled at the end of the last decade by the small group of vicarious billionaires listed below.[3]

	£ million
Prudential	7,470
Legal & General	3,809
Post Office pension fund	2,742
Standard Life	2,471
National Coal Board pension fund	2,367
Commercial Union	2,337
Norwich Union	2,235
British Rail pension fund	1,668
Guardian Royal Exchange	1,392
Scottish Widows	1,386
Electricity Supply Industry pension fund	1,359
Eagle Star	1,294
Cooperative Insurance	1,247
Sun Life	1,148
British Steel Corporation pension fund	1,076

The £1 billion threshold is obviously arbitrary and there are other billionaires outside the ranks of the life assurance and insurance companies and pension funds. At the start of 1980 the government-controlled Crown Agents held investments worth just under £2 billion; the Church Commissioners managed just over £1 billion; and the biggest unit trust groups, Save and Prosper and M & G, also handled around £1 billion apiece at that date.

It would be surprising, too, if the secretive Kuwait Investment Office, an off-shoot of the Kuwait Ministry of Oil and Finance which invests heavily in British shares and property, were not in the billionaire category. And if the non-life funds of composite insurance companies were included – that is to say, those that insure against accidents and misfortunes as well as undertaking life assurance business – the list would be longer still. The degree of centralisation of the ownership of investments in Britain nonetheless remains unusually striking. The top ten billionaire insurance companies account for over half the total long-term funds of the British insurance industry – that is, funds invested to provide life assurance, pensions and annuities. Half a dozen nationalised industry pension funds are responsible for around a quarter of all pension fund investments. And with this concentration of money in the hands of insurance companies and pension funds has come a marked change in the balance of power in the City. The élite of the merchant banking fraternity has long since been overtaken by the two largest groups of institutional investors.

At the turn of the decade the Prudential managed funds from its redbrick neo-Gothic head office in London's High Holborn amounting to twice the combined gross assets of N. M. Rothschild, Baring Brothers, Hambros and Lazard Brothers, financial houses that used to dominate the world's capital markets. Events in the recent history of these four merchant banks perfectly illustrate the shift in City fortunes.

The freehold of a merchant bank's premises is sometimes regarded in the City as its birthright. Yet in the late 1970s, when Barings wanted to have its offices redeveloped, it was forced to concede a majority interest in the site to the Electricity Supply Industry pension fund, which carried out the development. At much the same time Berkeley Hambros Property, an affiliate of Hambros, was obliged to sell an interest in the site of Hambros' head office in Bishopsgate to the GEC pension fund; it then leased the premises back.

Lazards suffered a rather different kind of upset. It saw its own parent and client, Lord Cowdray's conglomerate S. Pearson, rebuffed by a group of institutions when it tried to buy the outstanding shares in its partly-owned newspaper and publishing subsidiary Pearson Longman; Lazards had advised Pearson on the terms of the bid, which the institutions – none too wisely in the light of Pearson Longman's subsequent depressed trading performance – regarded as unduly mean.[4]

A final telling indication of how the climate had altered came in the shape of a change of ownership at that most tightly controlled of family banks, N. M. Rothschild. In 1979 Eagle Star Insurance became the first non-family shareholder in Rothschilds Continuation, the holding company of the merchant bank founded by Nathan Rothschild in 1804. The insurance company's entrée into the Rothschild inner sanctum was marred, however, by an argument over the degree of consultation (or lack of it) that took place between members of the Rothschild family when the shares changed hands. This became one of several causes of friction between the bank's chairman, Evelyn de Rothschild, and his cousin, Jacob Rothschild, who would have preferred the family to retain control over the shares. Late in 1980 disaffection erupted in an acrimonious public row which culminated in the resignation of Jacob Rothschild.

Ownership of shares is not necessarily synonymous with control, however. And the merchant banks have been able to wrest back some of their former power by acting as investment managers for the pension funds, most of whom delegate at least a part of the management of their funds to outsiders. The leading banks in this area, such as Kleinwort Benson, Hill Samuel, S. G. Warburg or Robert Fleming (to name four at random) individually control or advise on funds worth well over a billion apiece; the pension fund trustees exercise varying degrees of supervision, but in most cases the professional manager enjoys autonomy in deciding which company to invest in.

More than half the externally managed funds of insurance companies and pension funds are generally thought to be managed by less than a dozen merchant banks.[5] Some of the bigger stockbrokers also manage large sums of institutional money, particularly in the gilt-edged market – though not always without incurring the wrath of merchant banks, who dislike having to compete in investment management with people to whom they pay brokerage commission.

Investment managers in insurance companies and pension funds, ever sensitive to the accusation that they troop *en masse* around the capital markets like so many sheep, argue that bare figures showing who controls how much money give a misleading impression of the number and diversity of institutional managers taking investment decisions. In a single insurance company, for example, several investment managers may be investing different funds in different ways to satisfy different ends. Because the manager of a general insurance fund (which covers fire, accident and other calamities) might have to allow for the possibility of sudden and unexpected claims for, say, hurricane damage, he will take more trouble to invest in securities that are readily saleable than the manager of a life assurance fund.

Fund managers are, however, working in the same general ethos. And while they often hold different views on, for example, the technicalities of the government's monetary policy, their common interest in protecting the value of other people's savings leads many of them to share an overriding preoccupation with 'sound money' in assessing broader economic issues. In practice, moreover, a consensus view about the level of prices in particular markets tends to emerge all too easily, as we shall see later on. So it is hard to escape the conclusion that control of stock market investments, like ownership, is narrowly concentrated, and that the securities markets are not working as freely as a liberal economist might wish.

Left-wing and liberal academics and journalists started to worry about the accumulation of these large sums in the hands of institutional owners in the 1950s, when Richard Titmuss, Professor of Social Administration at the London School of Economics, attacked what he claimed was an irresponsible use of power by insurance companies and pension funds. In a prophetic essay[6] he argued:

> It is a power, a potential power, to affect many important aspects of our economic life and our social values. . . . It is a power concentrated in relatively few hands, working at the apex of a handful of giant bureaucracies, technically supported by a group of professional experts, and accountable, in practice, to virtually no-one.
>
> From other points of view, it is a force making for greater centralization of decision-making power reminding us again . . . of Disraeli's warning, 'centralization is the death-blow of public freedom'.

Yet for most of the post-war period the institutions deliberately shunned any role in national politics and they intervened directly in the affairs of only a handful of companies. Outside the City few people were aware of their investment activities, so warnings about insurance companies and pension funds being inadequately accountable appeared academic. Far from using their position as legal owners of stocks and shares to influence events, the institutions seemed determined to remain passive. The beneficial ownership of British industry, now vested increasingly in insurance policy holders and workers contributing to pension schemes, was even further divorced from control than it was when capital was in predominantly individual ownership. It became fashionable, notably under Edward Heath's Conservative government in the early 1970s, to criticise fund managers for using their power not too much, but too little.

The inconspicuous and outwardly benign face of institutional capitalism started to give way in the second half of the 1970s under the pressure of rapidly accumulating cash. Institutional investors simply became so large that they could no longer move about the financial landscape without occasionally upsetting the prevailing political and economic balance. Not surprisingly, then, the financial history of much of the past ten years concerns the growing power of institutions both to stabilise and destabilise financial markets, sometimes to the point where government policy was affected.

The collapse of the stock market in 1974, which deprived most of British industry of the opportunity to raise new equity capital in one of the tightest credit squeezes since the war, was a direct result of the institutions withdrawing their buying power from the market. A full-blown collapse of the British banking system, which had lent excessive sums on the security of property in 1971–73, would probably have been impossible to avoid, had it not been for the willingness of investment institutions to buy hundreds of millions of poundsworth of property from overstretched property companies in mid-decade. If they had refused to co-operate with the Bank of England in its attempt to clean out the Augean stables of the banking system, much more of British banking might now either be defunct or in the hands of the state. And the institutions' loss of confidence in the Labour government's economic policies in 1976, together with their refusal to buy the government's gilt-edged stock, contributed to the crisis that led to the arrival of representatives of the International Monetary Fund in Britain later that year.

The government was by no means alone in having to come to terms with institutional power. Quoted companies began to find that individual institutions were acquiring disproportionately large chunks of their share capital: or disproportionately little – most notably so in the case of Lonrho, the international trading group run by Roland 'Tiny' Rowland which was the subject of Edward Heath's famous jibe about the unacceptable face of capitalism. In the second half of the 1970s, Lonrho suffered the financial equivalent of 'being sent to Coventry' when many of the biggest institutions resolutely refused to invest in its shares. As long as it remained poorly rated in the stock market it became harder for this acquisitive company to pay for the takeover of other companies with its own shares. Ironically, many of the fund managers concerned insisted that they had few objections to Rowland's face or to his capitalism. They were simply unable to see from where, in the future, his company was going to find the cash to pay a steadily rising dividend.

The institutions' presence was inescapable outside the City too. Farmers discovered that they were being outbid at auction by insurance companies and pension funds seeking to increase their holdings of agricultural land (although the institutions preferred, in the main, to buy tenanted rather than vacant possession land). In the nationalised industries, trade union officials sat on pension fund investment committees where they had to decide whether to invest in property or in South African gold mines – twin horrors in the demonology of the left. And the pension funds jumped smartly from the back to the front pages of the national newspapers when it emerged that British Rail's pension fund had been busy buying works of art, ranging from a rare twelfth century candlestick to a blue period Picasso.

Towards the end of the decade, the pension funds in particular put their power to more active use outside the market, as well as in it. Goaded on by the unwelcome attentions of Sir Harold Wilson's committee on the workings of the financial system, they noisily demanded a say in the strategic management decisions of a handful of big industrial companies. British management suddenly found itself potentially accountable to a powerful new bureaucracy of proxy capitalists. Wilson, retired from high office, appeared to have succeeded in prodding the institutions into action where the earlier Heath government had failed.

Fund managers also enjoyed growing personal power: like government ministers and officials, they were able to exercise patronage. In the financial markets this amounted to a power to make other individuals rich. The most eye-catching illustration of such patronage occurred when the Crown Agents, a semi-official government financial institution, offered lavish loans and guarantees to a private company that they owned jointly with two property dealers, Ramon Greene and Jack Walker. Greene was a Reading estate agent with a housebuilding and estate development business; Walker was a solicitor with some experience in developing residential flats. Neither had any track record in large-scale commercial property dealing and development. Yet the Crown Agents' backing, which was first offered in mid-1969, raised them from obscurity and allowed them to accumulate £100 million-worth of property in less than two and a half years. Early in 1973 the Post Office pension fund rounded off this remarkable undertaking by buying most of the property on terms that left Greene and Walker with a profit of more than £8 million apiece in cash, equivalent to over £20 million in 1980 pounds.

By now the day-to-day decisions of institutional investors influence everything from corporate plans in industry to the shape of the urban and rural landscape. And as the institutions continue to grow, the criteria they apply in making their investments, are becoming a matter of increasing public concern. Most fund managers believe that their overriding legal duty of trust to the beneficiaries of the funds they manage, prevents them from taking into account the common interest, however defined; they argue that their first priority is to protect the immediate financial interests of their present and future beneficiaries. This attitude was no doubt harmless enough when the institutions were a less significant force in the capital markets. But coming from the most powerful group of proprietors outside Britain's public sector it looks suspiciously like a plea of diminished responsibility.

The institutions do, nonetheless, face a genuine dilemma. In their well-meaning pursuit of the beneficiaries' narrow financial interests, they are bound, occasionally, to find themselves on a collision course with other powerful groups in society because they handle so much of the nation's savings. But if fund managers try to find some broader social criterion for investment, they risk becoming more directly embroiled in the political debate on behalf of beneficiaries whose social and political values might differ from their own.

As long as the insurance companies and pension funds are responsible for such a high proportion of personal saving there is no obvious way of resolving this dilemma. But in practice, when the dilemma becomes acute, fund managers demonstrate a degree of flexibility that they rarely exhibit in public discussion, as we shall see in later chapters.

Perhaps the oddest feature of the wholesale transfer of shares from individuals to institutions in Britain is that it is not the result of any conscious act of political will. The financial mandarins of the insurance companies and pension funds happened on power almost by default, because politicians and civil servants failed to foresee the financial consequences of their actions when they introduced (or failed to introduce) new social security legislation, or when they tinkered with the tax system and restructured state industries.

As standards of living rose in the advanced industrial nations in the 1950s and 1960s, a growing number of people naturally looked for a better income on retirement. But whereas many continental European governments responded by improving the level of state pensions and giving the private sector a subsidiary role in topping up the pensions of the well-to-do, the British became enmeshed in adversary politics: neither party could agree on how best to look after the aged. As a result, the history of state pensions in Britain is strewn with might-have-beens such as the unimplemented pension system over which the late Richard Crossman toiled in the second half of the 1960s, or the state reserve scheme got up by the Department of Health under Sir Keith Joseph in the early 1970s and put down by the same department under Barbara Castle on Labour's subsequent return to office.

While the politicians argued, free enterprise attempted to remedy the state's omissions as best it could and occupational pension schemes mushroomed in both the public and private sectors of industry and commerce. By the time Mrs Castle introduced her new, and not conspicuously generous, state pension scheme in the

Social Security Pensions Act of 1975, it was deemed expedient to allow what was by then a thriving private pensions business to come into partnership with the state.

Had more of the burden of providing pensions for the aged fallen on the state, the land would not now be peopled with institutional giants. For state pensions are run on a 'pay-as-you-go' system in which portfolio investment plays no direct part. Retired workers' pensions are paid out of the government's current revenues (which of course include contributions from future beneficiaries): no attempt is made to build up a fund from which to pay pensions in future.

Occupational pension schemes in the nationalised industries, local authorities and private sector companies, however, rely mainly on the alternative 'funded' system. Here companies and employees meet the cost of pensions by saving up in advance. Over the course of the employee's working life, contributions are paid into a fund which is invested, either by an insurance company or by investment managers appointed by the trustees of the company's own self-administered pension scheme, in stocks, shares and other investments. When the employee retires, the pension is paid out of the fund which generally remains secure even if the employer goes bankrupt.

There is no need, at this stage, to go into the relative advantages and disadvantages of the two systems. All that need be said is that the way in which different nations finance the cost of pensions is a fairly accurate reflection of the degree of sophistication of their stock markets. In France where the Bourse does not play a central part in channelling savings into investment, virtually all pensions are paid on a pay-as-you-go system. The Germans, whose relatively undeveloped stock markets are dominated by the larger banks, operate a variant of the funded system in their private sector pension arrangements, whereby pension contributions are often invested in the employing company's shares; the pensions are independently insured to protect workers from the bankruptcy of the company. The Americans, whose securities market is second to none in size, operate mainly funded schemes, but while the growing power of the pension funds has attracted considerable attention in the United States, private investors still own twice as many company securities as financial institutions and the pension funds remain relatively passive investors.[7] Events such as the move by New York City pension funds to help rescue the financially troubled municipality in the mid-1970s, stand out by virtue of their rarity.

As for the British, whose stock market has traditionally played an important role in the nation's affairs, they are more heavily committed to the funded system than anyone else. In 1975 the Government Actuary estimated that half Britain's working population of 23 million was covered by occupational pension schemes. Outside central government, where these schemes operate on a pay-as-you-go system and where benefits were put on an index-linked basis in 1971, virtually all the occupational schemes are funded. The commitment to funding was, if anything, reinforced by Barbara Castle's new state pension scheme, which gave employers a choice in the way they met the level of pension benefits laid down by the Social Security Pensions Act. Either they could leave it to the government to provide the earnings-related part of the state pension; or they could contract out of the scheme provided they agreed to match the inflation-proofed minimum earnings-related pension provided by the state. The decision to jump one way or the other turned heavily on whether companies thought their pension funds' investments were likely to show a real return. Employees had no effective say in the matter; the act required employers merely to consult them before making the decision unilaterally.

All public authorities contracted out of the scheme. And instead of welcoming the opportunity to offload index-linked pension obligations onto the state, private sector companies contracted out to a far greater extent than the Government had expected. Yet by contracting out, many were committing themselves to a far more rosy view of the future than the one portrayed in their own corporate plans.

No doubt this was partly a gesture of faith in the market system. But in some cases companies were heavily influenced by the advice of insurance companies and pension consultants who were hardly impartial advocates since their income stood to be reduced if people contracted into the scheme. In the end only a handful of big companies, among them BAT Industries, GEC, W. H. Smith, ICL and the John Lewis Partnership, chose to swim against the tide by contracting in. Many of those who had contracted out had to improve benefits to meet the new standards laid down by the legislation and these improvements had to be financed. As a result more money poured into pension funds and into insurance companies that administered pension schemes.

Having passed the pensions buck so extensively to the private sector, successive governments felt obliged to subsidise it on an ever-increasing scale by allowing contributions into pension funds, together with capital gains and investment income on the funds' assets, to remain free of tax. This brings us to the second most important factor behind the growth of financial institutions in Britain, which lies precisely in a tax system that favours investment in an arbitrarily selected range of assets including houses, plant and machinery, life assurance policies, pension fund investments, computers and government stock. And the value of the long-standing tax reliefs on these assets has dramatically increased as a result of inflation.

Between 1945 and 1970 a standard rate taxpayer could usually put his cash on deposit at the bank or invest in a local authority deposit and expect to see a real return – that is, the interest after tax would generally be greater than the loss due to inflation. In the stock market a well diversified portfolio of equity shares also appeared to stand a sporting chance of showing a real return. For much of the 1970s, however, the rate of inflation exceeded the rate of interest on many kinds of investment. And it became much more difficult to match the returns on a government-subsidised investment in an insurance policy or pension scheme by investing directly in stocks and shares.

As a result, the middle class now protects the value of its savings by investing collectively, in much the same way as it has taken to collective organisation in white-collar unions in order to protect the real value of its income. Young people spurn stock market investment in favour of the building society deposit or life assurance policy; for capital appreciation they rely mainly on the purchase of their own home. Richer members of the older generation turn increasingly to tax avoidance. With the help of ingenious accountants, they have found that investment returns can perfectly legally be doubled, trebled or even quadrupled without risk to the investor. The trick is to make maximum use of tax reliefs available on institutional forms of saving, including those on life assurance premiums and pension scheme contributions, so that the government pays for part of the investment.

This fiscal patronage has changed the face of the financial system. The tax reliefs on mortgage interest, for example, helped bring about the explosive growth of the building societies, together with the rise in owner-occupation in Britain from little over 10% before the First World War to well over 50% today. In the view of some economists, it also exacerbated house price inflation, though the building societies naturally argue otherwise. Without tax relief on life assurance, it is doubtful whether savers would have contributed so extensively to the growth of the life assurance giants, because the investment returns on endowment policies are not notably impressive.[8] (It is worth pointing out in passing that in the United States, where there is no comparable tax relief and where inflation has recently whittled down investment returns, life assurance companies have seen a sharp decline in the demand for endowment-type policies; they are being forced to rethink their role in the financial markets.) And the pension funds, as we have seen, were affected in the same way as other forced plants in the fiscal hothouse: they grew and grew and grew.

In 1979–80, the cost to the exchequer of mortgage interest relief was estimated at £1.4 billion, while the equivalent figures for relief on life assurance and occupational pensions were put at £400 million and £800 million respectively. The grand total of £2.6 billion amounted to more than 30% of the borrowing requirement of Britain's public sector that financial year. The cost of subsidised thrift will, moreover, continue to be high, for collective saving remains overwhelmingly attractive at present rates of inflation.

A further devastating contribution to the growth of the pension funds came as a result of bureaucratic muddling over the financing of public sector pensions. The biggest muddle undoubtedly stemmed from the decision in the late 1960s to set up a pension fund for the Post Office. Within ten years this single act had added over 8% to the value of all Britain's pension funds and played havoc with the Post Office's profits and its pricing policy. Less intrepid seekers after financial truth should probably skip the next page or two, but for those who are interested in the way financial decisions are taken in Whitehall, the history of the Post Office pension fund makes a dumbfounding case study.

The trouble originally started when a Labour administration transformed the Post Office from a government department into a state-owned corporation. At the same time it was decided that the

Post Office should abandon the government's pay-as-you-go method of meeting pensions and establish an independent fund. In itself, the decision to set up a fund was not unreasonable. Nationalised industry employees do not necessarily need the same degree of security for their pensions as private employees. But a funded pension scheme forces nationalised industries to provide for pension costs as they are incurred and to adjust their pricing policies to reflect those costs. At the Post Office, however, the fund was set up in a manner almost perfectly designed, in a period of inflation, to guarantee chronic insolvency and thus to undermine the point of the exercise.

The obligation to pay pensions relating to Post Office workers' service before 1969 was passed to the new fund, which was set up under the chairmanship of a former Post Office official. In exchange the government agreed to pay regular sums into the fund to help meet the obligation. The Treasury decided that this should be done by pretending that the fund was entitled to repayments of capital and interest on a fictitious £1.4 billion holding of government stock. The fund was to receive whatever would have been paid on an equivalent real holding of $2\frac{1}{2}\%$ Consols.

It was an unhappy piece of financial management from the Post Office's point of view. Even in 1969 fixed-interest gilt-edged stock was regarded as a risky investment for pension funds because a fixed income, government guarantee notwithstanding, could not be expected to keep pace with any unexpected inflation in the cost of future pensions. Six and a half inflationary years later, the fund was reckoned to need a huge additional sum of £1.2 billion to meet the inflated cost of pension rights relating to the period before 1969. This, according to the Post Office, was equivalent to about $\frac{1}{2}$p for every inland letter sent and 0.3p of the unit cost on every inland telephone call in its 1975–76 financial year.

Not surprisingly, the government refused to accept moral responsibility for this shortfall; the Treasury's initial manoeuvre had been designed precisely to protect the government from any open-ended financial commitment. So the Post Office sought to increase its prices. Meantime the unwelcome £1.2 billion deficit stalked the corridors of the public sector for three years in search of a home. Its forlorn odyssey came to an end when the profitable telecommunications side of the Post Office was told to accept responsibility for the whole amount, so sparing politicians any embarrassment or loss of votes arising from the increase in postal charges that would otherwise have been needed to cover the deficit.

Customers of the Post Office's telecommunications business thenceforth contributed multi-million sums towards the pensions of postmen as well as electrical engineers. At the same time the government sanctioned some imaginative accountancy to ensure that the Post Office did not have to take into account any of the deficit in trying to meet its financial targets. But the seeds of a new bureaucratic muddle (and a battle between management and unions) had been sewn for the 1980s: what was to become of the deficit, and the whole pension fund, for that matter, when the Conservative plans to split the Post Office's telecommunications business from the postal business were put into effect?

Similar difficulties arose at British Rail, where the pension funds had been required by statute to make long term deposits with the rail board at pre-inflationary rates of interest. In this case the government did accept partial responsibility. Several hundred millions of public money were pumped into British Rail's pension fund until a Conservative transport minister, Norman Fowler, decided that the simplest way to meet the public spending cuts required of his department, was to put part of the pension fund onto a pay-as-you-go basis.

One final ingredient in the mixture of design and accident that has turned insurance companies and pension funds into such a powerful group of proprietors is the trend towards concentration in industry and commerce. Nationalisation has led to the merging of pension funds. So, too, has the unending boom in company takeovers. And insurance companies have been as prone to the desire to merge as industrial companies. If Britain had had an effective competition policy in the past two decades, three-quarters of its billionaire financial institutions would not now be billionaires.

Control of a significant proportion of the nation's wealth cannot be transferred from one group in society to another without tacit or overt political approval. Why, then, were politicians content to see the investment institutions acquire such a big strategic hold on the means of production? One reason is that the shift in owner-ship was so discreet that most politicians failed to notice until the institutions were already well entrenched; and it is possible that those who did notice were genuinely bemused by a phenomenon which blurs hallowed distinctions between right and left.

In the Conservative party, landowners feel instinctively unhappy when they see insurance companies and pension funds buying agricultural property. Some economic liberals, with a less funda-mentalist belief in the inherent virtues of ownership, dislike the loss of personal choice that institutionalised saving entails. Others such as Sir Keith Joseph, seem to feel – in theory if not in practice – that while subsidies to industry are an anathema, subsidies to different parts of the savings movement are perfectly acceptable. (When I asked him why, Sir Keith hedged; the answer to the question, he felt, was really the subject for a book.)

Many Conservatives also believe that the best way to sell capitalism to the workers is through the medium of collective savings, whereby small sums are parcelled together by middlemen for investment in the stock market in larger, more economic blocks. Several, including Sir Geoffrey Howe, until he became Chancellor of the Exchequer after the 1979 election, are or have been directors of insurance companies; others are merchant bankers and stockbrokers, for whom the management of pension fund investments has been a lucrative business.

On the Labour side, those politicians who are aware of the existence of financial institutions often regard them as the same old capitalists in new clothes. The fact that pension funds are the custodians of the savings of British workers does not seem to have affected their views of profits, taxation or dividends. And who can blame any Labour politician for feeling bemused when public corporations that were created in the socialising spirit of Clause Four of the Labour Party constitution, turn out to have spawned some of the most powerful engines of modern finance capitalism, in the shape of nationalised industry pension funds – pension funds, moreover, which are legally bound to pursue objectives entirely independent of those of the public corporations whose employees they exist to serve?

A further indication of how the issue of institutional saving cuts across political boundaries can be seen in the way it sometimes unites politicians of otherwise opposing points of view. There are economic liberals on the Conservative benches who would like to scrap tax reliefs on life assurance premiums and mortgage interest payments to promote 'fiscal neutrality', whereby different kinds of saving compete with each other on equal terms. On the left of the parliamentary Labour party Frank Field, former director of the Child Poverty Action Group, would like to see similar changes because he regards the existing reliefs as a government subsidy that could sensibly be directed to areas of more pressing social need.

The overwhelming response to the rise of financial institutions, however, is one of apathy – which seems odd, given the recent resurgence, among leading British politicians, of the belief that changes in the ownership of the means of production are urgently needed to bring about desired social and economic goals. Both Harold Wilson in 1974, and Margaret Thatcher in 1979, turned to the extreme wings of their respective parties to fill the post of industry secretary, and the ministers concerned came to the job arguing that a prerequisite of industrial and social regeneration lay in a change of proprietors. Anthony Benn nationalised ship-building and aerospace and argued for nationalisation in other key sectors of the economy; Sir Keith Joseph argued for the return of various enterprises, including part of the capital of British Aerospace, British Airways, and the telecommunications side of the Post Office, to the private sector.

The recent change in the pattern of ownership shows these political aspirations in a rather curious light. The private investor, as we have seen, is a net seller of shares while the institutions are net buyers. Anthony Benn's demand, made at the special Labour Party conference in June 1980, that no Labour government should compensate 'private speculators' when renationalising assets that the Tory government had denationalised, would adversely affect many of the $11\frac{1}{2}$ million British workers who are members of occupational pension schemes – as Sir Keith Joseph is quick to point out.

Yet any Tory move to transfer the ownership of public corporations back to the private sector would, by the same token, be less likely to set the people free than to shift a measure of power from Whitehall mandarins to pension fund mandarins. The relationship between ownership and power is obviously more complex than one might conclude from listening to the huffing and puffing of politicians as they shunt the nation's assets from private to public sector and back again. Most parliamentary politicians' pensions, incidentally, have been index-linked, like those of public servants, so ministers have been protected financially from some of the ill consequences of their restless manoeuvring of industrial assets.

Trade union leaders and managers are more conscious of the importance of investment institutions because they bargain over pension rights and sit on pension fund investment committees. But like the government, they have given the funded pensions' bandwagon a helpful shove without always recognising the longer-term consequences. The trade union movement is committed first and foremost to improving the state pension system. But in the period of pay restraint, introduced by the Heath government in the early 1970s, trade union leaders were quick to see – as the government no doubt intended – that pensions were exempted from the freeze. In lieu of higher wages, union negotiators obtained better pension benefits for their members.

By giving pensions increased priority in the collective bargaining process, however, the unions allowed their members to be swept into a savings medium that embodied the most sacred of middle class political values: capital. And they failed to retain full control over that capital when it went into the pension fund.

For their part, managers have been happy to go along with the boom in occupational pensions for much the same reason as the unions. In periods of pay restraint it gives them a convenient backdoor method of remunerating workers, so they are happy (if only temporarily) to accept the argument that pension contributions represent workers' deferred pay rather than the sophisticated modern equivalent of a gold watch. But the managers were also slow to recognise the nature of the beast that they had helped create. For if a pension fund is badly managed it can put a whole business at risk if the company is obliged to dip into its own profits to make good the insolvency of the fund.

Insurance company management is dominated by actuaries, members of a small but powerful profession that concerns itself with the mathematical study of probabilities both in relation to life expectancy and portfolio investment. Though not infallible, actuaries are highly trained and their presence guarantees a reasonable level of managerial competence. In contrast, pension funds are managed by people of widely different qualifications and backgrounds (though actuaries are to be found among them).

In many nationalised industry pension schemes the trustees are drawn half from the management, half from the workers. In the private sector, management more often has a majority on the board of trustees, though 50% worker representation is not uncommon. This is the case at Unilever, the Anglo-Dutch food and detergents group, for example, where maintenance fitters, meat-boners and lathe turners, as well as the odd economist and accountant, have been represented on the board of trustees. When it comes to investment management, however, common sense and a background on the shop floor are poor substitutes for financial *nous*: big risks have been taken needlessly by the pension funds of some of Britain's biggest corporations in both the private and public sectors in the 1970s (of which more in later chapters) without serious objections being raised by worker representatives.

Trustees have usually delegated the task of investing the fund to a professional manager, such as a merchant bank or a firm of stockbrokers. But in the larger pension funds management is increasingly carried out in-house. And the status of the in-house fund manager may not have kept pace with his ability to wreck his own company's profits. Many who spend more on stocks, shares and property in a single year than most managing directors in industry lay out on plant and machinery in ten, are not seen as meriting the trappings of high office in the corporate hierarchy.

Responsibility for pension funds in smaller companies sometimes falls on a personnel officer or overstretched company secretary, for whom the challenge of actuarial arithmetic may prove overwhelming. Pension funds are also a convenient place to put people out to grass: many a failed financial executive has been shuffled sideways and put in charge of sums that nobody would have dreamed of letting him handle in his previous position.

Having seen in the 1970s how inflation can affect pension obligations and investment returns, and having been forced to pump money into their pension funds as a result, larger companies now attach more importance to the quality of pension fund investment management. But there remains a marked sense of unease among the stockbrokers and bankers in the City over the variable skills of the fund managers looking after the British pensioner's £40 billion porfolio. Moreover, the risk of mismanagement is compounded by a serious lack of accountability.

The activities of pension funds are governed by trust law, which was designed to cope with the needs of families and charities, not those of huge impersonal savings institutions. As yet, there are no statutory requirements about the form of pension fund accounts or for their audit, no statutory definition of the duties of pension fund trustees, no obligation to make the accounts public, no certainty even, that beneficiaries have a right to information. In discussing the duties of pension fund trustees and their obligation (or non-obligation) to disclose financial information, the government-sponsored Occupational Pensions Board pointed out in a report in 1975 that 'quite apart from the lack of any statutory authority, it is by no means clear that an assembly of lawyers would be able to agree on what these duties or items of information are, or indeed should be'.

In practice the constitution of a pension fund is governed by the terms of its trust deed. This usually lays down broad rules for calculating pension benefits, preparing accounts, and investing in specific types of security. The trustees are then left to make up their own minds about what is in the best interest of the beneficiaries of the fund, without being subject to any discipline of disclosure or publicity. There is no statutory obligation to file accounts with a registrar, as there is with companies, and the number of pension funds that send their reports and accounts to the press as a matter of course, can be counted on the fingers of one hand.

In areas of commerce and finance where profits are not of paramount importance, such as co-operative retail societies, investments have sometimes been appallingly managed. Even in large companies investment errors are easily compounded because they are hard to detect. Fund managers and trustees can always justify poor performance by arguing that the short term gyrations of the stock market or property market are irrelevant to a fund where the average period to retirement for the workforce as a whole is more than twenty years. By the time poor performance is properly identified, they themselves may have retired.

The combination of undreamed of sums of money, management of variable quality and negligible accountability looks an unbeatable one for promoting incompetence and encouraging fraud. And at least one big fraud has already taken place. In 1980 Andrew Macfarlane, an investment manager at the £400 million Universities Superannuation Scheme, was sentenced to five years after transferring more than £1½ million of the fund's money to his own account at a firm of investment brokers, who were instructed to buy a large number of Krugerrands (South African gold coins) on his behalf. Before the transaction was completed, someone smelt a rat: when Macfarlane was caught by the police, he had air tickets to Malta in his pocket. Not all of the money was recovered, however, and the pension fund was forced to provide for a loss of £300,000 in its accounts. Macfarlane had earlier served eighteen months after being convicted for dishonesty while working for Barclays Bank Trust Company in Bournemouth.

The British have traditionally been among the world's least enthusiastic savers. Since the mid-1960s, however, contractual savings – those made regularly through life assurance, pension schemes and other savings contracts – have more than doubled to over 5% of gross domestic product. This creates an unusual opportunity, for a huge and stable pool of cash is now available to finance the much increased level of productive investment that Britain badly needs.

In practice, however, there is a potential shortage of new investments for the institutions. In the second half of the 1970s, the institutions' demand for investments was met from three main sources. Private shareholders sold them existing company securities, as they continued to swing from investing directly in the stock market to investing via the institutions themselves; the government sold them large amounts of new gilt-edged securities, in order to finance public spending; and overborrowed property companies sold them offices, shops and industrial premises, as they tried to restore their shaky finances after the excesses of the property boom.

In the 1980s the institutions are being forced to look to different sources of supply. The private investor cannot go on selling shares for ever; at the present rate of sales, there would be no more for him to sell by 1994, and in practice, sales would dry up much earlier than that. Sound companies are not issuing new shares on a scale to absorb as much cash as the institutions would like them to do. And while the government has augmented the supply of equity by selling part of its own holdings in quoted companies like

British Petroleum and by returning shares in nationalised industries such as British Aerospace to the private sector, it has sold less than originally intended.

As for gilt-edged, Mrs Thatcher's government sold far more, in its first two years of office, than City Tories would have wished. But if the government has any longer term success in bringing down public spending and in financing more of its borrowing by selling investments direct to individuals instead of institutions (through the issue of index-linked savings certificates, for example), the institutions face a potential shortage here too.

Property, meantime, is scarce now that property companies have put their finances back in order. As the founding entrepreneurs behind individual property companies retire or die, they will no doubt sell out to insurance companies and pension funds. But few entrepreneurs are otherwise keen to sell what they know to be a scarce commodity. The only other significant holdings of property are owned by the government and by property-rich companies such as retail chains.

So far, however, the government has only sold a fraction of its properties that are suitable for institutional investment. Buildings in new towns are for sale, but valuable Whitehall office blocks are not. The most that the institutions can hope for from retailers, meanwhile, is the occasional sale and leaseback transaction such as the deal whereby House of Fraser sold its D. H. Evans department store property in London's Oxford Street to Legal and General in 1981 for £29 million. So where will the institutions' money go? And will the institutions themselves retain the freedom to decide where it goes?

Under a Conservative government the professional fund managers have already been granted freedom from exchange controls and they are reacting to the shortage of attractive domestic equity and property by investing more in equity and property overseas. No doubt they will go on doing so as long as the Tories remain in power.

The government, meantime, hopes that its policies will ultimately lead to lower inflation, lower interest rates and a more favourable climate for business enterprise, which would encourage both new and established businesses to take more of the institutions' cash and put it to productive use.

If Labour (or a new government of any other political complexion) comes to power before the decade is out, however, investment choice may partly be removed from the institutions. Left wing politicians, the Trades Union Congress and a minority group on the Wilson Committee of enquiry into the workings of the financial system, argued that part of the £10 billion that flows into insurance companies and pension funds each year should be compulsorily directed into productive investment in industry.

Any move towards compulsory direction of investment would be stiffly resisted in industry and the City. It would also be resisted by many in the Social Democratic Party and on the Labour right. The struggle between management, unions, politicians and professional fund managers for control of the financial institutions' £100 billion crock of gold, promises to be one of the fiercer political battles of the 1980s.

2

Unwitting saboteurs

'Ownership confers a legal right of sabotage, and absentee ownership vests the owner with the power of sabotage at a distance . . .'

Thorstein Veblen, *Absentee Ownership and Business Enterprise in Recent Times: The Case of America*

BY THE EARLY 1970s the enormous buying power of the financial institutions was well recognised in the stock market. Invariably the biggest institutions – the insurance companies and pension funds, together with the merchant banks and stockbrokers who invested money on their behalf – bought more shares, on balance, than they sold in the course of any given year. In the previous two decades, their appetite for equity shares had scarcely wavered. It never occurred to anyone that the institutions might one day lose that appetite; still less that they could undermine the whole stock market simply by sitting on their hands.

An awareness of what could happen if the institutions ceased to buy shares dawned in 1974. While private investors continued to sell shares in publicly quoted British companies, they found fewer and fewer takers among the institutions. Professional investors chose instead to put unprecedented sums on deposit at the bank. Between January 1973 and December 1974, insurance companies, pension funds, investment trusts and unit trusts together increased their cash holdings by over £2 billion – more than 150%. And in the fourth quarter of 1974, for the first and last time during the decade, they sold more shares than they bought.[1]

This institutional vote of no confidence in equity shares caused a devastating plunge in the Financial Times industrial ordinary index, the most popular indicator of stock market confidence: it fell from 344.0 to 161.4 over the year. At 31 December 1974, all the quoted industrial and commercial companies in Britain were valued at only £17.3 billion, or less than a third of their market value two years earlier. It had been virtually impossible for most industrialists to raise new equity capital for much of the year.

Fund managers argued that the stock market was simply acting like a barometer in the face of unusually foul political and economic weather. To outsiders it looked more like a sinking ship in which panic-stricken passengers ran en masse from bow to stern and back again with each new rumour of another leak. The collapse of the stock market in 1974 demonstrated clearly, for the first time, how the rapidly growing financial institutions had become a potentially destabilising force within the economy.

If equity shares had remained predominantly in private hands, a collapse on this scale could only have been brought about by thousands of positive decisions by individual investors to exchange their shares for cash. But since the private individual was a persistent net seller of quoted ordinary shares, it took a much smaller number of institutional decisions to refrain from buying, to undermine the market. And unlike the private investor, the professional investor could not shut his eyes and hope that bad news would go away. The process whereby personal saving was giving way to institutional saving meant that over £3½ billion of new cash poured into the lap of the managers of insurance companies and pension funds in 1974. They had to do something with it, and doing something meant taking a view of the stock market.

It is doubtful whether a comparable collapse could have happened in any other major industrial nation. In the mid-1970s, life assurance companies in the United States, Canada, Japan, Germany and France held less of their investments in the form of equity than their British counterparts.[2] In Germany and France, as we have seen, few companies had independently funded pension schemes; in the United States and Japan, institutions did not account for such a large proportion of the market. In most of these countries institutional investment in equities was hampered by statutory restrictions. The British financial institutions were not similarly inhibited, and it is worth looking back at the history of their investment in equities to see how the conditions that led to the 1974 collapse were created.

In fact, institutional investors developed their appetite for equities early in the post-war period, thanks mainly to the advocacy of a far-sighted actuary, George Ross Goobey, who ran the pension fund of Imperial Tobacco (now called Imperial Group) for nearly three decades. When George Ross Goobey went to Imperial Tobacco in 1947, conventional wisdom dictated that insurance companies and pension funds should put their money into gilt-edged stock, debentures, preference shares and ordinary shares in that order, with ordinary shares very much at the bottom of the list. Gilt-edged yielded around $2\frac{1}{2}\%$, while ordinary shares showed a return of about 5%. The extra yield on equities reflected a belief that they were riskier than government stock and should show a higher return to compensate for the additional risk; investment thinking was heavily coloured by the dismal economic circumstances of the 1930s. Ross Goobey decided that the financial institutions had got their priorities upside down.

This view was not based on any broad macro-economic judgements or sophisticated forecasts about inflation. Ross Goobey simply thought that Dalton's $2\frac{1}{2}\%$ fixed interest government stock was a swindle when inflation was running at more than 4%, and that an investment in ordinary shares yielding 4%–5%, with some prospect of growth in income, looked absurdly cheap in comparison. His problem was to persuade the conservative top management of Imperial Tobacco that the accepted wisdom of the day was rubbish.

City folklore has it that he bought a second-hand Bentley he could barely afford, joined the same golf club as the chairman of the company, and launched a propaganda campaign from there. The truth, so Ross Goobey told me, was more prosaic, although the Bentley was real enough. When he arrived at the company, pensions were regarded as a necessary evil and the fund of £12–13 million was managed by the chief accountant in his spare time. Part of the reason why the directors wanted an in-house actuary was that they needed someone to interpret the advice given by their own consulting actuaries

The trustees were obtaining a return of around $2\frac{1}{2}\%$ on their (mainly fixed interest) securities, while guaranteeing pension benefits on a scale that called for a return of 5% on the fund's investment. The actuaries had declared that Imperial would have to put £5$\frac{1}{4}$ million – a huge sum in 1947 – into the pension fund if it was to meet its liabilities. Ross Goobey's preferred solution was to stop all investment in government stock and put the money into ordinary shares, which he expected would produce a growing income with which to meet rising pension payments.

This suggestion was regarded by most of Imperial Tobacco's top management as outrageous, as it would have been in almost any other large company at the time. But it elicited a more sympathetic response from the chairman of the company's investment committee, Sir James Grigg. Grigg was an unusually able ex-civil servant, who had held a number of key economic posts in Whitehall before serving in Churchill's cabinet as Secretary of State for War between 1942 and 1945. He eventually steered a proposal to increase the investment in equities through the trustees of the pension fund, who consisted of the top five directors of the company.

Thereafter Ross Goobey submitted a monthly report to the two junior trustees who, he says, spent so much time raising objections to the investments he made in individual companies, that they took a long time to notice that he was making no investment at all in gilt-edged. Later he persuaded the trustees to let him do something that no other manager of any large British pension fund has done before or since: he sold every gilt-edged stock in the portfolio and devoted the whole of the fund to equity investment.

Ross Goobey's supremely confident gesture was thoroughly vindicated over the next twenty years. An equity share carries the right to whatever income is left when all other claims on the company – bank interest, employees' pay, tax and other charges – have been satisfied. A right to the residual income of Britain's corporate sector was well worth having in the 1950s and for much of the 1960s and the success of the Imperial pension fund attracted widespread attention. While one or two other fund managers had come more tentatively to the same conclusions at much the same time, Ross Goobey was credited with founding 'the cult of the equity'. A majority of private shareholders was, by definition, excluded from the cult since the institutions' enthusiasm for equities could only be satisfied as long as individuals were willing to sell.

The change in investment thinking inspired by the actuary of the Imperial Tobacco pension fund led eventually to the enactment of the Trustee Investment Act 1961, which allowed general trust funds to invest up to half their money in equities, thus accelerating the shift towards institutional investment in ordinary shares; local authority pension funds, among others, had previously invested only in local or central government securities. And by 1963, every professional money manager was climbing aboard the bandwagon: the institutions owned over a quarter of the ordinary shares of British companies listed on the stock exchange, according to the Diamond Commission's estimate. By 1973 they owned nearly half. The received wisdom of the early 1970s was that pension funds should invest first in equities, and last in fixed interest stocks, which were regarded as being among the more risky investments for funds trying to meet rising pension commitments.

Enthusiasm for equities was by this time based on shaky arithmetic. In every year between 1964 and 1974 the increase in dividends paid by companies in the broadly-based Financial Times 500 share index consistently failed to match the increase in the retail price index. Insurance companies and pension funds, and their advisers in the City, turned a blind eye to this poor performance because their shares continued to show capital growth. Investors were looking for a store of value to protect their money from inflation. Yet in reality the capital growth only reflected the institutions' own willingness to go on buying equities; they were providing the impetus behind the rise in share prices to a level which could only be justified if companies managed, in the long run, to produce a flow of dividend income that outstripped the rate of inflation. It can be seen, with hindsight, that the institutions' expectations were pitched too high and that the stock market was expecting things of British industry that it was in no condition to provide.

Professional fund managers recognised as much in 1974. This time, however, they went to the other extreme. Insurance companies and pension funds usually insist that they invest for the long term and that they are not interested in attempting to out-guess market indices on a day-to-day basis. But in 1974 a majority of them took the unusual and apparently self-defeating course of putting much of their incoming cash on short-term deposit. As the biggest group of investors in the market, institutions collectively could not hope that delay would enable them to buy shares more cheaply at a later date since the weight of their buying orders would automatically push share prices back up against them.

What, then, was the point of depressing the FT industrial ordinary index to its lowest level since 1954 and thus undermining the value of the shares they already held?

An unusually severe fall in the equity market was, in fact, justified on several counts. The Organisation of Petroleum Exporting Countries (OPEC) had just administered a devastating blow to the world economy by imposing a fourfold increase in the price of oil after the Arab-Israeli war. Together with the simultaneous explosion of other commodity prices in 1973, this was pushing the world towards a combination of high inflation and deep recession. For much of 1974 America was in no condition to offer the western world political or economic leadership: each month President Nixon was sinking deeper into the mire of the Watergate scandal. In Britain, the year started with the three-day week, following the Heath government's confrontation with the miners.[3]

The confidence of institutional investors had already been shaken by the Heath government's blithe attack on one structural prop of market capitalism after another. Under the Tories there had been a relentless regime of dividend and price controls, together with widespread intervention in industry after the collapses of Rolls-Royce and Upper Clyde Shipbuilders. There was also a direct attack on property, first through a commercial rent freeze, then through a new tax on unrealised profits arising on the first letting of commercial buildings. Worst of all, from the point of view of financially conservative institutions in and out of the City, was the government's seeming unconcern at the rapid expansion of the money supply in 1972 and 1973.

It was the combination of price control and inflation that hurt British industry most, and thus undermined the value of the institutions' equity portfolios. As commodity price increases and wage inflation began to hit industrial companies in 1973–74, industry was statutorily prevented from passing on the full cost to its customers. It also faced an excessive tax bill because conventional accounting was throwing up profit figures which did not reflect the impact of inflation. Tax was effectively being charged on paper profits that represented 'stock appreciation', the difference between the original cost of inventory and the current cost of replacing it. Since the so-called profit was immediately used up in paying for higher priced inventory, companies were running out of cash and coming close to the borrowing limits set by their bankers. They knew that institutional investors could not be expected to put up new capital unless the outlook for real, inflation-adjusted profits improved.[4]

When Labour returned to power in March 1974 price controls remained in force, while the attempt to restrain wages was largely abandoned. Denis Healey's first budget tightened the screws by raising employers' national insurance contributions, establishing a higher than expected rate of corporation tax at 52% and proposing a 50% additional pre-payment of advance corporation tax. Further powers were given to the Price Commission to delay price increases for three months. In effect, British industry was being required to shelter the government and the consumer from the painful impact of the OPEC oil price increase, the 1973 commodity price explosion and the hugely inflationary wage rises that followed the new government's deal with the miners, while simultaneously shouldering an additional heavy burden of taxation and submitting to the sharpest credit squeeze since the war.

As weaker companies fell victim to the liquidity squeeze and the rate of inflation went over 20% – well above the statutory 5% ceiling on dividend increases – professional fund managers started to ask whether the equity market could survive. Similar questions were asked about the market in government stocks, which were also yielding a negative real return at the then rate of inflation. An anonymous investment manager wrote in the *Investors Chronicle* in May: 'So great has been the movement to the left in the policies of the two principal political parties over the last few years, that it is no more than commonsense to question whether dividends and rents will ever again be allowed to rise in a totally unfettered fashion.'

At the end of May, Jim Slater, the well-known financier, announced that cash was the most attractive form of investment. It was, he argued, the least risky of the options open to investors. Gilt-edged would be a dismal investment in anything other than a full-scale depression. Equities were hampered by dividend control and would come into their own only if there was a Weimar-type hyper-inflation. And property was undermined by the rent freeze.

Slater's views attracted enormous publicity, which in the short term probably did his own business no harm. Slater, Walker Securities was no less a secondary bank for having Jim Slater, the stock market wizard, at the helm; unknown to most people in the City, the deposits of its banking subsidiary were ebbing away and the value of the bank's increasingly unmarketable assets was waning as the share and property markets went down. To be thought of as sitting on a mountain of cash was, in the circumstances, no bad thing.

Yet Slater, whose bank was later to be rescued by the Bank of England, was articulating the thoughts of many institutional money men. Wage-related pension liabilities were accelerating at 15%, 20% or 25% a year. Pension fund managers were beginning to ask whether there was any point in continuing to invest today's money in assets that showed a negative real return to meet pensions payable in tomorrow's confetti money. Life assurance companies were wondering how the idea of a 'with-profits' endowment policy could survive when there were no real profits with which to pay the bonuses. The equity cult was well and truly dead. Its founder, George Ross Goobey, had in fact given up buying equities in the late 1960s and turned to property instead. In 1974, however, he was telling anyone who cared to listen that undated government stock, yielding 17%, was outstandingly cheap. The advice of the well-known actuary, which did not make headlines in the newspapers, proved better than the advice of Slater, the stock market wizard who was subsequently convicted of offences under the Companies Act for share dealings carried out during the boom. Any pension fund that acted on Ross Goobey's advice (Imperial Tobacco's did naturally) would have been showing a handsome real return on its investment by the end of the decade.

At the end of June 1974 the Financial Times industrial ordinary share index stood at 225.1. Had the market slide stopped there, the institutions whose failure to buy shares had precipitated the fall, might have been credited with uncommon foresight. Dividends and rents were controlled; British industry was going bankrupt. The market was telling anyone who cared to listen that something was desperately wrong.

In the event the free-fall continued. Part of the responsibility lay with the Labour government, which was slow to recognise the intensity of the cash squeeze that it had imposed on British industry. Nor was it disposed to pay attention to messages relayed by the financial markets, where the low level of share prices made it virtually impossible for most companies to raise fresh equity capital. The extent of the government's failure to grasp what was happening was underlined in September when the Chancellor Denis Healey announced that there was 'no evidence of any serious liquidity problem in industry'. The electronics firm Ferranti promptly foundered; British Leyland was soon to follow.

Equally important, many investment institutions feared that they were on the brink of insolvency. This was particularly true of the composite insurance companies. While their life funds frequently went on investing in equities, the general funds were selling shares, mainly because they were required by law to maintain an adequate surplus of assets over liabilities; this surplus is expressed as a percentage of their annual premium income.

In normal times, insurance companies do not like to let the surplus slip below 40% of premiums (well above the statutory minimum now set by the European Community, which is about 16% for most companies); at that level they could take on £10-worth of business for every £4 of capital. The 40% figure, known as the margin of solvency, provides a cushion against unexpected risks. In 1974 solvency margins throughout the insurance sector were being squeezed on two fronts. Premiums were rising because of inflation (people were having to pay more, for example, to insure against the inflated cost of rebuilding a home that burned down); and asset values were falling because of the collapse in the world's stock markets. As Commercial Union director John Linbourn pointed out to me, if a company's investment in equity shares is equivalent to twice its total share capital and reserves, the equities have only to halve in value to wipe out the company. Commercial Union and other leading British insurers had rather less invested in equities than that, but they still felt obliged to sell shares to protect themselves against a further fall in the stock market and to look for other means of bolstering their solvency margin.

Commercial Union's predicament was more exteme than most. In a dash to raise cash it sold 80% of its head office property in the City for £66 million, partly to a consortium consisting of Legal and General (whose business was primarily in life assurance and pensions) and the pension funds of the Post Office and British Rail, partly to the oil-rich Abu Dhabi Investment Board. Then, in the autumn, Commercial Union sold 40% of every United States common stock holding in its portfolio, causing an outcry on Wall Street where prices were depressed by the sales. Finally, after its attempt to boost its solvency margin by bidding £75 million for St Martins Property Corporation was thwarted by a counterbid from the Kuwait Investment Office, the big insurance company asked its shareholders to put up £62½ million of new capital. Without this cash call, its solvency margin would have fallen below 20%. This was above the legally permitted minimum, but most insurers regard 20% as the bottom limit of financial probity.

Other types of institution were similarly agitated about their finances. Unit trusts felt a need to build up their cash balances in case unit holders started to withdraw their money. Banks liquidated investments because they were worried that depositors would take out their money. Yet while these actions appeared to make sense from the point of view of individual investment institutions, the logic behind them was circular when looked at from the point of view of the institutions as a group. The further share prices fell, the more the institutions would feel a need to sell to protect themselves. Their own selling would then depress prices further. If the biggest buyers, the life funds and pension funds, lost their nerve and stopped mopping up everyone else's shares, there was a risk that the plunge would become self-perpetuating.

The final ingredient in any 'bear' market is fear. And in 1974 there was much for the institutions to be fearful about. For a start, the British banking system was close to collapse. Earlier in the decade, at the behest of the Heath government, the Bank of England had set in train a reform of the banking system. In a consultative document called *Competition and Credit Control,* published in May 1971, the Bank suggested that the previous system of monetary control, which put direct quantitative ceilings on bank lending, should be scrapped. The Bank proposed instead to control lending indirectly by requiring banks to comply with pre-ordained balance sheet ratios and by having them make special deposits with the Bank of England itself. Together with a number of other measures, these proposals were put into practice in September, 1971.

The new system proved disastrous. Between 1971 and the end of 1973 there was a rapid acceleration in bank lending. New money markets sprang into being as credit expanded. And a group of young, thrusting merchant banks, known as 'secondary' or 'fringe' banks, grabbed a growing share of banking business. The secondary banks obtained their deposits mainly from the money markets in the City – markets where banks, companies and financial institutions put their cash out at interest overnight, for a week, for a month, or for longer periods. They then lent much of this volatile, short term money to financial and property groups that were investing in longer term assets like property developments, which can take years to complete and let to tenants, or shares in medium and small sized companies, which cannot easily be sold in a falling market.

Under the new system the Bank of England was not technically responsible for regulating all the fringe banks. It operated a hierarchical system of control whereby the banks gave the Bank of England more information about the state of their finances in exchange for the freedom to do business in the different markets supervised by the Bank.

One flaw in this arrangement was that the Bank regulated less and less of the banking system as new banks and new markets sprang up on the back of the wave of monetary expansion in 1971–73. An Alice in Wonderland system prevailed whereby the bigger and more reputable the bank was, the more closely it was monitored. Another flaw was that the subtle distinction applied by the Department of Trade and the Bank of England to different kinds of banking businesses were entirely lost on the general public, and even on many more sophisticated members of the financial community. This was particularly true of secondary banks that had been granted a certificate under section 123 of the 1967 Companies Act, which exempted them from some of the more onerous provisions of the moneylenders acts. While they were not allowed to call themselves 'banks', there was nothing to stop them describing themselves in their title as 'bankers'.

These weaknesses of control were exposed when London and County Securities, which numbered the then Liberal leader Jeremy Thorpe among its directors, suffered a run on its deposits. From London and County, the crisis of confidence spread to Cedar Holdings (Bankers) – which was not in fact a fully-fledged 'bank' in the private language of the Bank of England – and to smaller financial groups like Cornhill Consolidated and Moorgate

Mercantile. Subsequently it spread to Cannon Street Investments, Triumph Investment Trust, First National Finance Corporation, Keyser Ullmann and numerous others. Although the Bank of England had set up a joint 'lifeboat' committee with the clearing banks, whose job was to pump money back into the secondary banks as deposits were withdrawn and to reorganise or wind down individual banks, confidence did not return. Financial institutions and others ceased to renew their deposits with the big finance houses, UDT, Mercantile Credit and Bowmaker. The Crown Agents, a semi-official government body, became insolvent as several of its investments in secondary and tertiary banks, and in speculative property ventures, turned out to be worthless.[5] Each government department that dealt with the Crown Agents had assumed that the other departments were responsible for supervising its financial activities.

This severe domestic financial crisis naturally played on the nerves of the investment managers of insurance companies and pension funds as well as the merchant banks and stockbrokers who helped invest their money. For most, at one time or another, had put money on deposit with fringe banks. And if the heavily-flawed system of bank regulation had opened the door for the expansion of the fringe banks, the insurance companies and especially the pension funds could claim much credit for propelling fringe bankers through the door and beyond. In 1969, for example, the Electricity Supply Industry pension fund joined with merchant bankers Robert Fleming and the Crown Agents in pumping large amounts of new capital into Pat Matthews's First National Finance Corporation. In the 1970s the National Westminster Bank pension fund (whose parent was chief banker to First National) subscribed for a large chunk of convertible loan stock in First National's investment trust off-shoot, Direct Spanish Telegraph; the holding was equivalent to 12% of the trust's equity capital on conversion of the loans. The electricity pension fund's other investments in fringe banking included large stakes in Cedar Holdings, which had also been backed by the pension funds of Unilever and the National Coal Board and by Phoenix Assurance.

At Tom Whyte's Triumph Investment Trust, the Courtaulds pension fund provided much of the capital for expansion in the 1960s, while the ICI pension fund put up money to finance property deals for the same financial group in the 1970s. The pension fund of Britain's biggest manufacturer was one of the more active financiers of the secondary banking sector: in the mid-1960s the ICI fund had taken a large stake in the (subsequently much-troubled) Rodo Investment Trust, run by French-born financier John Gommes, and had also been a backer, alongside the electricity fund, of Jack Dellal's Dalton Barton Securities while this fringe financial outfit was still a private company. Meantime Prudential Insurance helped increase the capital of Keyser Ullmann, which subsequently swallowed Dalton Barton, and the big insurance company also acquired more than a quarter of the ordinary share capital of United Dominions Trust when the stock market was close to its peak in 1972.

As for London and County, it had enjoyed the support of the United Drapery Stores (UDS) group pension fund, which subscribed for 22% of the ordinary capital just before it was floated. London and County was involved with UDS itself in operating banks inside UDS's stores. (More surprisingly, London and County's property dealing activities had been financed to the tune of £590,000 by the Staffordshire-based Leek and Westbourne Building Society.)

A handful of top pension funds and insurance companies had, then, played a crucial part in building up this small group of secondary banks that together made a very large dent in the British banking system when they collapsed in 1974. And they could not escape all responsibility for having done so. Where it was able to, the Bank of England manoeuvred them into putting large sums into the rescue of banks they had backed. Their confidence was further impaired when three big property companies, William Stern's Wilstar Securities, the Lyon Group and Guardian Properties, crashed at about the same time, leaving the many insurance companies, pension funds and banks that had backed them financially exposed.

There was more concern when two fair-sized broking firms, Mitton, Butler, Priest and Chapman and Rowe, went out of business. (Bizarrely, partners' share dealings at Chapman and Rowe had been financed by the Moscow Narodny Bank; this outpost of Russian state capitalism in the City had backed several highly speculative ventures in finance and property which turned sour in 1974.)

Insurance companies that had sold guaranteed income bonds were also in trouble. As interest rates rose throughout the year, investors cashed in their existing bonds and took out new ones elsewhere at a higher guaranteed return; companies which had failed to invest in assets that exactly matched the commitment to pay up on surrender of the policies, included Welfare Insurance, which had, among other things, advanced money personally to Jim Slater, and Jessel Securities' subsidiary London Indemnity and General Insurance, whose difficulties brought about the collapse of Oliver Jessel's shaky financial empire.

No one was immune from the effects of the general panic. On Wednesday, 30 July, Prudential Assurance, Britain's biggest private sector financial institution, the very symbol of solidity, probity and power in British finance, saw its share price collapse 10% in the space of the morning. The bear raid was partly sparked off by the difficulties of UDT, in which the insurance company had a 26% stake. In November, it was the turn of National Westminster Bank, which had lent more than most to ailing financial and property companies. The bank's shares sank below par (face value), and Sir John Prideaux, the chairman, was forced into an unprecedented public statement in which he denied that the bank's liquidity was under pressure. To many institutional investors it seemed as if capitalism was on its last legs and that the conspiratorial Left, with industry secretary Anthony Wedgwood Benn in the vanguard, had set up the new state-owned National Enterprise Board expressly to gather in the corporate ninepins as they came tumbling down. Outside the City, there were plenty of people who thought that the values of a property-owning liberal democracy were imperilled. Former military officers with quirky political views organised private armies whose every move was chronicled at length, and from different points of view, in the pages of the *Guardian* and the *Daily Telegraph*.

It was, in the end, the Labour Chancellor Denis Healey who put capitalism back on its feet. Before the February election, Healey had promised, in a memorable phrase, to squeeze the rich until the pips squeaked. Then, in his first budget, he assured himself a permanent place in the rogues' gallery of the Right by raising income tax to a penal top rate of 98% and by launching his assault on corporate liquidity. But the Chancellor also had the ability – mercifully for British industry and those employed in it – to change his mind. In November Healey introduced for companies a crude but effective form of relief from tax on stock appreciation. Price controls and restraints on bank lending were relaxed. For the rest of the Labour government's term of office, the manufacturing sector enjoyed a tax holiday as never before.[6]

Healey's November mini-budget paved the way for a stock market recovery and set the pattern for the rest of his chancellorship. For those who could read the signals, private ownership of capital was no longer a lost cause under the Labour government. Thereafter Denis Healey arguably fought a better rearguard action for the rich and for investors, institutional or otherwise, than any other holder of the chancellor's office since the war.[7] Yet in the panicky atmosphere of November 1974 few professional money managers saw Healey's measures for what they were. The insurance companies, then still the biggest investors in the stock market, were particularly nervous and in the final quarter of the year their long term funds sold no less than £60 million-worth of ordinary shares.

In Whitehall there was one government minister who did follow financial markets closely – Harold (now Lord) Lever, a genial and intellectually unorthodox financier who was Chancellor of the Duchy of Lancaster and special financial adviser to Harold Wilson. As the year progressed he became so convinced that share prices had fallen too far that he even tried to persuade his civil servants to put every spare penny they had into shares, with the caveat that they should be in companies that had no dealings with the government. Most, he told me, were faintly shocked. Lever also felt that there was a case for government intervention in the stock market. For years he had been keen on the idea of a government-sponsored unit trust to encourage wider ownership of equity shares in British industry. But he had hesitated to push it, partly because the government would risk being accused of selling the voters a pup if its own financial institution were launched when the market was high.

When the FT industrial ordinary index fell below 160, Lever decided that there was no risk at all that the voters would come away with anything but a bargain-basement price for their investment. He put his suggestion for a state unit trust to the Prime

Minister, Harold Wilson, pointing out that the government had a ready-made retail outlet in the Post Office, whose branches could sell the units over the counter. The government would buy an initial stock of several million pounds-worth of shares which would then be put into a trust whose units would be sold to individual investors. The attraction of the idea was that the trust would not only raise share prices through its own buying activity; it would also help break the vicious circle of uniformly pessimistic expectations among the institutions, who would see that the government could hardly risk selling equity shares to the public if it expected them to go down further. Once share prices were restored to more sensible levels, industrialists might be tempted to invest directly in plant and machinery. For there would be less opportunity to buy existing plant and machinery on the cheap by means of takeover bids in the stock market.

Harold Wilson's response to Lever's nostrum was sympathetic. And since the case for a state unit trust had long been argued by Anthony Crosland and other members of the reformist right wing of the Labour party, the idea looked capable of attracting a measure of political support. The plan (which was never made public) proved too unorthodox, however, for the Whitehall bureaucracy, which put up a barrage of objections. In the end the civil servants deprived British working men and women of the chance to grab the greatest investment bargain of the century through a government-sponsored investment institution. What the City would have made of this curious mixture of state intervention and popular capitalism in the highly-charged political atmosphere of 1974 is impossible to gauge. But it is worth noting that an earlier similar attempt by the Japanese government to prop up the Tokyo market had met with success.

There were some in the private sector who shared Lever's view that share prices had fallen too far. As the end of the insurance companies' financial year came closer, the two top investment men at the Prudential, Peter Moody and Edward Hatchett, started to ask whether the institutions could, or should, bring their enormous buying power into play to support the market. They felt that institutional investors had allowed share prices to become needlessly depressed, in view of the government's apparent change of heart in the November mini-budget, and of the recent downturn in world interest rates. They were also worried about the effects on the financial system of the downward plunge in the stock market, as the selling pressure from the institutions became self-feeding.

If any institution was well-equipped to lead a stock market rescue, it was the Prudential. Yet the idea of supporting the market was a surprising one to come from the heart of the insurance establishment, not least because it involved discussing investment policy with the company's competitors. If word leaked out, the Prudential might be accused of rigging the market. And the historical precedents were not encouraging. In October 1929, a group of New York's most powerful banks, led by J. P. Morgan, had tried to prop up Wall Street's collapsing market by placing several million dollars-worth of orders for ordinary stock. Although they announced their intention publicly, they succeeded in stabilising the market only for a couple of days before prices plummeted downwards again, leaving the bankers publicly embarrassed and financially over-committed.

The pros and cons were heatedly debated at high level in the Prudential; some thought an attempt to support the market would achieve nothing. There was also a risk that if word leaked out that someone was trying to support the market, others would grab the opportunity to sell as much stock as possible while the going was good. But in the end the directors agreed to let Moody and Hatchett go ahead. In the second week of December a group of top investment managers from Legal and General, Commercial Union and Sun Alliance, were invited to discuss the state of the economy and the stock market over lunch at the Prudential's head office in High Holborn.

According to Peter Moody, most of those present agreed that the market was too gloomy and in the course of the lunch the men from the Prudential suggested that each institution should put £5 million into the market, starting in mid-December. There was to be no publicity, but the jobbers could be relied on to detect that the buying was coming from some of the best names in the market.

Accounts of both the lunch, and what happened after it, vary. John Linbourn of Commercial Union told me that his company had already started buying equities and that the lunch simply reinforced its existing intentions. The Prudential certainly put £5 million into the market, while Sun Alliance admits to having put £5-10 million mainly into less marketable stocks outside Britain's top 100 companies; these were likely to respond more readily to buying pressure from a single institution. Legal and General, according to its chief investment manager Peter Simon, did not regard itself as being involved in any hard and fast agreement to support the market. His recollection is that people went away from the Prudential and did different things. What is clear is that the buying orders placed as a result of the meeting at the Prudential did not stabilise the market. Although the FT all-share index staged a mild recovery in the ten days before Christmas, the FT industrial ordinary index, covering thirty leading shares, continued to fall throughout the month; there was some disappointment among the institutions who bought.

The market finally picked itself off the floor in January 1975. After it had risen fast and furiously for three weeks, the *Investors Chronicle* got wind of a meeting between the institutions and published an article attributing the sharp rise to organised institutional buying.[8] In fact none of those involved believes that the institutions' rescue attempt triggered the rise. It was impossible, anyway, says Moody, for institutions of their size to buy shares when the market started to soar in the second week in January. The most he claims for the institutions is that they cleared much of the loose stock in the market out of the way, so that when the market lurched upwards, there was not enough selling pressure to put a brake on the rise.

The turn in the market could not have been harder to judge. On 31 December 1974, fund managers were shaken by an announcement that Burmah Oil, in which most major funds and countless widows and orphans held shares, was in trouble. No one in the City had expected the news (least of all the unhappy City Editor of the *Daily Telegraph*, whose column that morning had contained a glowing tribute to Burmah's management). It appeared as though a wave of corporate collapses might be imminent. Yet immediately after the FT ordinary index touched 146.0 on 6 January, 1975 institutional buyers started to emerge for reasons that no one has since been able to explain. By the end of January the FT industrial ordinary index had reached 236.9, to show a phenomenal rise of over 62% in just over three weeks. By the end of February it had more than doubled to 301.8. The more optimistic institutions were having difficulty buying stock since prices kept racing ahead of them; the jobbers accelerated the upward movement as they adjusted their books to cope with the first buying boom in months. It was the start of the sharpest bull market within living memory and a salutary lesson for most of the fund managers who thought they could outguess the stock market indices.

The most conspicuously flat-footed of the institutions were, once again, the insurance companies. In the first quarter of 1975, their long term funds sold nearly £30 million more ordinary shares than they bought. Quickest off the mark as buyers were the unit trusts and the private sector pension funds. Between them they bought over £220 million-worth of shares in the first three months of the year, thanks, in the case of many pension funds, to the good offices of their merchant bank and stockbroking advisers.

In 1975 the institutions completed the second half of the rescue that had been set in train by Denis Healey's November mini-budget. In the years 1975, 1976 and 1977, as the market rose, investors put up more than £2½ billion of new equity capital for British industry and commerce. During those three years, private individuals made net sales of more than £4 billion-worth of company securities; it is probably safe to assume that a majority of the new capital came from institutions.

In 1974 the corporate sector had borrowed heavily from the banking system (where the institutions had deposited their spiralling cash balances) to finance the inflationary increases in the value of its stocks and debtors. Against that background the rights issues had a significant effect on industry's solvency, which is measured by relating companies' net assets to their borrowings in a 'debt-equity' ratio; if the ratio goes too high lenders can call in their loans, renegotiate the terms or ask for a receiver to be appointed if the company cannot comply. As a rough indication of what industry's finances might have looked like without the additional capital, removing £2½ billion from the share capital, reserves and minorities of the 729 listed companies in the Department of Trade's balance sheet survey for 1977 would raise the average ratio of debt to equity from 36% to 48%. If insurance companies and banks featured heavily in the queue to raise money, this reflected their continuing fear about solvency margins. And, unlike industry, they had not received any tax relief against the effects of inflation on their own (monetary) working capital.

The institutions, then, were protecting their investment in industry and commerce by subscribing new capital, and their resolve was no doubt strengthened, in the case of insurance and pension funds, by the thought that their own companies might want to join the queue. They were encouraged in this by the Treasury, which had discretionary power to bend dividend controls when rights issues took place.

Who suffered most as a result of the investment institutions' earlier failure to keep equities afloat in 1974? The biggest sellers in the market, when prices were at their lowest level for two decades, were private investors: their net disposals of company securities during the year amounted to £1.2 billion. But if the official statistics are any guide, private investors did not sell at the very bottom. In the final quarter of 1974 they were net buyers of company securities for the first and only time in the 1970s. It was the professional investors who lost their nerve in the final giddy plunge – the life insurance companies, the investment trusts (which sold more heavily and consistently throughout the year than any of the other institutions), the private sector pension funds and the unit trusts. All sold more shares than they bought in the final quarter.[9]

But the several billions of pounds that were wiped off the value of equity shares in the bear market of 1974 were not lost in any absolute sense. In the stock market, one man's loss is another man's profit. And 1974 was one of the greatest years for bargain-hunting that the stock market has ever seen.

The identity of the biggest group of successful bargain-hunters can be gleaned from official statistics. Overseas investors – doubtless including several from the OPEC countries that had helped destabilise world share markets in the first place – bought just over £1 billion-worth of company securities in 1974, almost as much as private individuals sold. The heaviest buying was recorded in the last quarter of the year.[10] Even allowing for any element of unreliability in the figures, it seems that British investment institutions paved the way for the oil sheikhs to pull off the biggest stock market coup of the decade.

3
Investors or owners?

'Possession without obligation to the object possessed
approaches felicity.'

George Meredith, *The Egoist*

IN DEPLOYING THEIR CASH the pension funds' and life assurance companies' chief concern has always been to achieve the best
possible return for pensioners and policyholders. As long as these
institutions controlled only a small proportion of the nation's
savings it hardly mattered, from a wider economic point of view,
how they went about the job. What emerged from the chaotic
events of 1974, however, was that the pension funds and insurance companies had reached a size where they could no longer go
innocently about their own business without having a profound
influence on everyone else.

Apart from portfolio investors, the people most heavily affected
by the institutions' failure to maintain their appetite for equity
shares in 1974 were the managers of quoted companies in industry
and commerce, for whom the level of share prices in the stock
market affects the availability of equity capital and the price at
which businesses can be bought and sold.

So peculiar was the combination of circumstances that led to
most companies being deprived of ready access to risk capital in
1974, and so traumatic the experience for the institutions, that
fund managers will probably contrive to prevent a repeat performance in the foreseeable future. But industrialists continue to
be affected in other ways by many of the same institutional attitudes that led to the excessive slide in prices. Even though the
institutions control well over half the shares of all quoted companies and buy most of the shares that come onto the market, the
more traditional among them still see themselves as investors,

whose responsibility to industry does not extend much beyond buying and selling shares in individual companies, rather than owners, who retain shares for the long term and hold industrialists accountable for their management of assets which belong to others. Is this really the most sensible way for financial institutions to behave towards the quoted companies in which they invest?

Not in the view of one powerful group of critics whose arguments carried weight with the Heath government of 1970–74 and continue to affect thinking on both sides of the House of Commons today. If insurance companies and pension funds could only be persuaded to use their voting power to help revitalise the management of big inefficient companies, runs their argument, British industry might come closer to matching the levels of productivity seen in faster-growing Western economies like West Germany, where banks exert considerable influence over industrial management because they exercise voting power on behalf of their shareowning customers.

The institutions are reluctant, however, to be treated as unpaid national enterprise boards. Unlike politicians, for whom the exercise of power carries its own justification and reward, fund managers tend to regard their own effortless inheritance as an unwelcome by-product of the job. Neither temperament nor experience equips them to fill the gap left by the disappearing owner-manager in an age of giant corporations. And even those who are tempted by the idea of direct intervention in industry are inhibited because their power can rarely be exercised without painful repercussions around the City.

Many industrialists act as non-executive directors of insurance companies; it is not easy for an insurance company's fund manager to ginger up the management of an industrial company whose chairman sits on his own board.[1] Industry also gives valuable business to insurers, so unwelcome intervention in the affairs of a client company could well encourage the client to take his business to another insurer. As for the merchant banks, many complain that insurance companies constantly side with client companies in takeover bids. Yet merchant banks, too, can use the voting power they enjoy by virtue of managing pension fund investments to support their own company clients. They are similarly inhibited when it comes to intervening in badly managed companies. A reputation for meddling in industry would rapidly sour their relationship with sensitive corporate clients.

The stultifying effect of these connections partly explains why institutions have been so slow to ginger up industrial management in the past. And a less overwhelming set of City connections among the larger pension funds helps explain why they have been more aggressive interventionists than other institutional shareholders. This is particularly true where nationalised industry pension funds are concerned. Public sector pension funds, of which the state industry funds are the biggest, controlled investments worth more than £13 billion at the beginning of 1980. This is less than the sum handled by the private sector pension funds, but investment management of nationalised industry funds is less often delegated to stockbrokers and merchant bankers, and the money is more heavily concentrated in few hands. So the managers of the top six public sector pension funds below, which probably accounted for over two-thirds of the total public sector pension fund investments (apart from local authorities) and nearly 15% of the total annual cash flow of life assurance companies and pension funds at the turn of the decade, are in a position to wield disproportionate influence.[2]

	Fund £m	Cash flow £m
Post Office	2.448	472
National Coal Board	2.042	204
British Rail	1.525	179
Electricity Supply Industry	1.315	151
British Steel	970	164
British Gas	665	86

Some, like the Post Office pension fund, do have well-known City names on the board of trustees, and delegate part of the investment management. The merchant banks that are fortunate enough to advise the Post Office fund are J. Henry Schroder Wagg, S. G. Warburg and Morgan Grenfell. At others, outside influence is more limited, which opens the door to more assertive (and sometimes more risky) investment policies than the average merchant bank would normally pursue.

The public sector pension fund investment manager does not enjoy complete freedom, however. Apart from the restrictions imposed by his trust deed and by trustee law generally, the manager is inhibited by an important bureaucratic constraint. Anything that causes a nationalised industry chairman public embarrassment, or which provokes a parliamentary row that rebounds on him is likely to lead to a change of job for the man who causes the embarrassment. There are similar pressures in the private sector, where the pension fund manager who damages the company's image or gives the chairman a sleepless night could find himself out on the street. Pension fund managers in both the public and private sector are often employed by the company, not the pension fund. Their claim to act independently on behalf of beneficiaries has to be seen in that light.

No conflicting interest or bureaucratic constraint is as inhibiting, however, as the belief still held by many, that a falling share price exercises an adequate discipline on company management (because it leaves the company vulnerable to an unwelcome takeover) and that direct involvement in the affairs of the companies they own is potentially harmful to the beneficiaries' interests.

Once an investment institution starts discussing a company's problems with the management, runs the argument, it becomes privy to inside information – facts and figures which could be expected to influence the share price if they were publicised. The investment institution then forfeits its right to sell the company's shares, even where the fund manager believes that it would be in the beneficiaries' interest to do so, because it cannot deal on inside information, a practice that recently became a criminal offence under the 1980 Companies Act. The beneficiaries then sustain a loss, if the share price falls, which could have been avoided if the institution had kept the company at arm's length.

The idea that the beneficiaries' interests are best satisfied by adopting this narrow approach rests heavily on two assumptions. One is that investment managers are able to sell the shares in the companies whose share prices are about to fall. The other is that fund managers are capable of out-guessing the market and identifying potentially troubled companies before their share prices fully reflect the problems that they face. Neither assumption necessarily holds true in a stock market dominated by institutions.

The investment institutions, as we have seen, are the chief buyers of ordinary shares in British industry. If they wish to sell, who is to buy their shares? In practice, any institution that tries to sell out of a company that runs into trouble will be lucky to find a buyer except among its fellow institutions. So the institutions cannot, as a group, run away from the responsibilities of ownership. If they try, as many did in 1974, the attempt is self-defeating.

As for beating the market, a handful of institutions may be capable of outperforming the stock market indices consistently through active share dealing. But the institutions cannot, as a group, outperform a market in which they constitute a majority. Most investment managers who trade actively in the shares of their existing portfolios are doing little more than shuffle the returns on equity investment from one set of beneficiaries to another. If the whole group of institutions steps up its dealing activity, the chief effect is to give a fatter profit to the middlemen of the stock market – brokers, jobbers and (via stamp duty) the government – at the expense of beneficiaries.[3]

This goes some way towards explaining why a recent survey of pension fund investment returns in both the public and private sectors by actuaries Bacon and Woodrow, found that a majority had failed to outperform the FT-Actuaries all-share index over a number of years. But the survey also showed that no single investment manager had consistently outperformed his rivals; nor was there any correlation between the size of the fund, the level of its cash flow, or the type of manager (merchant bank, stockbroker or internal manager), and its performance.[4]

Similarly unimpressive results appear to emerge from confidential, unpublished performance figures collated by Derbyshire County Council for local authority pension funds. This survey shows each local authority fund's results under an anonymous number. The idea is that each authority can compare its performance with all the others, without anyone knowing who the others are (a system perfectly designed, incidentally, to protect the incompetent from public pressure to perform well). The returns show that some local authorities turn over shares in their existing portfolios at up to three times the rate they invest their cash income in new shares – and to little purpose. In the 1978 return, for example, only eight out of seventy-eight local authority pension funds managed to outperform the market indices, and the worst performers included many of the more frenetic dealers. The cost of poor performance here may ultimately fall on the ratepayer.

Where the level of share trading is concerned, the interest of the industrialist may conflict with that of the beneficiaries. For if pension fund managers were suddenly to become more sceptical about their own ability to beat the market and restricted their activities simply to investing new money as it flowed in, industry might be deprived of the stable and fairly priced flow of new capital that an active market in existing shares helps guarantee. Institutional share dealing could probably be scaled down dramatically, however, before the market became unduly thin. One of the more startling findings of the Wilson committee was that the average period over which insurance companies and pension funds held their shares had fallen from around twenty-four years in 1963–67 to eight years for insurance companies and six years for pension funds in 1973–77.[5] Admittedly the second period took in the freakish circumstances of 1974; it also took in a higher rate of inflation, which forces investors to shorten their time horizon. But it remains astonishing that the transfer of a huge part of the nation's savings from individuals to genuinely long term professional investors should have been accompanied by such a switch towards short term dealing activity.

Interestingly, levels of share dealing are higher among private sector and local authority pension funds than among nationalised industry pension funds and insurance companies. Is it merely coincidence that merchant banks and stockbrokers, who stand to gain financially from a high level of dealing in the portfolios they manage, are particularly strongly represented in the management of private sector and local authority pension funds? How closely, one wonders, are pension fund trustees monitoring their fund managers' share dealing activities? And to what extent is this preoccupation with the short term reinforced by the use of excessively narrow criteria for performance measurement? Fund managers who are judged by their ability to outperform either the stockmarket indices or their fellow pension funds have a powerful incentive to grab the bird in hand. They are an easy target for the corporate predator intent on a takeover bid, or a 'dawn raid' in which the predator rapidly acquires a large stake in another company by approaching a limited number of institutions with a seemingly attractive offer for their shares. But how else is investment performance to be measured? If a plausible alternative exists, it has yet to attract the attention it deserves.

Among the larger insurance companies and pension funds there is a growing awareness that professional investors cannot continue to keep industry at arms' length. John Linbourn of Commercial Union, for example, told me:

> We are not interested in trying to second-guess the market. When funds are as large as ours, the chances of beating the index by a substantial amount are close to nil. The dealing costs are such that it is more likely that too much trading will result in underperformance. Although we do sell from time to time, we prefer to stick with investments – we are long term investors in the life fund. So it obviously makes sense to intervene instead of dumping stock in these circumstances. Too much can however be expected of this involvement. The trouble is that we don't know anything about widgets. The most we can hope for is to influence a widget-making company to try to make sure that they have people that do.

The Prudential is also committed to closer involvement with the companies in which it invests. As Britain's biggest investment institution it is more than usually conscious of the practical difficulty of selling shares in companies that are going downhill and is less wary than some of confronting industrial management. The first recorded example of the Prudential standing up to a board of directors was at Birmingham Small Arms, the Midlands engineering concern run by the flamboyant Sir Bernard Docker, in the 1950s. Largely as a result of the Prudential's intervention, Sir Bernard lost his job and a tremor went through boardrooms around the country.

Since then the Prudential has been involved in most of the better-known cases of institutional intervention, including those at Vickers, the big engineering group, in the early 1970s, at Fodens, the lorry manufacturer in 1975 and at steel group Dunford and Elliott in 1977. At any given moment, I was told by Peter Moody shortly before he retired as the Prudential's chief investment manager at the end of 1980, the giant insurance group expects to have up to half a dozen equity investments that call for some direct involvement; only rarely does this activity reach the newspapers. It sees the management of all the 600-odd companies in which it invests at least once, often twice a year, and hopes to establish the kind of relationship that will encourage management to make early contact with the Pru in the event of financial trouble.

The Prudential and the Commercial Union are in the vanguard, however, and many fund managers prefer to cling to past orthodoxies. And while the Wilson committee commented on 'an impressive degree of unanimity' in the evidence it received on the desirability of institutions taking an active interest in companies whose shares they held, some of the evidence to the committee was, at best, lukewarm. The British Insurance Association (BIA), for example, declared that it could see no theoretical reason why insurance companies should shoulder any direct responsibility for the companies in which they invested. The most the BIA would concede was that 'practical considerations demanded a broader view'.

Throughout the 1970s leading insurance companies, in fact, fought doggedly against attempts to prod them into less passive share ownership. When Sir Leslie O'Brien, the Governor of the Bank of England, tried in the early 1970s to set up an institutional ginger group to identify companies that were running into difficulty and initiate changes on behalf of the institutional shareholders, he was firmly rebuffed by a majority of the insurance companies. Only a race of super-managers, they felt, would be capable of doing the job, and they argued that the publicity that the committee would attract, if it poked its nose into the affairs of individual companies, would be damaging. The governor was forced to retreat from his original suggestion. What finally emerged under the title of the Institutional Shareholders' Committee, after a protracted and secret debate, was an emasculated organisation, lacking any proper secretariat or research staff. The bodies representing the four major institutional groups (insurance, pensions, investment trusts and unit trusts) are members, and where more than one group has a significant interest in a problem, the case is dutifully referred to the committee for joint action.

The Bank of England suffered a similar rebuff in the second half of the 1970s when it pressed the idea of a new investment intermediary: an equity fund, designed to channel institutional cash into the hands of companies that were assumed to be having difficulty raising new capital on reasonable terms. This idea originated in the Central Policy Review Staff (the government's 'think tank'), where the putative equity bank was initially known as the

British Industrial Finance Fund, or BIF for short. As well as providing a way of channelling money into small and medium sized companies that were having difficulty raising equity capital, it was seen as a possible vehicle for financing very long term investments in areas such as high technology where a lack of income in the early years acted as a deterrent to the stock market. Other possible functions for the fund included identifying potential lame ducks (the Rolls-Royces, British Leylands and Alfred Herberts of the future), intervening on behalf of institutional shareholders and monitoring performance.

The idea was then taken over by the Bank of England, which set out to sell it to the institutions under a new name, Equity Capital for Industry. But the Bank was only able to dragoon the institutions into supporting the fund at the cost of jettisoning its more innovative functions.

When it was finally launched in 1976, Equity Capital for Industry looked like a bureaucratic response to the last crisis but one. Its first big investment in a financially troubled company, the carpet group Bond Worth, was disastrous; the company went into receivership within the year. By the end of the decade, its own managers were arguing that it was trying to plug a gap that did not exist; more than half its capital was sitting on deposit at the bank. The experiment generated remarkable heat for an investment that absorbed less than 1% of the insurance companies' and pension funds' combined cash inflow in the year of the flotation.

Despite the increasing pressure to establish closer relations with industry, many fund managers remained obsessively concerned with the need to preserve their right to sell shares in the market even in the second half of the 1970s. The National Association of Pension Funds, which represents most of the larger occupational pension schemes, pointed out to the Wilson Committee that the collapse of share prices in 1974 had caused many of its members to pull in their horns:

> There is emphasis now on investing in companies with a proven track record and financial strength. This has tended to result in investment in those companies with a large market capitalisation. There is a natural tendency to avoid investing in those companies where one may become 'locked in', given a marked change in prospects.[6]

This preoccupation can be seen more directly in the investment policy of some of the largest funds. George Dennis, investment manager of the Post Office pension fund, told the Wilson committee that 'we cannot own more than 5% of the total issued capital of any one company, and no more than 5% of the portfolio can be invested in companies with a market capitalisation of less than £20 million . . . ideally no investment in the UK will be less than £100,000.' In late 1977 when this remark was made, these criteria would have eliminated well over half the companies quoted on the stock exchange from the Post Office fund's portfolio, and heavily limited investment in a further quarter of the market.

Most institutions set similar parameters on the size of their investments in relation both to the company in which they invest and to their overall portfolio. Since investment management is increasingly narrowly concentrated in the hands of a small number of insurance companies, pension funds and merchant banks, the rigid application of these percentage limits leads institutional money to chase large companies at the expense of small. The dice then become loaded against the Marks and Spencers and ICIs of the future, for whom access to equity capital is made more difficult.

Smaller companies could equally find themselves at risk, however, if more institutional fund managers abandoned their preoccupation with marketability and decided to build up larger stakes in individual businesses. The dangers inherent in this approach can be seen by looking at the investment policy of Britannic Assurance, one of two major insurance groups based in Birmingham (the other is Wesleyan and General).

Britannic, which manages investments worth more than £500 million, started life in 1866 as the British Workman's Mutual Assurance Company. It still has a big industrial – that is, door to door home collection – life assurance business and it prides itself on having been the first industrial life company to give workers a contractual right to a surrender value on its policies, and on having employed Philip Snowden, the disastrously ineffectual pre-war Labour Chancellor of the Exchequer, as an agent. Unlike many institutions, Britannic is willing to build up big shareholdings in small companies and at the end of the 1970s, it held more than 5% of the capital of over eighty individual companies. In several cases these stakes amounted to more than 10% and occasionally more than 20%. And Britannic's grip on the companies is tighter than at first appears, because it also manages the investments of its own pension fund, together with a quoted investment trust, the Midland Trust. These, too, invest in some of the same companies in which the insurance company itself has large stakes. Britannic's views therefore carry disproportionate weight in takeovers affecting these companies – which brings us to another unusual feature of its investment policy: it opposes on principle virtually all hostile takeover bids for companies in which it invests.

At first sight this distaste for takeovers seems unobjectionable, even attractive, in a country where Conservative governments have shown only half-hearted interest in competition policy and Labour administrations have actively encouraged monopolistic industrial concentration through agencies like the IRC and the NEB. Britannic's recently retired chairman John Jefferson was also an outspoken champion of the small company in a decade when the odds were heavily stacked in favour of the big: Britannic did not hesitate, for example, to cock a snook at GEC by announcing publicly, at an early stage in the electrical giant's (in the event, successful) takeover pursuit of weighing machine makers, Averys, that it would prefer to preserve the existing management.

But consider the wider implications. A considerable number of the eighty or so companies in which Britannic has a disproportionately large influence are in the West Midlands. And the West Midlands contain a fair share of Britain's declining industries, some of which are represented in Britannic's portfolio. What encouragement does the presence of an institution committed to rejecting aggressive takeover bids give to management to confront problems of decline?

The judgement of Britannic's managers on individual companies, however good, cannot be infallible. And to whom are they accountable? Nearly 10% of the Birmingham insurance group, which has itself been the subject of frequent takeover rumours, is owned by its own pension fund – a practice that many pension fund managers regard as bordering on incest. Nearly 6% of the capital is owned by the Manchester-based Refuge Assurance, another provincial company with a big industrial business, in which Britannic has a 7% cross-holding. Other independent institutions hold Britannic shares, but it is almost unheard of for institutional investors to call fellow institutions to account. And throughout the 1970s Britannic's auditors were a small local firm, Flint and Thompson; Britannic was the firm's only quoted company client.[7]

As for the directors, their own holdings are small. But John Jefferson, one of whose forebears rescued Britannic from near-collapse in the 1890s, belonged to the third generation of his family to run the company. A fourth generation Jefferson, has recently been appointed joint general manager. In short, Britannic is a family fiefdom, and an inward-looking one at that. When I asked to visit the company on behalf of *The Economist* shortly before Mr John Jefferson retired at the age of sixty-nine, I was told that he would rather not be visited. Nor was the company willing to discuss its investment policy. One can only marvel that such a dynasty has not only survived into the final quarter of the twentieth century, but remains free to put its stamp on the industrial Midlands with half a billion of other people's money.

Other investment institutions are now treading the same path as Britannic in building up large stakes in individual companies. They will continue to do so as long as their cash flow rises and the supply of new British equity shares falls short of their requirements. The risk here is that the creeping monopolisation of private industry's share capital by giant institutions will lead to a tyranny of big decisions. Only a small proportion have to go wrong to cause large economic distortions.

On other occasions investment institutions appear to have been as anxious to use their beneficiaries' cash to make political points as to support the company in whose affairs they were taking a close interest. When a group of institutional shareholders came to the rescue of Fodens in 1975, for example, by no means all of them were convinced that the ailing lorrymaker's troubles were temporary or that there was a rosy longer term future for the company. The more recalcitrant of the big shareholders parted with their money only after vigorous prompting by the Bank of England's determined industrial adviser, Sir Henry Benson, a former senior partner of accountants Coopers & Lybrand, and some of them came into line partly because they wanted to demonstrate that private sector finance was not selling British industry short. Five years later Fodens went into receivership. It had fought off a take-over bid from Rolls-Royce Motors, with the support of its larger institutional shareholders, only a short while before.

An even more overtly political gesture was the decision by large institutional shareholders in Dunford and Elliott to team up with Equity Capital for Industry in 1977 to offer fresh capital to this financially stretched Sheffield steelmaker. The institutions had been incensed that the management had gone directly to the National Enterprise Board for cash without approaching its share-holders first, so they told the Dunford management that they would not vote in favour of the increase in authorised capital needed to allow the NEB to subscribe for shares. They offered Dunford an alternative financial package in order to rebuff any suggestion that the NEB could do something for a potentially viable company that was beyond the capacity of the private sector to provide. In the event, support was not required from either source because successive takeover bids were made for Dunford by Johnson and Firth Brown and Lonrho. But the institutions had made their political point.

Another danger in closer institutional involvement in manage-ment decisions is that institutional shareholders will impose their own risk-averse, narrowly financial preoccupations on industrialists who are already overprone to caution. Significantly, the two most bitter confrontations between institutions and industrialists in the 1970s did not turn on the efficiency or otherwise of the underlying business. The first battle arose when Coats Patons, the Glasgow-based multinational textile group decided, without sounding out institutional shareholders in advance, to pass its final dividend in 1975; it announced that, in order to preserve cash during the economic squeeze, it would give its shareholders new shares in lieu of the dividend. The institutions wanted none of it. After a bruising public row, they agreed to vote in favour of an increase in capital to permit Coats Patons to go ahead with its proposal only on the understanding that it would not happen again. Industrialists elsewhere duly took note that dividends could not be cut or passed without incurring institutional wrath in the absence of an overwhelmingly powerful excuse. Private investors, mean-time, began to wonder whether the institutions were not seeking the best of both worlds: a right to be consulted about dividend policy while preserving the right to go on dealing in the shares.

The second, equally aggressive, exercise of institutional power arose in 1978 over Allied Breweries' £64 million bid for J. Lyons, the food group whose fortunes were originally founded on the

famous tea shop chain. Some time before making the bid, Allied
Breweries had asked its shareholders to sanction an increase in its
authorised capital. The increase had been subject to an important
(but quite normal) condition. No part of the new capital was to be
used in a way that altered the nature of the company's business
without the prior approval of shareholders at a general meeting.
When Allied came to make its bid, stockbrokers' analysts argued
that Allied was altering the nature of its business by moving from
drink into food, even though it was technically within the letter
both of the law and of the Stock Exchange rule book on this point.
Hostility to the move was such that a committee of the National
Association of Pension Funds, whose members owned 14% of
Allied Breweries' shares, was set up under Hugh Jenkins of the
National Coal Board pension fund to consider what was to be
done.

Jenkins had already established himself as a hawk in earlier confrontations with Wilkinson Match, over a controversial deal with
the American group Allegheny Ludlum, and with Barclays Bank,
over its takeover of the Investment Trust Corporation. And his
committee decided that Allied ought to put the Lyons acquisition
to the vote at an extraordinary general meeting. Its demand was
flatly rejected by Allied chairman Keith Showering and his board,
who rightly perceived that in a confrontation the pension funds'
voting power was too blunt an instrument to be wholly effective.
The pension funds could hardly oust the whole board and run
Allied Breweries themselves. Both sides seemed deaf to any
suggestion of compromise.

In the end a face-saving compromise did emerge: the pension
funds were offered the chance to vote on a tame resolution to 'note
with approval' the acquisition of J. Lyons – in other words, to
pass a vote of confidence in the management. Approval was duly
granted. Jenkins had demonstrated, however, that even Britain's
larger quoted companies could no longer afford to ignore their
institutional owners. Yet here, as at Coats Patons, the institutions
were effectively compelling a company to conform with their own
portfolio requirements. It was a curious way of extracting a
better managerial performance from Allied Breweries.

All this appears, by default, to strengthen the case of those like
Peter Simon, chief investment manager of Legal & General, who
argues that the market can do a better job, in many cases, than an

interfering fund manager. Simon points to EMI, whose financial troubles in 1979 arose partly from its heavy investment in electronic scanners. Booming sales in the United States, the biggest market for the product, were abruptly curtailed when the Carter administration cut medical care spending programmes, in the mid-1970s. With the benefit of hindsight, everyone can see that EMI would have been wiser to sell the scanners under licence to an American company instead of courageously going it alone in North America. It is ridiculous, says Simon, to argue that the institutions were capable of making a better decision on the handling of the scanner than the management of EMI. And intervention would have been pointless because the deterioration in EMI's finances, together with the collapse of the share price in the stock market, led to boardroom changes in which chairman Sir John Read was replaced by Lord Delfont, and subsequently to a takeover bid from Thorn Electrical Industries.

Yet for every company like EMI where a direct role for institutional shareholders may not make obvious sense, there is another whose problems are readily identifiable and where simple remedies have not been applied. For years an ageing board presided over the fortunes of electrical group Decca, for example, while the company was sliding downhill. Every well-informed stockbroker in the City knew the extent of Decca's problems. Yet only when the chairman, Sir Edward Lewis, had reached the grand age of seventy-nine and when heavy losses were announced early in 1980, did the institutions start asking questions that should have been asked long before.

The board, it is true, had been protected because a majority of the company's ordinary shares carried no voting rights. But the institutions did hold some of the voting shares and could, at the very least, have registered a protest by voting against the re-election of directors. Few boards of directors, however many votes they control, sleep easily when the larger institutions decide to take up the cudgels. Why was this company, whose electronic warfare equipment and navigation systems were products of some national importance, allowed to sink to its knees, before it found salvation in the arms of a bidder, Racal Electronics, when Sir Edward Lewis was on his deathbed?

Decca is one of several companies where the insurance companies and pension funds knew that things were wrong, but waited a long time before giving the market mechanism a helpful nudge. Others where pressure might have been applied earlier include Reed International, which was widely criticised in the City in its period of over-expansion under Sir Don Ryder, later Lord Ryder of the NEB, in the late 1960s; Burton Group, the menswear chain which tried unsuccessfully to diversify away from the problems of its manufacturing and retailing business and ended up with unexciting new businesses and the same old problems; and Westland Aircraft, the helicopter and hovercraft concern where weak financial and labour management resulted in huge losses and write-offs on stocks and work in progress, in the late 1970s.

Institutions plead that it is not easy for them to find good new management to replace a deficient management in an ailing company. Far better, they sometimes argue, to use experienced non-executive directors to do the job. But while non-executive directors have a valuable role to play, their past performance has been mixed. A whole army of them failed to prevent National Westminster Bank from becoming uncomfortably heavily committed in property and secondary banking in the late 1960s and early 1970s. And they were unable to prevent disasters at British Leyland, Burmah Oil and numerous property companies and secondary banks at much the same time. This may partly reflect the fact that non-executive directors are powerless unless they are given adequate information by management. But it is also true that non-executive directors usually owe their position to the chairman and the executive directors. And since the legal liabilities that apply to executive and non-executive directors are identical, the relationship between the two is inclined to be cosy. Resignations by non-executive directors on points of principle are rare, as are contentious arguments between executive and non-executive directors that surface in public.[8]

Tinkering with the structure of the boardroom may not, in the long run, amount to more than a modestly useful device in helping improve productivity in British industry. Nor is it a satisfactory answer to the question of how institutions should tackle the responsibilities of ownership. Their problem, as A. W. P. 'Cob' Stenham, financial director of Unilever, pointed out to me in his capacity as chairman of the Unilever pension fund investment committee, is that they are under increasing pressure from government, unions and the general public to intervene in industry, yet they are better equipped by training and experience to improve industry's morals (on, say, insider dealing) or capital structure (by, for example, calling for the elimination of non-voting shares) than to stimulate its business performance. 'It is a terrific act of arrogance,' he says, 'for the institutions to think that they have anything other than money to contribute to British industry.'

Stenham sees no easy answers to the institutions' dilemma. But he feels they will have to shed their reluctance to experiment with different methods of backing small and medium sized companies. They could also, he argues, make a greater effort to identify and act on troublesome companies much earlier – a task in which the financial press can make a positive contribution by extending its coverage to look more deeply at management problems and corporate strategies in industry. The key to all this, however, says Stenham, lies in securing good new management for companies that need it. Though a pension fund manager can often spot that a company is running into trouble, it is most unlikely that he or his staff will be able to tell that company how to sort out the problem.

The politicians' ideal of productivity-conscious money men hounding quoted British companies into greater efficiency is not much closer in the early 1980s, it seems, than it was in the early 1970s. And professional fund managers are still some way from agreeing where the true interests of their beneficiaries lie or how their cash should be invested in a predominantly institutional market, which is perhaps understandable, given that the issue is much more complex than many politicians appreciate: there are indeed no simple solutions. What can be said is that the change from a market characterised by widely dispersed private shareholdings to one in which shareholdings are more narrowly concentrated in institutional hands, has resulted in a small but perceptible shift in the balance of power between the managers of Britain's quoted companies and their legal owners. In the 1980s industrialists can no longer take it wholly for granted that the shareholders will leave them free to run the business as they see fit.

4
The elegant financier

'He thought he saw a Banker's Clerk
　　Descending from the bus:
He looked again and found it was
　　A Hippopotamus.

"If this should stay to dine," he said,
"There won't be much for us." '

Lewis Carroll, *Sylvie and Bruno*

THE PROFESSIONAL FUND MANAGER who puts his beneficiaries' money into the small business sector is not cushioned
by the stock market from responsibility for the companies in
which he invests. Instead he is protected by the laws of investment arithmetic. The bigger the financial institution, the smaller
the damage an investment in a small business can inflict on its
portfolio. Secure in this knowledge, many investment managers
failed adequately to monitor their interests in small unquoted
companies, in the 1970s. The resulting investment mistakes were
so numerous that the unquoted company sector of the capital
market came to be regarded in the City as a graveyard for the
reputations and aspirations of some of Britain's biggest insurance
companies and pension funds. This was unfortunate, since the
small business sector has traditionally been a fertile breeding
ground for industrial innovation. It also accounts for around a
quarter of private sector employment. If the nation's most powerful group of capitalists adopts a once-bitten-twice-shy attitude
towards unquoted companies, Britain's economic future will be
bleak.

　　The man who unwittingly exposed the institutions' vulnerability in this area was Charles Gordon, an entrepreneurial financier
who saw early on that a financial gap was opening up as rich

investors with an appetite for high risk and high reward, and with a willingness to take a personal interest in small businesses, were being replaced in the financial system by risk-averse professional managers who invested simultaneously in hundreds of companies whose fortunes they were unable to monitor closely. It is probably not an exaggeration to say that Gordon was responsible for originating a majority of the unquoted company investments that found their way into pension fund portfolios in the 1960s and early 1970s. The history of his business dealings is worth exploring because it illustrates very clearly the problems institutions face in backing entrepeneurial companies. It also shows how easily the under-regulated pension funds can run into trouble when they stray away from the comfortable world of the stock exchange.

Charles Gordon first became aware of the importance of the institutions when he was a financial journalist on the *Investors Chronicle* in the late 1950s. There he specialised in property investment, an area in which insurance companies and pension funds were closely involved through mortgage lending to property companies. He rapidly built up valuable contacts with property entrepreneurs and fund managers, which were to stand him in good stead when he later moved to Hambros Bank as a financial consultant. At Hambros, Gordon started to advise property developers on raising finance. The most important of them was Jack Cotton, perhaps the most flamboyant of the post-war property entrepreneurs. He also established an unorthodox venture called Bentworth Trust, in which both he and Hambros, along with the pension funds of Unilever and Barclays Bank, took a stake. Bentworth set out to back small and medium sized private unquoted companies in industry and commerce. Its more successful interests included investments in television rentals, car parking and a joint company with J. Lyons, the food and tea shop group, which ran a Wimpy food operation in Europe.

Today there would be nothing unusual in such a venture. But in the early 1960s insurance companies and pension funds rarely put money directly into private industrial and commercial companies. Many pension funds had only recently started investing in quoted equity shares. Gordon also saw something that took many others in the City several more years to recognise. For all their glamour, the merchant banks had more financial talent at their disposal than money; many institutions, on the other hand, had more money than talent to manage it prudently. This was particularly true of the pension funds, whose managers were rarely to be seen at the lunch tables of leading merchant banks. Charles Gordon, according to one of his friends, was the first person in the City to treat pension fund managers like human beings.

Few men were more persuasive than Gordon when it came to raising money. He also entertained well. Fund managers, bankers and businessmen were whisked off to Covent Garden. With them went Gordon's attractive wife Nadia Nerina, the well-known ballerina. They dined with him at some of London's best hotels where everyone from the manager to the doorman seemed to know him. And they were made to feel like men who controlled several millions of pounds – which, more often than not, they did. One former colleague recalls a trip to Covent Garden at which part of the crush bar had been specially roped off for Gordon's party in the interval of the performance. Others remember being introduced to celebrities and peers at expensive restaurants.

In the mid-1960s Gordon left Hambros to set up a more sophisticated version of Bentworth Trust called Spey Investments. The pension funds of Barclays and Unilever followed him from Hambros. He also won the support of Fund Holdings, a trust of the Salmon family that helped found J. Lyons. (He had met Sir Julian Salmon through the joint Wimpy venture that Lyons had had with Bentworth Trust.) Later came Boris Marmor, a property entrepreneur whom Gordon had also met at Hambros: Marmor took charge of a joint property venture called Spey Westmoreland. Gordon also found new and powerful institutional support in the pension funds of Imperial Chemical Industries and the nationalised Electricity Supply Industry.

It was not just charm and flattery that coaxed this formidable group of institutional shareholders into Spey Investments. Gordon had an interesting argument about the capital market which was novel at the time and which still has some relevance today. The City's methods of raising capital, he claimed, were archaic. The stock market was an unreliable guide to the real worth of any company that wanted to raise capital, and the institutions could not collectively outperform it when their own investment decisions dictated the level of the market. In the 1960s the clearing banks advanced money mainly on overdraft, leaving small and medium sized companies in a state of permanent insecurity since the banks could pull the rug from underneath them when their overdrafts came up for annual review. The banks relied heavily on the security of a company's stock, debtors and factory premises instead of attempting a serious assessment of the business's likely cash flow. When I went to see Charles Gordon in 1979 (he chose, characteristically, to be interviewed over tea at the Ritz) he told me that one of the chief flaws of the capital market was that finance was tailor-made for the lender, but rarely for the borrower. 'Only if the needs of borrower and lender are directly related,' he argued, 'do you have elegant financing.'

Spey Investments was intended to give insurance companies and pension funds an opportunity to extend elegantly tailored financing to industry and commerce, and dispense with stock-broking and banking middlemen. The way to build up good small and medium sized businesses, Gordon argued, was to provide them with stable, long term institutional finance and to monitor their performance through an intermediary company that acted on behalf of the institutions. The vast cash resources of the insurance companies and pension funds would allow the intermediary to outbid the rest of the market for the best companies on offer.

The theory was more impressive than the practice. Spey's industrial interests, which ranged from new industrial processes starting from scratch, to mature but financially troubled businesses that were bought for their recovery potential, were an ill-assorted collection of investments in unconnected areas, such as plastics, retail fashion wear, brush products and taxi services. Few performed well; some performed disastrously. Amazingly, none of the institutions noticed that several of the investments were losing money at an awesome rate.

Gordon had set up a prudent system for vetting acquisitions whereby none of Spey's institutional backers were ever required to commit money in advance. The fund managers were always given a specific memorandum for each proposed acquisition and asked whether they wanted to invest. If any two of them disliked the proposal, they were empowered to veto it for the whole group. But once they had given their fiat, the laws of investment arithmetic took over: they never demanded any further detailed management information and relied, in so far as they relied on anything, on informal contacts with Gordon.

Spey's accounting practices at this point were so quirky that the annual accounts failed to reveal the trading performance of the underlying companies in which it had invested. Auditors Cooper Brothers (now called Coopers & Lybrand) raised no objections until late in the day. When one of his colleagues expressed concern about the deteriorating profitability of the trading subsidiaries Gordon assured him that the amounts involved were so trivial, from the institutions' point of view, that there was no need to worry. And he was, in a sense, right. Although Spey was a large company spending huge amounts of money, it was still only a small investment in the portfolios of most of its backers. As the industrial ventures ran into deeper trouble, Spey channelled its institutional shareholders' money increasingly into property and finance. In 1969 and 1970, Spey Westmoreland laid out £27 million on the acquisition of two quoted property companies, Allied Land Holdings and Hallmark Securities.

Spey's overheads raised the eyebrows of everyone other than its institutional backers: there were Rolls-Royces and premises in the City which, in the words of one fund manager who resisted the temptation to sign up, looked more like a showroom than a place of business. Gordon had decorated Spey's offices in Old Jewry with more than £50,000-worth of ultra modern art that appealed not at all to conservative City tastes. Then the former journalist, who used to regard a surfeit of press publicity as an early warning sign of corporate trouble, started talking to the press in extravagant terms. (In this, he was oddly similar to his former colleague, the property entrepreneur Jack Cotton, who suddenly became publicity conscious, after years of reticence, just when his business was getting out of hand.)

And in 1970 ambitious plans were launched for a new merchant bank, Spey Finance, into which the pension funds and insurance companies would pour more capital. Many of them, according to one former Spey executive, could hardly wait to sign the cheques for the £20 million that was asked of them. With such capital backing, Spey Finance would start on much the same financial footing as long established merchant banks like Baring Brothers or N. M. Rothschild. But it would have a crucial advantage over them. Future access to new capital, which these family banks lacked as long as the family wished to retain control, was almost certainly guaranteed. Yet Gordon would not necessarily lose control of Spey and its bank. He had managed to persuade the institutions to accept a capital structure for Spey under which he owned a majority of the votes without having to put up more than a fraction of the money. The new merchant bank was to become the lynchpin of a financial conglomerate that would embark on further investments in banking, property and industry.

Even at the time, the enthusiasm of some of the institutions for this would-be super-bank seemed misplaced. Once again Gordon had enlisted impressive names. Sir Paul Chambers, the former chairman of ICI who had recently been appointed chairman of Spey Investments, became chairman of Spey Finance and Sir Joseph Lockwood of EMI became deputy chairman. (Chambers had also brought Royal Insurance, of which he was chairman, into Spey Investments.) But the chief executive was Lord Chalfont, an ex-minister in the 1964–70 Labour administration. Chalfont was expert in defence and foreign affairs, but his qualifications to run a bank were obscure. Nor had Gordon himself much direct experience of commercial banking. A respected French commercial banker, Albert Gabizon, who was hired because he did have experience, came and went within the week. His whirlwind departure from Spey was never properly explained.

As Spey's industrial interests ran into deeper trouble, rumours started to go round that all was not well with Charles Gordon's empire. They were only temporarily quashed by Sir Paul Chambers' arrival in April 1970. Outsiders noticed a series of rapid exits and entrances. Gordon paid his managers well and sometimes offered them shares in the subsidiaries which they ran as an incentive. But he did not hesitate to sack them. Others left of their own accord. One subsidiary alone had five managing directors in three years. Then Gordon started to lose confidence in Boris Marmor, who was not liked by all Gordon's City friends.

In the end one of the institutions did start to worry. In October 1970 Unilever's finance director, Jasper Knight, retired and became chairman of a Spey subsidiary. He was not impressed by what he saw. The further he delved into Spey's affairs, the less he liked them. The other institutions did not take his reservations seriously. They thought that the trouble stemmed from a clash of personalities between Knight and Gordon. But they did see that Spey's management needed strengthening to cope with the flood of recent acquisitions. Malcolm Bates, an experienced industrialist who was then working at the Industrial Reorganisation Corporation, was appointed. He arrived in April 1971. Soon after came Philip Ralph, then head of corporate finance at merchant bankers Hill Samuel. By the time Ralph arrived, Unilever's pension fund had decided to pull out, much to the annoyance of the other institutions, who complained that Unilever was needlessly rocking the boat.

Bates and Ralph found on arrival that Spey's state bordered on chaos. And despite the backing of cash-rich, powerful insurance companies and pension funds, it had achieved the remarkable feat of running short of money. The capital structure had been tailor-made for the institutions, in such a way as to give Spey a permanent financial problem. Because the institutions wanted an income which was not taxable, they advanced cash mainly in the form of loan capital instead of ordinary shares. The loans carried an obligation to pay interest come what may, year-in year-out. Had they put up equity capital, which would have been more appropriate in view of the risky nature of the underlying businesses, Spey would only have had to pay dividends (from which tax is deducted at the standard rate and accounted for to the Inland Revenue by the company) as and when it was able to do so.

The result was that the parent company of the group faced a crushing burden of overheads, of which the interest on the institutions' loans was the most punitive. Nobody, Bates told me, had bothered to chivvy profitable subsidiaries into paying dividends to the parent, whose only source of income was from the sale of businesses. There were no adequate management accounts and no real management infrastructure. Gordon was chief executive and had a majority of the votes in the company. Since few people had been prepared to cross him, nothing had been done to put the organisation into shape. Even when Bates and Ralph had slimmed the head office staff from over 80 people to nearer 20, they found it hard to establish what many of the former staff had been doing.

On 4 June 1971, Gordon's old employer, the *Investors Chronicle*, published a critical article which questioned whether Spey's management was as good at selecting and managing businesses as it was at finding money to buy them. It also pointed out that the accounts of both the parent and its key subsidiaries were badly out of date. The threat of bad publicity finally roused Spey's institutional backers, in a way that the company's own poor performance had failed to do. By the end of the month, the institutions, led by Norman Freeman, manager of ICI's pension fund, had decided to take a firm grip on Spey and to curb Gordon's wilder ambitions. A proposal was put to him that the group should sell Spey Finance to First National Finance Corporation, the 'fringe' banking group run by Pat Matthews, whose chairman was Viscount de L'Isle of Phoenix Assurance. The price was £8.5 million, of which £7.5 million was in First National shares and only £1 million in hard cash.

In a heated boardroom row that lasted for three days, Gordon resisted this and other proposals. With good reason as it turned out: First National sold the business for nearly £13 million in cash four months later, and its own shares were to become almost worthless later in the decade. But he lost the battle. Although he still had voting control of Spey, it gave him no real power once the institutions had decided on a course of action that he disagreed with. On 30 June a press release was put out announcing that Gordon had sold his controlling shareholding after 'amicable' discussions and that he was resigning all his directorships in the Spey group.

In the City it was rumoured that Gordon had been paid off handsomely. Yet if anyone was paid off, it was the institutions. In a settlement that was not made public at the time, Gordon agreed to buy some of the shakiest businesses in Spey at their original cost, as well as taking on works of art, chauffeurs and secretaries, for which he was to pay £666,000 in six half-yearly instalments, together with interest at $7\frac{1}{2}\%$. Bates, Ralph and the institutional shareholders had appealed to his pride when he was in no state to think about the financial consequences. The beneficiaries of Gordon's last, self-justificatory gesture were the pensioners and policyholders of the institutions that backed Spey. For Gordon the terms of the settlement, which required him personally to find $£\frac{3}{4}$ million in three years, were at the very least stringent.

Despite this setback, Charles Gordon moved into a suite of offices in the same building in Old Jewry that Spey occupied and established a property dealing group called Benedict Investments. In no time, clearing banks, merchant banks and London-based American banks were paying him court. His new offices looked smarter by the day, recalls Philip Ralph, as his former offices became more drab under less entrepreneurial management.

Gordon's luck finally ran out when the property market collapsed in 1974. His empire foundered leaving debts of more than £3 million. By then Spey had received all but the last £125,000 instalment of principal and interest on the outstanding amount owed by Gordon.

Whatever else may have been wrong with Charles Gordon's venture in Spey Investments, the underlying idea of channelling institutional money into unquoted businesses did have appeal for Bates and Ralph. Instead of winding the company down, as people in the City had expected, they soldiered on. One fact that never emerged when the boardroom battle was raging was that Bates and Ralph did not want to lose the services of Spey's founder. They tried to persuade Gordon to take a break for six months and go abroad. Afterwards, they suggested, he should return as a non-executive deputy chairman. Both men felt that Gordon's way with the institutions was too valuable to lose. And Bates had come to the conclusion that there was an industrial and commercial business in Spey worth preserving.

Before long, Spey's businesses started to recover and buyers began to knock on Spey's door. Lord Poole of Lazard Brothers the merchant bank owned by Lord Cowdray's S. Pearson group, was interested. So, too, was Sir Isaac Wolfson of Great Universal Stores, who thought that Spey might make a useful acquisition for his private Anglo-Portuguese Bank.

In the end William Brandt's, the merchant banking subsidiary of National and Grindlays, took a controlling interest in Spey Investments late in 1972. Spey still had to struggle with a very inelegant burden of debt, however, and when the stock market plunged in 1974 the value of its quoted investments plunged too. By the end of 1975 it was showing a deficiency of assets against liabilities of over £5 million and the institutions were forced to pull out at a loss.

Yet Bates and Ralph had demonstrated to the directors of Brandt's, if not to a wider public, that Gordon's idea of marrying institutional money to unquoted companies through an intermediary investment group could have potential, provided that the intermediary also had sound industrial and financial management. Brandt's was later able to nurse the business back to health. By

1980 the residue of the former Spey empire was being groomed for flotation on the stock market.

One of the more unfortunate effects of the fiasco at Spey Investments was that it reinforced the natural caution of the professional money managers, who became even less inclined to invest in unlisted companies than they were before. Towards the end of the 1970s, however, interest revived partly because the Wilson Committee helped focus political attention on the small business sector. In its interim report on the financing of small firms,[1] published in 1979, the committee pointed out that there were deficiencies in the availability of equity finance for small businesses and that this was 'putting undesirable constraints on their rate of creation and growth'.

The Wilson Committee was, in fact, rediscovering a gap that had originally been identified by a committee under Harold Macmillan in the 1930s. The same gap had subsequently attracted the attention of the Bolton Committee, whose report on small firms was published in 1971; its findings were largely ignored, first by a Conservative government under Edward Heath, then by a Labour government under Harold Wilson himself. What was new by the time that Sir Harold Wilson came to prepare his own interim report in the late 1970s, was that the neglect of small business had been exacerbated by the rapid growth of institutional giants which laid heavy emphasis on size and marketability in choosing their investments. Although they were the chief buyers of equity-type investments in the financial system, the pension funds and life assurance companies had been slow, with one or two honourable individual exceptions, to find effective ways of putting capital into unquoted companies.

In 1979 when the Wilson Committee's interim report was published, the accounts of the pension funds of the Post Office, British Steel and British Airways showed negligible interests in unquoted companies, except in property. The Electricity Supply Industry, ICI and Unilever appeared more adventurous, but many of their unquoted investments were left over from the days of Spey Investments, or were directed towards finance and property, rather than industry. And the National Coal Board pension fund, which had set up an organisation specifically to provide finance for smaller businesses, was having difficulty in finding takers. Other institutions made similar complaints about a shortage of suitable investments. No doubt this partly reflected the dismal economic climate, but it also raises questions about whether they were aiming for those parts of the market where new capital was most needed.

There could, however, be a further reason for the inadequate flow of equity finance into small business, stemming from the structure of the financial system itself. The chief financiers of small, high-risk businesses in Britain are specialist merchant banks such as the Industrial and Commercial Finance Corporation, which was set up in response to earlier worries about the small business financing gap, and the clearing banks which with their big branch networks are ideally equipped, in theory, to support small firms all over the country. Yet the business of banking is inherently unstable. One function of the banking system within the economy is to borrow short from depositors and current account holders, and to lend long to industry and commerce. So banks always live with the possibility that if depositors withdraw their cash, they may not be able to meet the withdrawals.

This should be little more than a minor psychological constraint for the clearing banks, which are too big to suffer (or to be allowed by the Bank of England to suffer) a run on their deposits. Yet some clearing bankers remain deeply concerned with the need for security, and none too keen on assessing the capacity of a business to generate future earnings, as the following exchange between Sir Anthony Tuke of Barclays Bank (then plain Mr) and the Wilson committee underlines:

Q: (Sir Harold Wilson) Could I put a type of case, it is not an individual case, that we have had in evidence once or twice? There is a chap, say, round about 40 who is highly technological, who worked for a big firm, who wants to go off and develop his ideas, and indeed make some money for himself and for his family by doing that. In some cases the firm itself that he has left, or some other firm, is going to be quite pleased that he is being hived off, they will have permanent relations with him, and it is not much of a headache for you, but this chap goes away, taking two or three people perhaps of his own department in the firm, it is very highly technological, he is out in the provinces somewhere, what about the problem of your bank manager who is highly trained in the normal work of a branch and in financial matters generally, but is inevitably unable to understand the technological significance? Do you have people at head office he can go to then, or in your regions, or perhaps in a big branch somewhere else in the country who can help? What happens when this man is really asking for money and his demand can only be backed and answered by a real understanding of the perhaps very sophisticated technology?

A: (Anthony Tuke) Speaking from my own experience in the past of this, I frankly do not think if you are talking of high-grade technology, the banks are likely to have available to them the sort of person who can base his lending judgement on the technological chance this particular enterprise may have. We would be much more likely to take a sort of balance-sheet banking view of this.[2]

For the founders of, say, a computer soft-ware firm whose most valuable assets are their own brains, this bankerly view is a major impediment. And since many other high-technology businesses on which Britain's longer term economic well-being depends, have no tangible assets to speak of in the balance sheet, the impediment could have far-reaching consequences.

In merchant banking the fear of withdrawals of deposits and of insolvency is a more serious constraint. The average merchant bank becomes insolvent if much more than 15–20% of its loan portfolio becomes irrecoverable. So merchant bankers are nervous about commitments in unquoted companies, which are by definition more risky investments than quoted ones, and they are forced to take a very short term view in the interest of self-preservation.

The rise of the pension funds creates an opportunity to counter-act this bias against imaginative risk-taking. The pension funds have a natural desire for equity-type investments. Since they can afford to think in decades rather than years, the lack of marketability in unquoted investments is less important to them than it is to banks. Unlike insurance companies, pension funds are not hindered in their investments in unlisted companies by Department of Trade regulations.

There is probably no more stable source of finance outside government than an 'immature' pension fund – that is, one where the contributions from members into the fund exceed the payments being made to pensioners (which is the case with a majority of British pension funds). Far from living with a worry about cash being withdrawn, the manager of an immature pension fund lives with the near-certainty that cash will continue to pour in for many years hence. So the impact of losses on the portfolio will automatically be reduced: they will represent an ever-diminishing percentage of a growing fund.

The risk in unquoted investments can be reduced further by spreading money over several companies and by restricting the money to a small percentage of the portfolio. The problem is not that the institutions face excessive risks but that a law of diminishing accountability applies as giant institutions extend their hold over the nation's savings: the bigger the fund, the greater its tolerance of investment error; the more heavily concentrated the institutions, the greater the system's overall tolerance of loss.

By the end of the decade, small companies were back in fashion with the institutions. Many were investing via intermediary companies operating on principles not very different from those that Spey had originally intended to apply. Others, such as the pension funds of the National Coal Board, the Post Office and British Rail, were investing directly.

Whether the pension funds, in their commendable new-found enthusiasm for unquoted companies, will ever be truly effective investors in this area, however, remains to be seen. Radical innovation in small business will always tend to appear uneconomic because it falls outside existing frameworks of assessment and it does not lend itself well to bureaucratic investment appraisal. The fund managers' natural desire to protect their reputations also makes it harder for them to invest imaginatively in small business. If the City has a categorical imperative it is, never be caught with egg on your face. This cynical ethic has some point in merchant banking, where it takes very little in the way of mistakes to send the banker to Carey Street. As a working rule for pension funds investing in small high-risk companies or new ventures, where the success of one investment in ten pays for the failure of the other nine, it may be needlessly inhibiting.

In the small business sector billionaire insurance companies and pension funds will always be condemned to steer a nerve-racking course between the Scylla of profligate and uncontrolled risk-taking and the Charibdis of antisocial hyper-caution. Far better, however, to make the attempt than to opt out entirely. The moral of Charles Gordon's misadventure with Spey Investments, which is as relevant in the early 1980s as in the early 1970s, is not that risks should be avoided at all cost, but that they should be taken more judiciously and within a more effective regulatory framework that ensures that the managers of small, unquoted companies are held properly accountable to the ultimate owners of the business.

5
Sold on property

'It's a good thing to make mistakes so long as you're found out quickly.'

attributed to J. M. Keynes

FEW OTHER NATIONS have as active and sophisticated a market in commercial property as Britain. And in few other nations do financial institutions invest so heavily in offices, shops, factories and warehouses. At the start of the 1980s insurance companies and pension funds not only owned more land, bricks and mortar than any other group apart from owner-occupiers, but were among the most active property developers as well. They were absorbing a growing proportion of the agricultural land and forestry that came onto the market. And they owned £16 billion-worth of land and buildings, accounting for 18% of their total investments, where at the start of the decade they had owned properties with a book value of only £2.2 billion, equivalent to 10% of their investments. Much of this increase came about at the expense of over-stretched property companies that were forced to sell off properties to repay heavy bank borrowings run up during the boom in the early 1970s. By 1980 property companies owned assets worth little more than £7 billion – a third less, in real terms, than they owned ten years earlier.[1]

Institutional enthusiasm for property has been a constant source of chagrin to environmentalists and to those whose communities have been broken up by the comprehensive re-development schemes that insurance companies and pension funds willingly financed; also to Labour politicians and trade unionists who regard investment in property as inherently unproductive. Yet few trade union trustees of the larger pension funds raise serious objections to the investment of their own members' retirement savings in land and buildings. And in some cases the property market provides a back door through which institutional cash sneaks into productive industry. In successive squeezes industrialists have been able to raise sorely needed capital by selling their offices, factories and warehouses to institutional investors and then leasing them back.

The people who have most reason to be thankful that insurance companies and pension funds had a considerable appetite for property, however, are the bankers who become overcommitted in property lending in the 1970s boom. Had institutional investors not been there to help stabilise the banking system by purchasing assets from troubled property companies, so enabling them to pay off their debts, the bankers would have suffered mortal embarrassment. Yet the rescue of the British banking system was a much less smoothly managed affair than might appear at first sight. Professional money men showed widely varying degrees of competence in a rough, entrepreneurial market where they were unprotected by City codes, stock exchange regulations or legislation designed to protect the less experienced from their own gullibility. While they did indeed play a pivotal role in saving the City, many had to be badgered and bullied into doing so by the Bank of England. In 1974 pension fund trustees and directors of insurance companies suddenly found themselves accepting just the kind of wide interpretation of their fiduciary obligations that they usually claimed they could not legally adopt.

The story of the institutions' involvement in property in the 1970s, which unfolds in the course of the next two chapters, is one of frequent over-generosity to property entrepreneurs and of frequent errors of investment judgement – particularly among the pension funds, whose standards of disclosure were so low that their members and the general public were rarely aware of what was going on. Yet their investment blunders turned out, as often as not, to be so much writing in the sand: the rising inflationary tide ultimately obliterated some of the biggest mistakes. As rents soared to unprecedented levels towards the end of the decade, the institutions became yet more enthusiastic about the merits of an asset which was once again in short supply.

The long tradition of institutional generosity to property entrepreneurs goes back to the period after the Second World War. At that time insurance companies and pension funds were more interested in lending money on the security of other people's property than in owning property themselves. The insurance companies, in particular, invested heavily in long term fixed interest loans and debentures. This suited the entrepreneurs, for if a property company borrowed 100% of the money needed to finance a development it enjoyed the whole of the benefit of any increase in the value of the developed property. The insurance company did not share in the increased value – the 'equity interest' in the property – at all. It got back only the money it had advanced in the first place. With inflation, the real value of its fixed interest loan was actually falling.

As the first post-war property boom gathered pace after the abolition of building licences in 1954, the institutions began to realise that they had turned a whole generation of property men into millionaires. From 1959 onwards they started to demand shares and options on shares in the property companies which they financed with mortgages and loans. By this time, however, the first boom was close to its peak. Most insurance companies overpaid for the equity interest they acquired in entrepreneurial property companies. They found soon after that their investments had plunged in value and that many of the options were worthless.

Yet property men had not, on the whole, consciously taken them for a ride. Most were congenital optimists who believed that property values would always rise and that they were doing the insurance companies a favour by letting them in on the act. They simply drove as hard a bargain with the financial institutions as they could. The period between 1954 and 1964, at which point the boom petered out because the developers had created more buildings than were needed to meet the existing demand for space, saw the creation of several enduring partnerships. The Cooperative Insurance Society helped the controversial developer Harry Hyams make his millions; patronage from Eagle Star helped turn the Freshwater family into one of Britain's biggest residential landlords; and Commercial Union played a key part in promoting Nigel Broackes, whose Trafalgar House property group became the hub of a conglomerate empire that subsequently acquired the Cunard shipping concern, Beaverbrook Newspapers and a host of other construction, civil engineering and housebuilding interests. These were just three of the countless relationships forged between financial institutions and property men in the boom.[2]

By the time the second post-war property boom started in the late 1960s, the insurance companies and pension funds had discovered that property was a sound investment in its own right and were buying large amounts of it in the open market. Their enthusiasm was understandable for property has excellent investment characteristics. Rent is paid quarterly in advance and is not subject to deduction of tax at source. Whereas dividends, which are taxed and paid in arrears, may be cut or passed at the directors' discretion, rents still remain payable even if the tenant company is making heavy losses. If the tenant goes bust, the landlord still has a building which he may be able to let to another company. The shareholder, on the other hand, is left with a worthless certificate. And though rents only rise at the date of periodic reviews, rent review periods on commercial property have come down, in the past ten years, from fourteen to seven, five or even three years, and most leases stipulate that rents shall be reviewed upwards only.

But the overwhelming attraction of property for the institutions (and anyone else who can afford it) is that land is in limited supply. And the shortage of it in this landlocked island has been made more acute by planning controls, land taxes and other government imposed restrictions. It was a combination of in-built scarcity, inflation and the active participation of entrepreneurs and financial institutions that transformed the British property market from a financial backwater, in which owner occupiers and specialist investors engaged in a humdrum commerce in bricks and mortar, into a uniquely important part of the financial system. Security, marketability and potential for a rising income made property an ideal asset with which to confront rising pay-related pension commitments or insurance policy bonuses. In the 1970s it became a substitute in the financial system for the index-linked government stock that successive governments refused to issue – that is, a stock on which the return is guaranteed to rise broadly in line with inflation.

From the professional fund manager's personal point of view, property was doubly attractive because of its capacity to absorb huge amounts of cash. For a pension fund that has to find a home for £100 million or £200 million a year, buying an office block for £20 million or £30 million comes as something of a relief. It is much easier than investing £30 million in second-rank companies whose shares the institutions cannot buy without pushing prices up against themselves.

Real estate is also a relatively undemanding investment in other respects. In Britain, unlike the United States, tenants of commercial property are usually responsible for repairing and insuring the building, so the landlord enjoys a quiet life. Because the investment is not quoted on the stock exchange, the investment manager does not have to worry about the performance of his investment from day-to-day. Investment appraisal is much simpler than with, say, a high technology company. And no one is likely to accuse the fund manager of failing in his responsibility to British industry if the investment turns out to be a poor one. Nor can anyone be sure whether the investment really is a poor one in the short term, because property, unlike an equity share, is not a uniform article; a valuer has to make a subjective judgement about its worth and there are no really adequate property indices against which to measure performance.

All these things provided an inducement to fund managers to plunge over-enthusiastically into property. But the institutions' buying was only a contributory factor in pushing up prices in the early 1970s. The second great post-war property boom, which reached its peak in 1972–73, was mainly the creation of bankers, for whom the existence of a hyper-active property market constituted an irresistible inducement to lazy lending practices.

Like institutional investors, bankers welcomed the capacity of property to absorb huge sums of money, thus enabling them to expand their business. And it also offered a convenient short-cut in appraising a client's prospects. Instead of lending money on the basis of projections of the future earnings of the business, British bankers rely more heavily than their counterparts elsewhere on the security the business offers in the form of land and buildings.

The usefulness of property as collateral for banks is enhanced by the willingness of British chartered surveyors to put a value on any given building by reference to comparable recent transactions in the open market, after assessing the position of the building, the scope for rental growth, the terms of the lease, the state of the structure and so forth. Even if there have been relatively few comparable transactions, the surveyor will still hazard a guess at a property's value. This carries the risk that bankers will place too much faith in the valuer's signature and spend too little time asking whether the valuer's judgement is credible, whether the values are likely to be sustained for any length of time and how the company will meet the interest and repay the capital. Or, to take the point one step further, that blind faith in the wisdom of the valuer will leave the British banking system vulnerable to collapse if property investment bubbles over into speculation. This is precisely what happened in the early 1970s, which witnessed one of the most remarkable speculative bubbles in financial history under the lax monetary regime of the Conservative Chancellor Anthony (now Lord) Barber. To understand the part the institutions played in creating the boom and in rendering the subsequent collapse harmless, it is necessary to look at the way the property boom itself was financed.

During the 1954–64 bull market in property, the financing of speculative property development was relatively straightforward. The simplest way for the developer to go about the job was to buy the development site – of which there were plenty in war-torn Britain – with money from his clearing bank. Construction was then financed either by the construction company or by the clearing bank again. On completion and letting, by which time most of the risk in the development was over, the developer would turn to an insurance company, friendly society, pension fund or other institution for a long term mortgage.

The financial institution would value the property at a multiple of the rent; it might, for example, have considered an office block to be worth fifteen times the annual rent – known as 'fifteen years' purchase' – which would imply that the property yielded an income of $6\frac{2}{3}\%$ of its capital value. The institution would then usually lend up to two thirds of the value of the completed building. Provided the developer got his sums right, this was enough to recoup the whole cost of the development and the rents paid by the tenants were sufficient to cover the interest payable on the mortgage advanced by the institution. The entrepreneur became the proud owner of a valuable asset, which was likely to yield a rising income when the rents came up for review at a later date as well as a steady rise in capital value. He rarely had to put up significant sums of his own to get the development off the ground.

By 1970, however, the economics of property development had

ceased to be quite so favourable to the developer, partly because inflation had driven up interest rates to the point where it was no longer possible to put up a building and cover the annual interest bill with rents from the completed project. The entrepreneur could still show a capital surplus on the completion of his development; the problem was how to retain his newly created investment, given that the initial income was exceeded by outgoings.

Among the increasingly speculative options open to the developer was the sale and leaseback, a form of finance that had first become popular in the credit squeeze of the mid-1950s. Under this formula, the institution bought the freehold of the site and usually shouldered the whole cost of the development. In return it granted a lease to the developer at a ground rent. The developer then hoped to extract a higher rent from the ultimate tenant when the building had been completed and let. The attraction of the deal for the property man was once again that he had to put up little or no money of his own and the higher the rent he achieved, the greater the initial income he obtained from the development. The disadvantage was that he had to run significant risks to obtain that extra profit. If the developer failed to let the building, or if he let it at a rent that failed to match the ground rent he had promised to pay the institution against a formal guarantee, he was left with a continuing drain on his company's resources.

Another option was to sell more developments to an institution directly on completion and to use the proceeds to finance other developments which could then be retained. But for a trading operation of this kind to succeed, development and letting had to run smoothly and the property market had to stay buoyant to ensure that a buyer would emerge to take the completed investment.

Most entrepreneurs, though, wanted the best of both worlds, so they turned increasingly to the banks for medium term finance. Accommodation from this source was expensive, but the property men were not particularly concerned if interest charges exceeded rents from the property they bought or developed; they were happy to 'gear up' – the City jargon for increasing the proportion of borrowed capital in the company – because property values were rising merrily. They could bridge the gap between rents and interest charges by borrowing more from the banks on the strength of the rising value of their existing portfolio. These new borrowings could then be used to pay interest on older borrowings. The more property prices rose, the larger became the gap between income and interest that property men regarded as acceptable. And the periods over which they were prepared to run an income deficit became longer and longer. The bankers were usually happy to live with this practice of 'deficit financing', as long as they had a certificate with a valuer's signature at the bottom.

Paying interest out of fresh borrowings was obviously risky; 'gearing' increased the potential for loss as well as profit. It was made even more dangerous by the willingness of the developers to borrow at variable, instead of fixed rates of interest, which meant that if interest rates rose sharply, the developer's finances might become unmanageable. A similar threat was posed where developers financed their activities in Britain with borrowings in foreign currencies. In 1972 and 1973 rates of interest on Swiss francs, Deutschemarks and Kuwaiti dinars looked cheap. But there was a danger, which some of the biggest property companies were happy to disregard, that if sterling plunged in the international markets, the cost of repaying foreign borrowings would soar.

The assumption underlying all this exceptionally risky borrowing was that rents would rise very rapidly, so that the gap between interest charges and rental income would narrow and disappear in due course. In the event of financial trouble in the intervening period, property men assumed that they could sell properties in the open market to reduce borrowings. Few stopped to think about the circumstances in which they might be forced to sell, or to ask whether the insurance companies and pension funds would still be willing buyers if the government introduced a financial squeeze or took other measures to dampen the speculative boom.

Investors, bankers and property men were also lulled into a false sense of security by the willingness of property company auditors to believe anything that the valuers told them. In many cases, chartered surveyors and other valuers with qualifications of varying suitability accepted instructions to value speculative, uncompleted and unlet developments – often just holes in the ground – on the assumption that they would be completed on time and let in full to tenants at current market rents. Property companies would then incorporate these hypothetical figures in their accounts; the only allowance many of them made for the fact that the development was months, or in some cases even years, from completion, was to deduct the estimated cost of putting up the building from the supposed value on completion. Valuers were equally willing to put fanciful guesstimates on virtually unsaleable interests in property arising from sale and leaseback transactions. Some of the most reputable names in the accountancy profession would pronounce favourably on the resulting figures in their audit reports.

The false sense of security was strengthened further by the willingness of developers to add interest charges to the cost of their developments in their companies' accounts, instead of deducting the interest from profits. Some of the biggest developers in the land were able, in this way, to expand their development programmes at greater and greater risk, without the disclosed profits of the business suffering at all.

It was not merely an excessive respect for professional valuers that encouraged British bankers to turn a blind eye to the way they were pouring money into companies that were running at a growing cash deficit. In the early 1970s Ted Heath and his Chancellor of the Exchequer Anthony Barber were anxious to encourage an upturn in industrial investment. They did not want to stand in the way of that upturn by keeping bank lending on a tight rein. Yet the industrialists had no great urge to invest, so banks turned to a more speculative clientele. When, in 1972, it became clear that too much money was going into property, the Bank of England publicly requested banks to restrain their lending to property and financial companies. Exhortation proved a poor substitute for the controls that had been scrapped on the introduction in 1971 of the Bank's new policy of Competition and Credit Control, described earlier in chapter two. Those banks that exercised restraint could not help financing the less restrained lenders via the impersonal mechanism of the money market. Secondary banks, whose overall supervision was technically neither the responsibility of the Bank of England nor the Department of Trade, took the spare cash that others were putting into the market and recycled it in ever increasing amounts to the property men.

A more fundamental reason for the banks' headlong plunge into property was that they could think of nothing else to do in the face of the most serious inflation since the First World War. Confidence in paper money was waning rapidly. People in and out of the City searched with increasing desperation for any currency or asset that showed some prospect of preserving its real value. Property seemed to offer a better chance of avoiding loss, in this atmosphere of near-panic, than most other forms of investment.

Insurance companies and pension funds were no less prone to this attitude than bankers. They had, after all, to find an outlet for their growing cash flow, so it was not surprising that they ended up putting money into the property market. The extent to which they contributed to the price spiral can clearly be seen in the activities at the time of the Post Office pension fund and Prudential Assurance, respectively the fastest growing pension fund and the biggest insurance company.

In the early 1970s the Post Office's problem in the property market was how to find an adequate number of suitable investments when property prices were soaring and the competition for the small quantity of property that came onto the market was fierce. So when merchant bankers S. G. Warburg approached the fund to ask if it wanted to buy a private property group with gross assets worth around £95 million, the trustees were naturally interested.

The potential acquisition was English and Continental Property, a group owned jointly by the Crown Agents and two entrepreneurs, Ramon Greene and Jack Walker. In 1971 and 1972, these two men had astonished the property market by paying what appeared to be exceptionally high prices for three large London office blocks – Burmah House and Cunard House in the City, and Bush House in the Aldwych. These had been bought mainly with money provided or guaranteed by the Crown Agents. The involvement of this semi-official body in the company had been the subject of criticism in the unpublished report of the Stevenson Committee, which was appointed to look into the Crown Agents' activities and status after an extensive investigation into their financial and property dealings by the *Guardian* newspaper.[3]

While denying that the Stevenson Committee's findings had anything to do with their decision to sell, the Crown Agents were none the less keen to dispose of their investment. In mid-1972 they had come to a tentative agreement to sell English and Continental to First National Finance Corporation, the secondary bank run by Pat Matthews. Warburgs were called in to provide independent advice on the terms of the deal because the Agents held 9% of First National and their finance director Alan Challis was both a director of First National and chairman of English and Continental. In the event the sale of English and Continental to First National fell through and Warburgs, who were one of the Post Office pension fund's investment advisers, offered the deal to the fund instead.

The trustees decided to buy most of English and Continental's commercial property portfolio for £34 million. One of the attractions of the purchase was that this £34 million was only a down payment. In due course the fund would pay off the borrowings of over £60 million with which the property company had financed its purchases. So this single investment could be relied on to absorb more than £95 million of the fund's money over a very short period.

The Post Office was not the only institution to buy property wholesale during the boom. The BP pension fund had bought Western Ground Rents, a quoted property group, for £19 million in 1969 and the insurance companies had been even more enthusiastic buyers of quoted property companies. Between 1971 and 1973 Prudential bought Edger Investments, Royal Insurance acquired Sterling Estates, Commercial Union swallowed Holloway Sackville and Legal & General bought Cavendish Land. What distinguished the Post Office fund's purchase was that it looked unhappy even at the time. Within days of the completion of the acquisition on 23 January 1973, the government announced that it was to introduce a freeze on commercial rents. This immediately knocked several millions off the value of the properties the fund had just acquired, because the buildings were, in many cases, let at below current market rents and the fund could no longer rely on those rents being allowed to rise to market levels when they came up for review. Other pension fund managers took a certain pleasure in the Post Office fund's misfortune. But many of them, had they been in the same position as the managers of the Post Office fund, would almost certainly have done the same deal on similar terms. An inexorably rising, multi-million pound cash balance imposes an urgent imperative of its own.

The Prudential's contribution to the boom was less direct, but arguably more powerful. In 1972 and 1973 the big insurance company was not an enthusiastic buyer of property in the open market. Its investment managers felt that commercial property prices had raced away too far and that it was wiser to commit more money to new developments and to agricultural property. But it did encourage others in the property market by pumping money enthusiastically into secondary banking. No less than £50 million of the £119 million that the Prudential invested in ordinary shares in 1972, went into just three financial groups: United Dominions Trust, Keyser Ullmann Holdings and Dawnay Day. As a result of this foray into the financial sector, it held 27% of United Dominions, 12% of Keyser Ullmann and 20% of Dawnay Day – significantly larger holdings than it was normally prepared to take in run-of-the-mill companies. All three groups were heavily committed, either directly or through lending activity, in property. And in the case of Keyser, the Prudential encouraged a series of speculative moves that were to increase that commitment substantially.

The Prudential's liaison with Keyser Ullmann started in January 1972. At that time Keyser was a respectable but undistinguished merchant bank which was seeking to establish a reputation. To do that it needed to grow, but growth in merchant banking could not be achieved easily without the approval of the Bank of England. After years of trying to impress the Bank by running Keyser very conservatively, the joint managing directors, Ian Stoutzker and Roland Franklin, had conspicuously failed to win authorised banking status for their bank, let alone to achieve a place on the exclusive accepting houses' committee. In frustration they decided to become too big for the Bank of England, and everyone else, to ignore.

Their first major coup was to persuade the Prudential to subscribe £7½ million of new equity capital in January 1972 and to do so on terms that valued Keyser's shares at more than the prevailing stock market price. The deputy investment manager of the Prudential, Ronald Artus, went onto the board. The stock market was naturally impressed that Britain's biggest insurance company had decided to back Keyser Ullmann on such a scale and the bank's shares rose rapidly. This paved the way for a huge takeover bid two and a half months later, when Keyser announced an agreed offer worth more than £70 million, payable in Keyser shares, for one of the larger quoted property companies, Central and District Properties. Keyser and Central and District shared a common chairman in the Tory politician Edward du Cann, and Stoutzker had known Barney Shine, one of the founding entrepreneurs of Central and District for some time.

The attraction of the deal for Keyser was that the property company's assets would increase the bank's capital base. And since the Prudential had also helped raise the bank's share price before the bid, the cost of the takeover was reduced. The more valuable Keyser's own shares appeared, the fewer it had to offer to shareholders in Central and District in exchange for their company. It had little difficulty in persuading institutional shareholders in Central and District to accept its offer, because the Prudential underwrote it: shareholders could take the Prudential's cash in lieu of Keyser's shares. Central and District's other founding entrepreneur, Jack Rubens, was astute enough to sell his total shareholding for cash.

Having bought a major property group, Stoutzker and Franklin were now rich in assets. But Keyser was short of earnings because the initial return on investment in property was low. A logical next step was to make another acquisition which showed a high initial return to compensate for the shortcomings of the Central and District deal. So Keyser Ullmann turned to Dalton Barton, another secondary bank run by two entrepreneurs called Jack Dellal (known as 'Black Jack' to his friends in the City) and Stanley van Gelder.

Dalton Barton, whose offices were in Knightsbridge in London's West End, was one of the wonders of the stock market. Though not regarded as being remotely within striking distance of the upper crust of British banking, this fringe financial concern had persuaded the pension funds of ICI and the Electricity Supply Industry to give it substantial backing while it was still a private company. It was also backed by Trade Development Bank, part of a Luxembourg-based group run by publicity-shy international financier Edmond Safra. After Dalton Barton was floated on the stock market its profits, deposits and advances had risen astonishingly fast. Yet few people in the City had a clear idea of where the business came from or how Dalton Barton made its money.

Stoutzker and Franklin had known Dellal and van Gelder for some time because the two groups shared a joint venture in Peureula Investments, a quoted residential property dealing company run by Peter and David Kirch, which was also extensively financed by Trade Development Bank. The Kirchs made their money buying flat blocks and houses wholesale and selling individual flats and houses to sitting tenants; alternatively they offered tenants inducements to leave, so that the property could be sold with vacant possession. They had not over-endeared themselves to tenants, community workers and the press. But their operation, in which Dalton Barton had played an important part, appeared to be enormously lucrative. Keyser Ullmann's managers had been duly impressed.

In mid-July 1972, with the support of the Prudential, Keyser announced that it was to merge with Dalton Barton. Within eighteen months the Prudential's backing had enabled Keyser to transform itself from a small-time merchant bank valued in the stock market at less than £10 million to a huge property and banking concern controlling assets worth well over £100 million. And it appeared to have found a partner with a brilliant capacity for generating dealing profits. Before the takeover was completed, Dalton Barton revealed that it had sold Paramount Realty, a property company acquired for £12½ million only three months earlier, at a profit of £2½ million – a remarkable speculative killing by any standards.

From then on it was impossible for anyone in the City to ignore Keyser Ullmann. But not everyone saw the deal in an enthusiastic light. *The Times*, in particular, argued that the combined group was unusually heavily committed in property and that this commitment was by no means free of risk. It also questioned whether the two banks would blend harmoniously over the longer term.[4]

Scepticism was well founded on both counts. To start with, the two secondary banks never merged themselves very thoroughly. Dellal and van Gelder continued to do business from their West End offices. People at Keyser's own offices in the City were not always sure what these consummate wheeler-dealers were up to. Yet Dellal and van Gelder were so successful at generating profits that no one was tempted to argue with them, least of all the Prudential, whose man sat on the board of the main Keyser Ullmann holding company, but not on the board of its banking subsidiary. Any inclination to argue with the two men was even further diminished when they put together an astonishing deal in August 1973 whereby Keyser agreed to sell Central and District Properties for no less than £97 million to Town & City Properties, one of the biggest property development groups in the country.

Town & City's purchase of Central and District epitomised everything that was unsound about the property boom. The company that Keyser was selling had recently disclosed pre-tax profits of less than £3 million; Town & City's bill for interest on the acquisition was expected to exceed this figure by well over £10 million, leaving a huge shortfall of income against outgoings. The idea behind the deal was that rents on Central and District's properties would rise as they came up for review and that Town & City would meanwhile help bridge the gap between rents and interest by selling off properties. The aim, so Town & City's chairman Barry East told a press conference at the time, was to close the financial gap by 1977. In the meantime Town & City would live happily with its enormously high gearing. No less than £95 million of the £97 million purchase price was financed by bank borrowings, most of which fell due for repayment between 1974 and 1980. And there was a further burden of debt, in that Central and District itself had outstanding borrowings of £45 million for which Town & City was accepting responsibility.

Perhaps the strangest thing about this, the most grandiose of the moves in the game of 'Monopoly' that was played out in the financial system in the first half of the 1970s, was that so few people saw anything odd about it. Barclays Bank, whose merchant bank subsidiary had put together finance for the deal jointly with N. M. Rothschild, was so enthusiastic about the transaction that it took a quarter of the equity capital in the Town & City subsidiary company through which the acquisition was made; it shared the investment jointly with the Barclays Bank pension fund. And several other banks, which were offered options on Town & City shares, flocked to participate in financing the deal even though it broke several of the canons of prudent banking.

Town & City was putting up only £2 million of its own money, while the banks put up £95 million. So if the value of Central and District's properties fell by much more than 2%, the security for the bankers' loans would be deficient. As for the Prudential, it was delighted to see Keyser Ullmann emerge with a profit of over £20 million and with nearly £100 million in cash available for investment elsewhere at higher rates of return.

The only discordant note was sounded in the press. In an article entitled 'Gearing with a vengeance', *The Times* declared that the risks in Town & City's acquisition were massive in the light of the huge deficit of income and the unparalleled degree of short term borrowings that the company had taken on.[5] It also warned of the dangers, for Town & City, if the government introduced tough anti-property measures later in the year. The *Investors Chronicle*, though more cautious, expressed similar misgivings about the effect future government measures might have on the assumptions underlying the transaction.[6] But at the peak of the boom, these views were regarded as eccentric. There was much mutual back-slapping over the way in which the British banking system had raised such a huge sum without a hitch.

In one sense the bankers' response was easy enough to understand. The thinking behind the deal was exactly the same as the thinking behind scores of other deals that bankers were financing elsewhere in the property market. But the scale was different. In the heady atmosphere of the time, people firmly believed that property values could only continue to rise. This was particularly true of the men from Keyser Ullmann. They promptly laid out much of their £100 million proceeds on advances to a string of poor quality property companies. In less than a year Keyser was to become dependent for its survival on the support of the Bank of England and the clearing banks; it was ultimately to make provisions and write-offs of over £100 million against bad debts, mainly incurred in property. Within months Town & City was to find itself at the mercy of its bankers. And part of the task of picking up the pieces after this fiasco was to fall on the Prudential, whose investment judgement had hitherto been widely respected in the City.

One way or another, a collapse had been inevitable because the property values on which the banking system was putting unlimited faith were absurdly high in relation to any realistic assessment of the rents that offices, shops and factories were likely to yield in future. The only question was how and when. In the event, politics took a hand because of public resentment at the way a tiny proportion of the population seemed to be growing richer by the day without doing anything that resembled honest toil. In December 1973 the pressure for action to curb what politicians and journalists had dubbed the grotesque profits from property dealing, became too strong for the Conservative government to resist. On the 17th of that month Anthony Barber announced that he was to introduce a tax on development gains and a tax on the first letting of newly developed property.

The political assault on property coincided with the sudden loss of confidence in the stability of the secondary banks. By the end of 1973 jumpy depositors were taking money out of the secondary banks and putting it into the big four clearing banks. What was needed, if the remaining depositors were not to end up with large losses, was for the money to be recycled from the clearing banks back to the secondary banks. Hence the Bank of England's move early in 1974 to set up a 'lifeboat' committee in which it joined forces with the clearing banks to confront the crisis of confidence that was enveloping the banking system. The original idea was to buy time, so that the secondary banks could call in loans and make orderly disposals of property and securities; the clearing banks would then be repaid out of the proceeds.

Neither the Bank of England, nor the clearing banks, had any notion late in 1973 that such a high proportion of the secondary banks' loans were secured on hopelessly over-inflated property values, or that the crisis was not simply one of confidence. But the Bank's officials did see that the support of outside financial institutions, such as insurance companies and pension funds, would be necessary if an orderly realisation of the secondary banks' assets was to proceed. It was determined, where possible, to protect the banking system by pushing as much financial responsibility as it could onto those institutions that had invested in or deposited money with individual secondary banks. This was most apparent in the rescue of Cedar Holdings, the second of the fringe banks to run into serious difficulty. The rise, fall and joint rescue of Cedar by its own clearing bank and its four main institutional share-holders is worth recounting in some detail because it illustrates perhaps more clearly than any other rescue the methods by which the collapse in the banking system and the property market was arrested. It is also curiously revealing about the way the institutions – and the Bank of England – responded to the biggest financial crisis since the 1930s.

Cedar had been started in 1958 by Michael Morrison, an entrepreneur who had been impressed, on a visit to the United States, by American-style banking methods. He felt that there was room for a more simplified form of consumer lending than British banks were then offering, not least because clearing bank managers were inclined to treat personal borrowers like aberrant schoolchildren, instead of profitable customers. So he decided while still in his early twenties to set up a banking operation that provided loans impersonally, on standardised terms, in much the same way, he explained to me, as a sausage machine turns out sausages. The average loan was usually about £500 and it was secured by a second mortgage on the borrower's home.

The beauty of the business was that it opened up a huge potential market by reversing the clearing banker's unspoken assumption that the personal customer is always wrong. The snag, from the customer's point of view, was that he had to pay a very high fixed rate of interest, by clearing bank standards, to be treated like an adult human being. What really launched Cedar in a big way, however, was the arrival on the scene in the mid-1960s of the financier Charles Gordon (see chapter four). Gordon introduced Morrison first to the Unilever pension fund, then to Phoenix Assurance and to the pension funds of the nationalised coal and electricity industries.

Despite the obvious financial attractions of an investment in Cedar, there was a social danger here for the institutions. If people who were dependent on them for pensions and life assurance also independently raised second mortgages from Cedar, they might find themselves thrown out on the street by a company of which they themselves were the beneficial owners, if Cedar ever came to enforce its security. Phoenix and the pension funds of Unilever, the Electricity Supply Industry and the National Coal Board nonetheless proved enthusiastic backers. When Cedar Holdings came to be floated on the stock market by Barclays Bank Trust company in January 1971, by which time Morrison was 36, it was forecasting profits of nearly £$\frac{3}{4}$ million; the business itself was valued at £8 million. The support of the four institutions, which had advanced £6.6 million of long term loans to the company, and owned 42$\frac{1}{2}$% of the ordinary share capital, was crucial in winning support for the new issue. It was widely assumed in the City that if the company continued to prosper, the institutions would put up further capital.

Cedar did indeed prosper and as it did so, the basis on which it financed its business changed. Charles Gordon, who had aimed to eliminate as much risk from Cedar's lending as possible by borrowing long from the institutions and lending over a shorter period to customers, left the board at the time of the row at Spey Investments. Soon afterwards, Cedar turned to the money markets to raise deposits, with the result that business grew even faster. By June 1973, with encouragement from its institutional shareholders, Cedar had tapped the money market for £60 million of short term, and thus potentially volatile, deposits. The institutions had arranged to put up yet more loan capital and three of them were now represented on the board and closely involved in the company's affairs. At the same time Michael Morrison succumbed to the fashionable idea that banking and property worked better in tandem. He and his father, Jack Morrison, who was chairman of Cedar, also ran a quoted property company called Amalgamated Securities. They decided to combine the bank's earnings and the property company's assets by merging the two concerns. The institutions once again gave their fiat.

By November 1973 the enlarged Cedar Holdings appeared to be poised for even more rapid growth. The institutional shareholders had introduced Michael Morrison to the Post Office pension fund, which liked the look of the business so much that it decided to become a substantial backer. As a preliminary to putting up longer term capital, the fund placed £10 million on deposit. Then, suddenly, before the terms of the deal with the Post Office fund had been signed and sealed, the bank was hit by the backwash of the troubles at London and County Securities. Cedar's larger depositors – there were close on thirty of them – started to withdraw their money. Instead of being able to announce that he had won the support of Britain's fastest growing pension fund, Morrison found that the men who looked after the British postman's pension were voting with their feet. The Post Office fund joined the mass exodus from Cedar.

In early December a series of increasingly fraught discussions took place with the Bank of England and with the four institutional shareholders, during which Morrison tried to drum up support for his failing business. Initially the institutions agreed to put up £25 million. They were prepared to do so because the money could be secured on properties that had come into the group through the acquisition of Amalgamated Securities earlier in the year. It soon became apparent, however, that none of the deposits from the money market were being renewed and that the company might need as much as £70 million to staunch the outflow. Then came Anthony Barber's anti-property measures on 17 December, which were directed specifically at new developments. Cedar's biggest property commitment was a £15 million development at Buckingham Gate, Victoria, in central London, which was a long way from completion and for which a tenant had yet to be found. The logic on which the original rescue had been built now began to look shaky.

At this point, the institutions decided that they had no option but to put Cedar into liquidation. But before any decision was taken, the Bank of England intervened. On 20 December 1973, Morrison and representatives of the four institutional shareholders were summoned to the Bank. The men from the Phoenix and from the pension funds of the National Coal Board, the Electricity Supply Industry and Unilever, together with Cedar's own clearing bank Barclays, went into a meeting with Bank officials led by the Deputy Governor, Jasper Hollom. Morrison, along with his fellow director and cousin David Fischer, was put in a room elsewhere in the Bank; they were joined later by other executive directors. What followed, according to one participant at the main meeting, was 'an immense arm twisting session' in which the Bank of England tried to persuade the institutions to participate in a £70 million rescue.

Hollom argued that the British banking system was in danger of collapse and that the effect of such a collapse on sterling and on the economy would be catastrophic. The institutions were told that they had a moral responsibility, in view of the explicit support they had given to Cedar over the years, to prevent it from going to the wall. And it was in their own wider interests to save the company, since a decision to let it fail would further undermine confidence in the City, thus depressing the value of their other investments. Cedar, moreover, had valuable properties which could be realised in due course to repay funds advanced to facilitate the rescue.

There was also a question about the responsibility of the fund managers in their role as non-executive directors of Cedar. By this time all four institutions were represented on the board: Hugh Jenkins of the Coal fund, which had not been represented on the board earlier on, had joined when the crisis blew up. While their chief motive in becoming directors of the company had been to protect their investment in it, they had nonetheless taken on wider legal responsibilities to all the other shareholders by becoming officers of the company. The men from Phoenix, Unilever and Electricity, who had, while they were on the board, whole-heartedly backed all the moves that had led to Cedar's downfall, were obviously open to moral pressure because they had allowed Cedar to overstretch itself.

And for all four investment managers on the board at the time of the crisis, there was a genuine potential conflict between their obligation to beneficiaries of their funds and the obligation to Cedar and its other shareholders.

Among the institutions, Lord de L'Isle, the chairman of Phoenix Assurance, proved the most susceptible to Hollom's arguments. This was, at first sight, surprising, for de L'Isle, a former governor-general of Australia and holder of the Victoria Cross, held strong libertarian views and was a leading light of the fringe right wing National Association for Freedom. He can hardly have relished being told by officials of a government-owned corporation to pump shareholders' and policyholders' money into a company that was, to all intents and purposes, bust. He did, on the other hand, have a strong sense of public duty and a different set of financial priorities to the pension funds. Phoenix was a com-posite insurance company; unlike the pension funds, it had to meet a statutory minimum level of solvency and its solvency margin had been declining steadily over the previous twelve months as the stock market declined. It was suggested at the meet-ing that if the secondary banking crisis was allowed to get out of hand, it might spread to the insurance companies. De L'Isle must also have been conscious of Phoenix's other commitments in secondary banking. He himself was chairman of First National Finance Corporation, in which Phoenix had a sizable stake. First National was to become one of the biggest casualties of the collapse.

The pension funds were less keen to save Cedar and the City. They believed that their trustee obligations prevented them from putting money into a company that could not offer adequate security for new loans. And their investment managers could not have been cheered at the prospect of justifying to their chairmen an investment of several more millions in a bankrupt company. They also defended their performance at Cedar partly by arguing that they had been misled, in some respects, about the business. The non-executive directors had not been informed about the purchase of an expensive jet aircraft and information had been withheld from them about the extent to which customers were in arrears on the repayment of loans. A heated argument developed and Gordon Richardson, the recently appointed Governor of the Bank, was brought in, when necessary, to lend authority to the officials' case.

The institutions gained the impression, in the course of the argument, that the Bank would go to considerable lengths to persuade them to comply with its demands. For the men from the nationalised industries, there was the fear that the Bank might bring pressure to bear through their ever-sensitive chairmen, or even through the government itself. And the institutions also gained the impression that they might have difficulty in any future dealings with the parts of the City that came within the Bank's jurisdiction.

The one thing Hollom was totally explicit about was that he expected everyone to hammer out the terms of a rescue for Cedar there and then, and that no one was to leave the Bank until the job was done. More than one of those present felt that the Deputy Governor's behaviour towards the institutions came closer to that of a scoutmaster in charge of a bunch of rebellious schoolboys than of a top central banker asking the representatives of some of Britain's biggest corporations to do him a favour.

In the end the nationalised industry funds acquiesced. But the Unilever pension fund proved a harder nut to crack. The fund's senior representative at the meeting was Unilever's finance director Cob Stenham, who argued strongly that it was no business of pension trustees to throw their money into public spirited, uncommercial ventures. But he must nonetheless have been aware that the Bank of England administered Britain's exchange control regulations and that a failure to comply with its request might affect the climate in which the multinational Anglo-Dutch group negotiated remittances of company funds from Britain to other countries. A further problem was that if Unilever itself was seen to respond to a patriotic call to save the City, members of the British management would have an awkward time trying to justify their actions to their Dutch colleagues.

In the end Stenham agreed to go along with the Bank. But he

did not allow the Unilever pension fund's money to be used in the rescue. Instead, the big multinational put its own money into Cedar and indemnified the fund against any loss on its existing investment – a compromise which both acknowledged the *realpolitik* of the situation and protected the pension fund members' interests.

For its part, Barclays Bank was exceptionally unhappy to be involved in a further commitment to Cedar. But in the end it felt it had no option but to go along with the rescue proposal. In the upper reaches of British banking, the authority of the Old Lady of Threadneedle Street was still unquestioned. Several hundred millions more were to be poured into the secondary banks before the clearing banks became truly rebellious. It was finally agreed that Barclays and the four institutions should together advance up to £72 million to replace the disappearing deposits.

Once Hollom had got what he wanted from the institutions, he left Jim Keogh, the Bank official then responsible for monitoring and regulating the banking system, in charge of a meeting to sort out the detailed terms. More lawyers and bankers were brought in to help. It then became apparent that none of those present had enough technical knowledge to put together the highly complex financial package that was required. So Kenneth Cork, senior partner of City chartered accountants Cork, Gully, was called in. Cork was an exceptionally experienced operator in the toughest area of accountancy – receivership and liquidation – and had an unrivalled knowledge of company rescues and reconstructions. On this, as on countless other occasions, in the course of the secondary banking and property crisis, he brought practical know-how and common sense into the proceedings.

While the finer points of the rescue package were being settled upstairs, Michael Morrison and his fellow executive directors were given no inkling, in their downstairs room, of what was going on. Cedar was represented at the negotiations by John Gillum, from its merchant bank Samuel Montagu, and Michael Richardson, from the company's stockbrokers Cazenove. And while the investment managers and bankers became increasingly convivial over a not ungenerous flow of whisky, Morrison and his colleagues were given a bottle of beer apiece and some fairly meagre refreshments to last them from three in the afternoon until late into the night.

Morrison was finally brought into the proceedings at 11 o'clock. He was, on his own account, thoroughly distraught. The eight hour wait at the Bank followed four emotionally charged weeks in which Cedar had come closer and closer to bankruptcy. He was then confronted with a document setting out an agreement which would deprive him of control of the business he had built up over fifteen years. He also thought it gave a raw deal to the non-institutional shareholders in the company.

In return for putting in a maximum of £72 million, Barclays and the institutions were to take control of the company and extract a rescue fee from it of up to £5 million. The Bank was also to take a fee for its services. Cedar's ability to take on new business was to be restricted and the institutions would buy its properties at an independent valuation if the management was unable to sell them in the open market. Failure to sign the document, Morrison was told, would mean that the business would be liquidated immediately.

The executive directors tried to contact Lord Goodman, the well-known lawyer, for advice. But at that late hour, they were unable to get hold of him. A similar attempt to reach Cedar's auditors, Cooper Brothers, failed. In the end Morrison was only able to talk briefly to David Eastham, the chief executive of Cedar's joint stockbrokers, Joseph Sebag. Then, under duress, as he saw it, he signed away his business. It was three o'clock in the morning when the main participants in this highly charged episode, of which only bare details later appeared in the financial press, finally left the Bank of England. As far as the Bank was concerned, the unorthodox means employed to keep Cedar afloat were amply justified by the end, which was to save the City.

Cedar's problems were in some ways less acute than those of other fringe banks. Its advances were chiefly made to personal customers and despite the rapid expansion of the business, the level of bad and doubtful debts was not high by the standards of secondary banks that had lent heavily to commercial property companies. Cedar's problem was simply that the loans were financed by short-term deposits that were rapidly draining away. The property interests, on the other hand, were of relatively poor quality, although it was to the sale of the properties that the institutions looked for the repayment of their advances. Under the terms of the rescue, the value of Cedar's properties now became the key to its future viability.

In that, Cedar was an accurate reflection of the state of the rest of the banking system. In the first three months of 1974, the property market was in a condition bordering on paralysis. Development property became virtually unsaleable while Anthony Barber's measures to tax developments remained unclarified. Interest rates were rising rapidly so that property companies suddenly found themselves paying over 20% on bank loans. And when Labour returned to power in the spring, the writing was on the wall for the more heavily borrowed groups. Among the quoted property concerns, Town & City Properties suddenly found itself in acute financial trouble, as did the smaller Guardian Properties. The private property empires of William Stern and Ronald Lyon were tottering. There were fears that investors in property bonds – a form of property unit trust for small savers – might try to sell their bonds, so precipitating liquidity crises. The big Abbey Life property bond group was particularly vulnerable because it had development commitments; and its bondholders did indeed start to bale out on an unprecedented scale. Secondary banks, Cedar among them, found that they could not sell property on the open market. The assumptions on which the property boom had been based – that bankers would continue to lend, that investment institutions would go on buying and that rents would continue to rise – had crumbled.

By April Gordon Richardson, the Governor of the Bank of England, was confronting a more serious problem than he had faced when confidence in the secondary banks had collapsed at the end of the previous year. The legacy from the boom years was such that at the end of 1973 banks had lent a total of £1.7 billion to property companies on the security of assets that were often grossly overvalued. But these figures were only part of the picture. The clearing banks, of which National Westminster was the most exposed, were in difficulty at one remove because they had lent money to construction companies, financial and other groups which had then committed money to the property market. And property represented collateral for bank loans to countless manufacturing and retailing businesses around the country which now faced an exceptionally stringent credit squeeze. The banking system's ability to pull itself out of this dangerous trough hinged mainly on the willingness of insurance companies and pension funds to buy property from troubled companies, and on the price at which they bought. Yet the peak annual investment the insurance companies and pension funds had made in property during the boom was only about £600 million – far less than the £2 billion, £3 billion, or more, that might have to be absorbed very rapidly in order to underpin the banking system.

As the troubles of individual property companies came to a head, Richardson turned, in April, to the government for help. But at that point he had yet to establish the rapport with Labour ministers that later became a hallmark of his governorship. Offering support to property companies proved too hot a political potato for the recently appointed Labour government to handle. So Richardson's officials were forced back onto their own devices. In the end they adopted a two-pronged strategy to support the property market and thus to underpin the collateral of the banking system.

On the one hand, Jasper Hollom and his team, with frequent assistance from Kenneth Cork and other City professionals, cajoled and bullied bankers into refraining from calling in their loans; this they did by encouraging moratoria on repayments of loans, schemes of arrangement in the courts and by applying pressure directly to banks and other creditors to persuade them not to appoint receivers and liquidators. On the other, investment institutions were badgered and coaxed into buying properties from beleaguered companies. The object was to prevent a flood of properties pouring onto an already weak property market, and to bring about an orderly transfer of assets from vulnerable companies to more stable insurance companies and pension funds. It was, in fact, a gigantic exercise in rigging the market and in directing institutional investment in what the Bank of England perceived to be the public interest.

The odds against a successful outcome in this bankerly evacuation from the property sector, were considerable. Among the more active lenders in the later months of the boom were foreign, and particularly American, banks. They had enthusiastically adopted native banking habits and pumped large sums into such risky companies as Town & City, British Land and the private Stern and Lyon groups.[7] Under pressure from their head offices, for whom the British financial crisis was a far-flung, parochial affair, the Americans were sometimes reluctant to go along with the Bank of England's plan for an orderly unwinding of property company finances. And there were other strains on the rescue operation nearer home. The clearing banks became increasingly unhappy with the calls that the 'lifeboat' was making on their resources. Some top clearing bankers felt that they were paying too high a price to protect National Westminster from a clientele that included many of the biggest casualties in the secondary banking and property markets.

The Bank also faced a serious problem with the insurance companies and pension funds. It had been able to railroad fund managers into supporting Cedar and other secondary banks mainly because they thought that the rescue would ultimately be paid for out of the sale of property assets. Once the investment institutions had recognised that the property market had foundered, their trustee obligations became a much more formidable obstacle to providing support than they did at the start of the banking crisis.

In the event, the chartered surveyors came to the trustees' rescue. For much of 1974 sections of the property market were so depressed that there were few transactions to provide satisfactory evidence of property values. Rent controls had cast a cloud over reversionary property, where investors could no longer rely on rents rising to market levels on the arrival of the next rent review or the reversion of the lease, and at one point such property was virtually unsaleable. Developments posed a similar problem. In the worst recession since the 1930s, nobody could be sure whether tenants would emerge to take space in the completed developments; construction costs were soaring. Development sites, for which companies had been prepared to pay millions in the boom, suddenly became next to worthless. In the absence of a proper market the valuers simply used their imaginations on a more extensive scale than they did in the boom and their inspired guesswork gave the directors of insurance companies and the trustees of pension funds a chance to pass the fiduciary buck.

Typical of the wide variations in opinion between professional valuers, and of the uses to which property valuations were put during the boom and the subsequent collapse, were those that arose in respect of Cedar Holdings' uncompleted office development at Buckingham Gate. In 1973 chartered surveyors Jones, Lang, Wootton had been asked by the directors of Cedar to value this speculative development as if it were completed and let. The company then put a figure on the cost of completing the development, using quantity surveyors' estimates. On this basis Buckingham Gate was said to be worth £9.2 million in its then state and the figure was incorporated in the balance sheet. So Cedar's net worth was boosted by property values that did not, at that point, exist. In a brief reference to the basis of the valuation in the small print of the notes to the 1973 accounts Cedar said that 'Properties in the course of development have been valued as being completed and let; the estimated costs of completion of such properties has been provided for.' Despite the inclusion of these hypothetical values which inflated the company's net worth, Cedar's auditors Cooper & Lybrand declared in their report that the accounts showed a true and fair view.

After the collapse of the market, the ultimate cost of the development, assuming that the institutions allowed the development to continue, was expected to approach £15 million. There was no tenant in sight and Cedar's own management had been unable to sell the uncompleted property in the open market. A further valuation was then undertaken by Jones, Lang, Wootton on the basis of which the property was estimated to be worth £1½ million. Meantime Healey & Baker, another leading firm of chartered surveyors acting for the institutions, produced a valuation that suggested a figure of minus £½ million. These widely diverging professional opinions provided the starting point for negotiations to establish the price at which the institutions would buy the property. There followed a protracted haggle between Cedar, its merchant bankers, Samuel Montagu, and the institutions and their merchant bank Hambros, over this and several other properties in Cedar's portfolio.

In the case of Buckingham Gate the institutions eventually adopted a conciliatory approach. When formal documents were sent to the shareholders of Cedar outlining the terms on which the institutions were to buy, no reference was made to the negative value put on the development by Healey and Baker: the deal took place on the basis of Jones, Lang's figure which pointed to a positive value for the property of £1½ million. As the saga dragged on, the institutions became noticeably less determined to squeeze Cedar for every last penny.

Similar haggling, often acrimonious, went on all round the property market for the next three or four years. In most cases only the barest details emerged in public. The Bank of England was reluctant to see a fragile boat rocked by too much publicity, and most of the participants in these transactions shared the Old Lady's sentiment. Under a Labour government, investment in property remained a potentially sensitive political issue. It was also legally sensitive, in that the fiduciary duties of investment managers were constantly being put to the test in awkward circumstances. And if people outside the City started to ask how banks and property companies had got into such a mess in the first place, the Bank's own regulatory performance in the early 1970s might have come under uncomfortably close scrutiny.

In some cases, however, the rescues and reconstructions were too big to escape public attention. This was certainly true of Town & City Properties, where a complicated financial package was put together, involving the takeover by Town & City of one of its biggest creditors, Sterling Guarantee Trust. The banks agreed to defer their demand for interest on loans, while the Prudential committed itself to buy £20 million-worth of property from Town & City. At the same time, Sterling Guarantee's management took control of the troubled company, in a role not unlike that of a receiver and manager.

Other transfusions of cash into ailing companies were more straightforward, as when Eagle Star bought thirty-nine properties from English Property Corporation for £55½ million in 1976. And there were countless similar transactions on a smaller scale in which insurance companies and pension funds bought property for cash, which was then used to pay off the property companies' bankers and creditors. Sometimes investment institutions themselves had to be rescued from over-commitments in property. Welfare Insurance, which had invested a high proportion of its beneficiaries' money in property development companies, was taken over by London and Manchester Assurance, in a joint rescue with the National Westminster Bank and the Brooke Bond Liebig pension fund (Welfare had originally been owned by the well-known tea company and continued to manage part of its pension fund). On other occasions property companies became involved in supporting fellow property groups – sometimes in highly unorthodox circumstances which did not call for the involvement of the Bank of England. The Freshwater family, for example, ran two separate property businesses, one publicly

quoted, called Daejan Holdings, one private, in which the biggest
company was Freshwater Family Holdings. In 1975 some of the
biggest companies in the Freshwaters' private group were close
to insolvency and an important American off-shoot had been
forced to file a petition under Chapter XI of the Federal Bankruptcy Protection Act after defaulting on its debts. With the
reluctant acquiescence of its biggest institutional shareholder
Eagle Star, which was represented on the board, the publicly
quoted company helped out by extending nearly £1 million of
credit to a private company owned by the Freshwaters and by
buying properties from the private companies for £6 million.[8]

The greatest difficulty, in the steady transfer of assets from property companies to insurance companies and pension funds, arose
over the poorer quality property, and particularly over developments. Where development had been financed in advance by an
institution, the insurance company and pension fund involved
could often be persuaded to buy out the developer on the basis of
a valuation. But where speculative development had been financed
by a bank, without any advance letting, there was little that could
be done except to complete the development and hope that a
tenant would take the space and thus turn the building into a
marketable proposition.

The biggest insurance companies and pension funds, however,
bought actively from companies in the open market. Many of the
best known names in property, such as Land Securities, MEPC,
Capital and Counties, British Land, Regional Properties, and
numerous others, were forced to sell good quality property in
order to put their finances onto a sounder footing. Office blocks
all over London and the provinces, prime sites in London's finest
shopping streets, town centre developments, factory and ware-
house estates poured out of entrepreneurial companies into the
hands of anonymous institutions. In all, between 1974 and 1978,
insurance companies and pension funds spent £5 billion buying
property from overstretched companies. Only three large quoted
property groups – Amalgamated Investment and Property, Town
and Commercial and Guardian Properties – went to the wall. But
the balance of advantage between institutions and entrepreneurs
in the property market had changed irrevocably.

The question remains: why did the institutions buy? And why,
given that the Bank of England had only the flimsiest of sanctions

against insurance companies and pension funds, did so few of them call the Bank's bluff in those cases where it tried to persuade them, against their instincts, to buy? The position was, after all, very similar to the one that was to arise when the institutions confronted the Bank in the gilt-edged market in 1976 and in later years (which will be discussed in chapter eight). The property companies, like the Labour government in 1976, were forced sellers. The financial institutions knew that if, as a group, they failed to buy the properties that the Bank was anxious to persuade them to buy, property prices would come down further and give them a chance to buy more cheaply.

The answer is that many of the larger institutions retained their faith in property as the best investment with which to meet rapidly inflating liabilities, even when the market was at its nadir. So they needed little prodding to buy in the open market at knock-down prices. Outside the market they were open to persuasion, once again, because they believed that investment in property was fundamentally worthwhile. And by supporting property prices in this way, they were protecting the value of their other investments.

But that alone cannot quite explain the institutions' readiness, in those instances where they participated in rescues that did not make obvious commercial sense, to abandon their traditionally narrow interpretation of their fiduciary responsibilities. It may well be that professional fund managers in insurance companies and pension funds are more willing to bend the rules to save the City than they would be to save a government whose political priorities they do not, in many cases, share.

6
Innocence and experience

'A man accustomed to think in millions – other people's millions.'

Arnold Bennett, *Journal*

THE MAIN REPORT of Sir Harold Wilson's committee on the workings of the financial institutions called for a new pension scheme act, similar in form to the existing Companies Acts. Among the things that the committee wanted the act to lay down were: requirements for regular disclosure of information to pension fund members and beneficiaries; a definition of the duties of employers, trustees and their advisers in relation to pension schemes; a definition of the rights of pension scheme members and beneficiaries, together with the methods of redress available to them in cases of abuse; a central registry of pension funds where financial information such as the annual accounts and the latest actuarial valuation of the fund could be filed and made available to the public.

These suggestions cannot be casually dismissed. They were the unanimous recommendations of a committee whose members included such financial and industrial heavyweights as Sir David Orr, chairman of Unilever, Sir Kenneth Bond, deputy managing director of GEC, Sir John Prideaux, former chairman of National Westminster Bank, Richard Lloyd, deputy chairman of Hill Samuel and Gordon Bayley, general manager and actuary of the National Provident Institution, as well as academics, trade unionists and others. Additional support for statutory disclosure requirements came in evidence to the Wilson Committee from the Bank of England, which had had numerous opportunities, in the course of the 1970s, to acquaint itself at first hand with the activities of individual pension funds. The Bank has traditionally been one of the most powerful advocates of self-regulation in financial affairs. Yet it argued to the Wilson Committee that the resources of the pension funds were so large that their activities were of legitimate public interest. Public scrutiny of the pension funds in the financial press, the Bank argued, would stimulate efficient management and help reduce the risk of 'undesirable practices'. Where, then, does the need for greater accountability arise?

From the point of view of the economy as a whole, the shift in the ownership of capital from individuals to investment institutions has dramatically increased the financial system's tolerance of loss-making investment. Money is concentrated heavily in the hands of a small number of billionaire funds. The bigger these funds grow, in real terms, the bigger the individual mistakes they can make without affecting the overall solvency of the pension fund.

From the point of view of the individual fund, the most obvious danger is that the trustees and managers may be tempted to take unjustifiably large risks in relation to the size of the fund on which employees are dependent for much of their retirement pensions. If this leads to heavy losses the fund may become insolvent. The deficiency then has to be met from increased contributions from the employer and employees. Alternatively the level of benefits may have to be reduced.

A rather different area in which there is a clear need for increased accountability and disclosure relates to the private share dealings of those who run the pension fund. It is a general principle of the law of trust that a trustee should not benefit personally from his fiduciary position. Yet there are no specific legal requirements governing the personal investment dealings of pension fund trustees or managers. Nothing, for example, prevents a fund manager from dealing for his own personal account in the same shares that he deals in for the fund. Yet there is an obvious temptation for the manager of a big fund to buy shares for his personal account in the knowledge that subsequent buying by the pension fund may push up the price of the shares; the manager would then derive an immediate personal profit. If the trustee or manager runs an active share dealing company for his own personal account, stockbrokers may be tempted to offer the private company attractive deals – potentially lucrative underwriting of new share issues, for example – in the hope of securing more of the pension fund's business.

Potential conflicts of interest can also arise where the trustee or fund manager takes a personal financial interest in a company which is backed by the pension fund. If the company threatens to collapse, for example, the trustee or fund manager may be forced to take a decision on the pensioners' behalf about whether or not to rescue the company, when the decision could have a dramatic impact on his personal finances. Alternatively, the trustee or manager may be tempted to take stakes in private companies backed by the fund. A mere £5-worth of shares in a private company whose total ordinary share capital amounts to only £100 may suddenly become very valuable if the pension fund decides to back the £100 company with £½ million of loan capital. Other potential conflicts can arise if the pension fund trustee or manager borrows personally from entrepreneurs whom the fund itself backs. For if the trustees or managers are personally dependent in any way on an entrepreneur in their personal business dealings, it could become much harder to turn down unsuitable investment propositions that the entrepreneur puts up to the fund. The conflicts are at their most frequent in the property market where, as we have seen, formal regulation is not much in evidence.

All this contrasts sharply with the regulatory arrangements covering the private business dealings of company directors. Directors are statutorily required, for example, to reveal publicly any material personal financial interest, however indirect, in contracts with their company in view of the potential conflict of interest. And where large transactions involving a potential conflict of interest are concerned, the directors of quoted companies are obliged to submit details to the stock exchange and may be required, under stock exchange rules, to obtain shareholders' approval for such proceedings.

The National Association of Pension Funds, which covers most, but by no means all, of Britain's larger occupational pension schemes, believes that self regulation adequately protects present and future pensioners from abuse and that the past record in pension fund management has been good. Since the full record is not publicly available, in the present state of pension fund self regulation, it is impossible for most people to assess this claim. The present chapter seeks to put it in context by looking at widely varying standards of investment judgement and personal investment arrangements by fund managers and trustees at some of

Britain's largest pension funds, often in circumstances where the beneficiaries might have questioned whether the trustees had taken adequate precautions to prevent conflicts of interest arising. The implication is not that personal share dealing by investment managers is necessarily reprehensible, or that situations which appeared to pose possible conflicts of interest necessarily gave rise to such conflicts in practice. But common sense suggests that fund managers should be especially careful in the way they go about their own dealings and in the personal financial associations they form with businessmen who have a financial connection with the pension funds they manage. These connections may be harmless enough for the businessmen concerned. But for the pension fund manager they could on occasion result in his being forced to confront awkward choices which might otherwise have been avoided. Nor should the cases discussed necessarily be regarded as typical; past standards of pension fund disclosure have been so poor that it is impossible to say what is or is not typical in this area. But they should give the reader enough information to judge for himself or herself where the balance should lie in the argument between the Wilson Committee and the Bank of England, on the one side, and the National Association of Pension Funds on the other.

One pension fund whose past activities give rise to a considerable number of questions is that of Britain's biggest industrial company, Imperial Chemical Industries. From the late 1950s to mid-1974 the ICI pension fund's investments were managed by Norman Freeman, who differed from many other fund managers in that he was more than usually keen for the fund he managed to back speculative entrepreneurial companies, both in and out of the stock market. It was perhaps only natural, then, that the ICI fund should have gravitated early towards investment in property. But where other funds preferred to obtain a high proportion of their investments through purchases of completed and tenanted properties in the open market, ICI, under Freeman's direction and with the support of the trustees, acquired much of its property by financing speculative development in which both the risks and the rewards were higher.

Another characteristic of the ICI pension fund, under Freeman, was that a number of its investment staff, in their personal capacity, embarked on private business deals with entrepreneurs that the ICI pension fund itself had backed with its members' money. And

Freeman himself, who was a trustee as well as being the investment manager, apparently felt no inhibition about establishing
private business arrangements with well-known entrepreneurs. In
the early 1970s he embarked on a number of private investments
which could possibly have led to conflicts between his own personal interest and that of the beneficiaries of the ICI pension
fund.

One such was a joint investment with half a dozen others in
the private company owning the 19th Club in Old Burlington
Street in the West End of London. Here Freeman and his deputy
investment manager William Dobbie (who was not a trustee)
became co-shareholders with, among others, Pat Matthews of
First National Finance Corporation and Stanley van Gelder of
Dalton Barton Securities. The ICI pension fund was one of the
biggest shareholders in First National at the time. Only months
before becoming a partner with Matthews in the 19th Club venture, Freeman was playing a key role in the board-room battle at
Spey Investments, in which there was a heated argument with the
financier Charles Gordon over the sale of Spey's banking interests
to First National. And the ICI fund had also been a major shareholder in Dalton Barton Securities.

Another of Freeman's investments which could have involved
similar potential conflicts of interest was a 5% stake in a private
company called Claytherm Hotels. The chief shareholders in Claytherm, which owned the Hotel Miramonte at Praia das Macas outside Lisbon in Portugal, were Ernie Clay, chairman of Fulham
Football Club, and Peachey Property Corporation, whose controversial chairman Eric Miller received a knighthood in Harold
Wilson's resignation honours list and subsequently committed
suicide before the publication of a Department of Trade report
that accused him of milking Peachey Property to finance his expensive way of life.[1] In this case the ICI pension fund held between
4% and 5% of Peachey's capital. And the relationship with Miller
was to prove embarrassing for Freeman. In evidence to the Department of Trade inspectors, Miller accused him of accepting personal favours from Peachey in return for offering the pension
fund's assistance to the company in a property transaction. The
inspectors concluded that the allegation was without foundation,
but the fact that it was made at all underlines the danger of not
keeping private and public business well apart.

A further unusual feature of Freeman's interest in the hotel company was that his shares were initially held under a nominee name. Nominee names are employed by stockbrokers and merchant banks primarily for administrative convenience. But they can also result in the identity of the broker's or banker's client being kept secret. In this case the nominee company, called Heribank Nominees, was administered by Heritable and General Investment Bank, a fringe financial concern owned by publicity-shy property entrepreneur, Instone Bloomfield, and his family. The link with ICI here was that the pension fund was the biggest institutional shareholder in Bloomfield's quoted property and hotel group, Oddenino's Property and Investment, with 13% of the equity capital. The fund had also financed Oddenino's, jointly with Pearl Assurance and the National Westminster Bank pension fund, in the development of the Royal Garden Hotel in Kensington, and was committed to putting up further cash for the company's property development programme in North America. The shareholding in Claytherm was re-registered under Freeman's own name shortly after he ceased to manage the ICI pension fund's investments.

The personal financial arrangements of Freeman and Dobbie that are of most interest to members of the ICI pension fund and to shareholders in ICI itself, however, relate to the fact that the two men controlled a private property and share dealing company called Dobman Property and Investment, which was active in the first half of the 1970s. Admittedly, for pension fund managers to run a personal dealing company would not necessarily have been considered unusual in the City at that time. But Dobman was no small-time investor. In 1972–73, Dobman Property and Investment was buying and selling between £500,000 and £1 million worth of shares a year. It also took on underwriting commitments, which amounted on 30 September, 1972, for example, to more than £70,000. Perhaps the most surprising feature of Dobman, however, was that certain entrepreneurs whom the ICI pension fund had backed became shareholders in this venture.

Among those who were registered as holding shares in Dobman Investment and Property were Cecil Attwood, chairman of Dufay Bitumastic, a quoted paint and protective coatings group, and David Berchanpour, an Iranian citizen who was a director of

Edinburgh Industrial Holdings. ICI pension fund had significant holdings in the early 1970s in both Dufay and Edinburgh Industrial. The identity of the larger outside shareholders in Dobman, however, lay behind nominee names. The biggest of them was Heribank Nominees, the company administered by Instone Bloomfield's private bank. It is not clear whether Bloomfield was directly interested in the shares, but there can be no doubt, on the basis of records filed at Companies House, that Bloomfield's Heritable and General Investment Bank was involved in the financing of a property deal with which Dobman was concerned; Dobman's mortgage register records a charge securing property in Bristol in favour of Bloomfield's fringe bank.

Another large holding in Dobman was in the name of Libra Nominees, a company registered in the Isle of Man. Libra's claim to fame is that it cropped up in the Department of Trade report on Peachey Property in connection with unexplained transactions involving property dealer, financier and self-styled socialist Judah Binstock. A search in the Isle of Man does not reveal the beneficial owners of Libra, but it does show that one of the three directors was Binstock; it seems probable that Binstock or his family were interested in Dobman through this holding. And Binstock's interest in Dobman is put beyond reasonable doubt by the appearance on Dobman's share register in 1972 of Mutual Loan Fund Association. Mutual Loan Fund was a finance company in which the major shareholding could be traced back, via companies in Liverpool, the Isle of Man and Kuala Lumpur, to Binstock. Mutual Loan Fund Association's investment in Dobman thereafter appeared as a trade investment in its balance sheet.

The involvement of Freeman and Dobbie with this elusive expatriate entrepreneur is of interest on a number of scores. The first is that Binstock's background makes him a surprising associate for the investment managers of the pension fund of Britain's biggest industrial company. Binstock is now a fugitive from British justice and enjoys the dubious distinction of having been the subject of anxious scrutiny or critical comment in no fewer than three separate Department of Trade investigations. The first and most critical of these examined the way in which the quoted New Brighton Tower Company, which Binstock and his then partner Leon Davies controlled in the 1960s, helped finance the develop-

ment of the Victoria Sporting Club in London's Edgware Road.[2]
The inspectors concluded that Binstock and his partner appeared
'to have given more thought to their interest and enrichment than
to those of the shareholders whom they were supposed to represent and protect'. The inspectors were also concerned with
apparent irregularities in the running of the club while it was
under Binstock's control, but were unable to arrive at more than
tentative conclusions because the controversial financier was by
then resident abroad and refused to give evidence. Later, a war-
rant was issued for Binstock's arrest in connection with currency
irregularities. Scotland Yard's criminal intelligence department,
known as C11, also suspected Binstock of having links with
organised crime, especially the Mafia.

These facts about Binstock could not, of course, have been
known to Freeman and Dobbie in the early 1970s. But even at the
start of the 1970s, Binstock's reputation was not high in the financial community; he had been strongly attacked in the press for the
way in which he had profited from his association with the New
Brighton Tower Company. In 1972 the ICI pension fund nonetheless became involved in a deal set up by Binstock that was later to
prove very costly for the fund.

Binstock, by this time, had taken up residence in the fashionable
Avenue Foch in Paris and had joined the growing band of British
property entrepreneurs who were buying development sites in the
French capital. He invited ICI, together with Triumph Investment Trust, a fringe bank run by the Hungarian-born entrepreneur Tom Whyte, to participate in a Luxembourg-registered
company called Orbisa. ICI had built up a holding in Triumph
and was keen to go into European property. The outcome was
that the ICI fund took 15% of the ordinary share capital of Orbisa
and became a joint promoter of the company, a small number of
whose shares were quoted on the Luxembourg stock exchange.
The idea was that ICI should provide guarantees for bank loans
advanced to Orbisa to build up a portfolio of French properties,
while taking a share of the profit on individual property transactions. In due course it was hoped that Orbisa could be floated on
the British stock exchange. Triumph and ICI pension fund also
established a similar venture in Belgium with the well-known
Brussels developer, Charles de Pauw. In addition Freeman con-
firmed to me that he believed Binstock had been in partnership

with Sir Eric Miller's Peachey Property Corporation in a transaction involving the sale by Peachey to the ICI pension fund of a property in Paris.

In the event, the partnership with Triumph proved short lived. Early in 1974 Triumph Investment Trust's finances were crumbling as nervous banks and investment institutions failed to renew their deposits with its banking subsidiary. So the ICI pension fund, together with other institutions that had been involved with the troubled secondary bank, was invited to a meeting presided over by Jasper Hollom at the Bank of England. As in the case of Cedar Holdings, forceful arguments were levelled at the institutions.

ICI's then finance director, Albert Frost, was not keen for the ICI pension fund to become involved in a rescue. But he felt that there was too much at stake, in the secondary banking crisis, to refuse to offer support, provided that it was arranged in as commercial a manner as possible. The trustees decided in favour of support. With a minimum of publicity, the ICI fund provided assistance to Triumph by buying its shares in Orbisa on the basis of an independent valuation of its properties. Given that many of the properties were little more than holes in the ground, at that time, and given that they were a long way from finding tenants to fill all the potential space, this valuation must have been unusually tentative all the same. And it was not an ideal moment to increase the fund's exposure in Europe, in view of the onset of the OPEC-induced recession, which was bound to make it harder to find tenants for the properties. To make matters worse, the French government had just imposed a rent freeze and put a ban on foreign companies borrowing money in the domestic market. The effect of the ban was to send the British, who had been partly responsible for the boom in French commercial property prices, back whence they came.

The timing of the deal was also unfortunate in that several of the ICI pension fund's other investments were suddenly turning sour. Because of the fall in the British and other stock markets, the value of the fund had fallen from £479 million to £382 million in the year to March 1974, despite its strong cash flow. And in addition to its associations with secondary banks, the ICI fund had been an enthusiastic backer of several quoted and unquoted property companies that were now running into trouble.

In the unquoted sector the ICI pension fund was heavily exposed in the Lyon group, where it had guaranteed £13¾ million of bank borrowings, in exchange for a fee and for a share of the potential profit on future sale of the property developments for which borrowings had been raised. This sounded a good deal during the boom, when the fund had hoped to extract a profit from Lyon's developments without having to lay out any cash. When the property market crashed and Lyon was unable to pay interest or principal on its loans, the ICI fund had to pay up under the guarantee.

Similar trouble had arisen at English and Continental Investments, a second incarnation of the property group run by Ramon Greene and Jack Walker. When the Post Office pension fund had bought most of English and Continental's portfolio in 1972, the two men had kept three big sites for future development and invited new institutional partners to join them in another spending spree in the property market, both in Britain and France. One was the ICI pension fund, which took its place alongside an off-shoot of Continental Illinois, the Chicago-based banking group, and the Crown Agents, who turned to Greene and Walker with renewed enthusiasm after making a profit of £16 million on the earlier sale to the Post Office fund. ICI took just over 11% of the equity capital of English and Continental in exchange for which it was expected to help finance a development programme whose estimated total cost, in mid-1973, stood at £93 million. English and Continental's main development sites in Britain were the former Westinghouse works behind Kings Cross in London; a large site bought from the Port of London Authority at Cutler Street on the fringe of the City; and a site originally owned by British Rail at Manchester Central Station. At the same time English and Continental became involved in the development of several properties in Paris.

The value of the developments plunged disastrously in 1974. Once again the ICI fund moved into the breach. It offered support by buying five French properties from English and Continental with a book value of around £7 million. This, however, was a less risky investment transaction than the earlier deal with Triumph because English and Continental was mainly refurbishing buildings rather than developing them from scratch. The letting problems were also less formidable. But the fund's intervention was not enough to save English and Continental Investments from subsequent liquidation any more than the earlier rescue package was enough to save Triumph, which collapsed within months of ICI's purchase of the shares in Orbisa.

Other investments of the ICI pension fund that were running into trouble included two private companies called Aquatels and Rentaplay (Aquatels), which were respectively set up to develop and operate a recreation centre at Basildon in Essex. The pension funds of ICI, National Westminster Bank and the Electricity Supply Industry were jointly involved here in backing an entrepreneur called Reginald Treble. So, too, were other investors, whose identities were concealed on the share registers of the two companies under the names of Impartial Nominees and Rodo Nominees. Impartial was administered by a small City stockbroking firm called Charles Spencer; it also featured as one of the larger shareholders in Dobman Property and Investment, the Freeman–Dobbie dealing company. Rodo Nominees was a company operated by Rodo Investment Trust, a financial and investment concern that was run in the second half of the 1960s (when the Basildon recreation centre was being planned) by the entrepreneur John Gommes. Gommes was also the chairman at that time of Dufay Bitumastic, whose managing director Cecil Attwood held shares in Dobman Property and Investment. And the ICI pension fund, along with the electricity pension fund, held a big share stake in Rodo Investment Trust until serious financial difficulties at Rodo led to Bankers Trust International taking control of it.[3] Before Bankers Trust took over, Norman Freeman had held a directorship in the Rodo group.

In the event, none of the shareholders in Aquatels or Rentaplay (Aquatels), anonymous or otherwise, did well over the long run with their investment. For between 1975 and 1978 the combined losses mounted progressively to over £1 million. The three institutions, which owned 27% of the ordinary capital apiece, felt obliged to take direct control over their investment, merge the two companies and pump more money into the enlarged concern, which was insolvent. Liabilities exceeded assets by more than £2 million.

In the quoted sector, one of the biggest casualties in the ICI portfolio was G. R. A. Property Trust, the greyhound racing stadium group which had plunged headlong into property dealing and development during the boom. The ICI fund was the company's biggest institutional backer; by 1974 it had invested over £10 million in G.R.A., which was struggling with an oppressive mountain of debt. In the following year the struggle proved too much and a moratorium was declared on its borrowings. ICI had little option but to agree to the moratorium.

To make matters worse the property crash was creating a backwash at some of the ICI pension fund's investments that were only indirectly connected with property. Through its involvement in Spey Investments, the fund had become the biggest single shareholder in National Car Parks, in which the pension funds of Unilever, Barclays Bank and the Electricity Supply Industry also retained an interest. Norman Freeman had gone onto the board. The private car parking company's finances had been badly affected by price controls on parking tariffs and by the effect of the oil crisis on motoring habits. It also had huge borrowings of nearly £8 million at the end of 1973, in relation to its net assets of only £$\frac{1}{2}$ million. And there were even doubts about the real value of those net assets because the two entrepreneurs who ran National Car Parks, Donald Gosling (who was later knighted in Harold Wilson's resignation honours list) and Ron Hobson, had arranged loans of more than £2 million from NCP to one of their own financially stretched property companies. So the pension funds, which had put £1 million of fresh capital into NCP only the year before, found that their investment was threatened from an unexpected quarter. As for the stake in Spey itself, there was little hope that the ICI fund would emerge with money intact.

All investment involves an element of risk and all fund managers are bound to back a loser from time to time. Freeman no doubt had winners to his credit as well. And his investment strategy, including substantial commitments to speculative property development, was approved by the ICI investment committee and by the pension fund trustees, among them a number of highly qualified main board directors of ICI. But the number of investments in the ICI pension fund that ran into difficulty in the mid-1970s still seems remarkably high by the standards of other financial institutions. While Freeman's approach to investment produced good results when financial markets were buoyant, it appears not to have stood up well when put to the test in the more demanding financial climate that set in after 1973. Freeman, however, was fortunate enough not to have to cope with the continuing problems posed by these investments of the ICI pension fund in entrepreneurial companies. In June 1974 he retired and went to live at Hyères in the South of France. Dobbie also retired before the full extent of the difficulties emerged. The two men did, however, face problems in Dobman, whose share dealing losses in the year to 30 September, 1974, amounted to £120,000; its highest-ever profit before tax had been £45,000. It was not an ostensibly rewarding investment for the entrepreneurial friends of Freeman and Dobbie, some of whom were anxious by that time to part with their investment. Freeman and Dobbie did not, however, buy out their fellow shareholders' shares. Instead, control of the company was sold, and the outgoing shareholders repaid from the proceeds. The purchaser was none other than Judah Binstock.

Freeman was succeeded as general manager of investments at ICI by Alwyne Conlong, who came to the job from the Church of England Board of Finance. Much of his time in the next three or four years was spent sorting out the more speculative investments. When I went to see Conlong at ICI in 1980 he was reluctant to discuss events that took place before his arrival. But it is probable that the French properties that originally came into the fund through the association with Judah Binstock and Orbisa were one of his most persistent headaches.

In the year to March 1977, the excess of interest and other outgoings over rental income on properties in France amounted to more than £10 million, equivalent to 19% of the total cash available for investment by the ICI pension fund that year. The fund had also guaranteed more than £68 million of bank borrowings for property developments, which was equivalent to nearly 14% of the book value of the whole ICI pension fund in March 1977. In the two subsequent years the deficit on the French properties declined as a percentage of the fund's rapidly growing cash flow. But by 1979 the fund had still been forced to provide a cumulative total of more than £22 million to cover the excess of outgoings over income arising from these property developments in Europe. Today the capital value of the properties has probably increased. to compensate for much of this deficit. But it has been a dismal investment for ICI, when measured against the return the fund could have obtained on many more orthodox investments. And by 1979 the fund had effectively run up borrowings on its overseas investments of no less than £164 million – a huge sum equivalent to more than 20% of the pension fund's gross book value at the time of £783 million and scarcely credible given that it is highly unusual for pension funds to incur large-scale borrowings. In 1980 the fund was still having problems in letting some of the remaining space in its French property portfolio. When I approached Norman Freeman, he did not wish to be interviewed. But he did reply to a letter in which I pointed out that I would be raising questions in this book about potential conflicts of interest that might have arisen as a result of his involvement in private business arrangements with entrepreneurs who had received financial backing from the ICI fund. In his letter he said that it was entirely wrong to imply that there was any conflict of interest for him. He added that his dedication to the interests of the pension fund and to his other responsibilities at ICI was total. As for Judah Binstock, Freeman made no reference to his personal links with the expatriate financier, but in relation to the ICI pension fund he argued that Binstock's connection 'was minor and indirect'.

Under Conlong the ICI pension fund goes in for more conservative types of investment than it did under his predecessor. And private dealings of the investment managers and staff are apparently more carefully supervised. Since the fund's income continues to be adversely affected by investments in companies run by entrepreneurs with whom Freeman and Dobbie were privately associated, the scheme's 140,000 members, who in 1980 put over £20 million of their annual pay into the fund, might nonetheless reasonably ask a number of questions.

Why should a trustee of the ICI pension fund, who was responsible for managing its investments, have sometimes used for personal account dealings the nominee services of a little known tertiary bank like Instone Bloomfield's Heritable and General, so potentially putting himself under a personal obligation to a client of the fund, in preference to those of a better known clearing bank or merchant bank? Why was Freeman's holding in a private company in which Peachey Property was one of the two main shareholders held in a nominee name administered by Bloomfield's bank? Whose identity lay behind the names of Impartial Nominees and Rodo Nominees, in the investments in Aquatels and Rentaplay (Aquatels)? Why did the trustees sanction the original investment in Orbisa, given that Judah Binstock's reputation even at the time fell some way short of what might have been expected of a client of the pension fund of Britain's biggest and most reputable private sector industrial company? And why did the trustees, who included at the time a future chairman of ICI, Sir Maurice Hodgson, disclose so little in the annual accounts of the pension fund about the nature and extent of the commitment they were undertaking by buying Triumph Investment Trust's shares in Orbisa in 1974?

In practice, present and future pensioners of ICI might not have come to much harm if the ICI pension fund had run into more serious trouble. ICI takes better care of its pensioners than most private sector companies and it even guarantees to keep the fund solvent. But this raises an important question for ICI's own share-holders. For if the pension fund's investments are badly managed, it is they who ultimately foot the bill. Between 1974 and 1979 the company's contributions into the staff fund went up from 12.2% of pay to 18.8% of pay – a rise of more than 50%. The comparable increase in the workers' fund was from 7.2% of pay to 12.3%, which is equivalent to a rise of more than 70%. In round figures the company contributed £59 million in the year to March 1979 compared with only £19 million in 1974. Would the contributions have had to rise so fast had the fund not been committed to the highly speculative investments in Orbisa, G.R.A., the Lyon group, Aquatels and the rest?

ICI's was not the only pension fund to find that backing British property entrepreneurs away from home could be a hair-raising experience. Perhaps the narrowest escape was that of the Unilever pension fund. In the case of the big Anglo-Dutch multinational there is no question of any potential conflict of interest between the trustees' public and private interests. But there is a question mark over how they came to sanction an unusually risky joint property venture in France and Germany in the early 1970s. This step was to involve the fund in heavy guarantees and borrowings in relation to property developments that ultimately cost little short of £100 million.

The property entrepreneur whom the Unilever fund chose to back in this instance was Howard Ronson, who had been intro-duced to the fund in the early 1970s by Chesterfield Properties.

Unilever pension fund had had earlier dealings with Chesterfield, a quoted property company run by Harold and Roger Wingate, and was anxious to increase the percentage of overseas investments in its portfolio. So in 1972 it was agreed that the pension fund should join forces with Chesterfield and Ronson. The Unilever fund effectively took 50% of the equity capital of the companies set up for the purpose and agreed to guarantee part of the borrowings raised to finance developments, while Chesterfield and Ronson were to provide the development know-how and take 25% of the capital each. A noteworthy feature of the partnership was that while Chesterfield had a sound reputation in property development in Britain, neither Chesterfield nor Ronson (who was still only in his late twenties) had a particularly lengthy track record overseas.

Unilever and Chesterfield were by no means alone in looking for commercial development opportunities abroad. At this point in the property boom numerous developers felt that prices had become so high in Britain that there were greener pastures elsewhere. Interest rates were lower and yields on commercial properties were invariably higher in the other major industrial economies. While British property developers owed much of their success in the domestic market to inept government planning policies and a lax monetary climate, most of them genuinely believed that they had some special 'expertise' – a word that was constantly on the lips of British property men in the early 1970s – which they could employ for the good of both themselves and the continentals. To that end they took their sometimes slapdash financial habits to Europe. They were preceded by estate agents who scoured the main cities for commercial property investment and development projects. The locals wisely took advantage of the British invasion to sell their less attractive real estate at prices which said more about conditions in the British property market than they did about the economics of property development in the countries concerned.

In this heady atmosphere Howard Ronson set off around Europe in search of developments. Between 1972 and 1974 he accumulated two projects in Paris and seven development schemes in big German cities including Cologne, Dusseldorf, Frankfurt, Hamburg, Munich and Stuttgart, for the joint venture with Unilever, as well as putting together other deals in which the Unilever

pension fund was not involved. The ultimate cost of the two
French developments was to work out at well over £20 million,
including interest; the equivalent figure for the German developments was around £70 million. It was a big development programme, even by the standards of the British property
boom.

When conditions in European property markets took a turn for
the worse after the oil crisis, the Unilever pension fund's adventure
across the channel appeared in an entirely new perspective. Very
little of Ronson's development programme was let in advance and
in 1975 when conditions in the property markets of both Germany
and France looked particularly bleak the prospects for letting were
depressing. Unilever had originally agreed to guarantee around
30% of the bank borrowings that Chesterfield and Ronson arranged for the development companies. But the banks were not
prepared to go on providing finance unless they were offered
further security or guarantees.

Chesterfield was not in a strong position, while the property
market was depressed in Britain, to help with finance. Though not
one of the worst hit property groups, it had a heavy burden of
short term debt. Had it been required to honour the guarantees it
had offered on the joint ventures on the continent, its own financial problems might have become serious. Nor could Ronson have
been expected to put up significant sums. So the Unilever fund
found that while it was legally obliged to guarantee only 30% of
the borrowings, the true position was that it would have to
guarantee very much more if the developments were ever to be
completed. As other investment institutions discovered at about
the same time, there was no such thing as a 30% commitment
when the going became hard. The biggest institutional backer of
a troubled property company normally had to choose between
offering 100% support and abandoning its investment.

In this instance the Unilever pension fund felt that it had little
option but to go ahead with developments where construction
was already in train. But in the case of a mixed shopping and office
development in Moncherbergstrasse in Hamburg, and a 180,000
square foot office block at rue Raymond Losserand on the Ilot
des Mariniers in Paris, there was an opportunity to pull out. After
taking independent professional advice, and deliberating at length,
the trustees decided to persevere. So at 31 March, 1976 the

Unilever pension fund, whose book value was only £245 million, had effectively underwritten a development programme that was ultimately to cost nearly £100 million. The risk was enormous.

For most of that year sterling sank inexorably against the French franc and Deutschemark, as it did against most other leading currencies, with the result that the sterling cost of meeting the guarantees of foreign bank borrowings was rising at a frightening rate. There was a nightmarish possibility that the Unilever pension fund might find itself burdened with a spiralling sterling commitment for an investment that would, in the absence of lettings, become a multi-million drain on the fund's resources for several years to come.

To make matters worse, the trustees were suddenly forced to confront a threat of an entirely different nature. In July, 1976, the Department of Trade published a report which was severely critical of Howard Ronson's conduct in managing the affairs of a group of housebuilding and residential development companies originally set up by his father Gerald Ronson in the early 1960s. (Although they are related, there is no business connection between this Gerald Ronson and the entrepreneur of the same name who runs the Heron filling station and property group.)

The report was concerned mainly with the affairs of Dwell Constructions, and Yorks and Lancs Construction Company. It was unusual in that none of the companies concerned was quoted on the stock exchange. The inspectors had been appointed after a chorus of complaints about the Ronsons' standards of construction and slowness in meeting their bills from housebuyers, building societies, subcontractors and creditors, in Yorkshire and South East England. Several high court actions had been pending against the companies when they had gone into liquidation and a deputation of creditors had gone to the Board of Trade to try to get something done about their plight.

The inspectors' conclusions, at the end of an inquiry which they said had been 'painfully and embarrassingly prolonged because of the complexity and disorder of these companies' affairs', were damning. The conduct of the companies under investigation managed by Gerald Ronson, a former East End furniture manufacturer, and his son Howard, was characterised for a long period, the inspectors alleged, by 'arrogance, callousness and inefficiency, and by a ruthless pursuit of profit without any adequate capital resources to justify it'. Both men were accused of gross mismanagement and the inspectors found that there was evidence from which a court might have inferred that for a period of months before Dwell Constructions and Yorks and Lancs Construction Company stopped trading, Gerald and Howard Ronson 'were knowingly parties to the carrying on of the business of both companies with intent to defraud the company's creditors'. Howard Ronson was criticised for his 'harsh and oppressive' handling of sub-contractors. And although he was still only in his mid-20s when the companies went into liquidation, the inspectors were not inclined to be indulgent. They considered that neither he nor his father was 'a suitable person at the present time to act as a director of a company'.

This huge report, which ran to four heavy volumes, did not attract much publicity in the national press. Few people connected the name of Howard Ronson with Unilever and interest among financial journalists was limited because none of the Ronson companies had been quoted on the stock exchange. It was arguable, too, that the inspectors were applying an inappropriately high set of moral standards; some of the country's biggest quoted property groups had spent most of the property boom pursuing profit on a thoroughly inadequate capital base without incurring censure. But the trustees were in an embarrassing position. For a pension fund to go on putting several millions of its beneficiaries' money into the hands of a man who had been condemned as unfit to be a director of a company by inspectors appointed by the Department of Trade, would have looked highly questionable if it ever attracted public attention. Yet if the trustees jettisoned Ronson, they would have had to find an alternative management team to see the development programme through to a possibly more expensive conclusion.

In the event, Ronson offered to resign from the board of all the companies involved, while continuing to manage the development programme. The Unilever pension fund agreed with this solution. At the same time the fund bought Ronson out of the German developments for an initial payment of £$\frac{1}{4}$ million, to be followed later by a further sum calculated on the basis of the net worth of the German interests in the early 1980s. Ronson did, however, continue to hold his shares in the French developments because his interest there was held indirectly through a joint company with Chesterfield Properties. Unilever could not get rid of him on its own initiative.

Had details of these arrangements ever been made public at the time, they would almost certainly have raised eyebrows. To start with, the severing of connections with Ronson was little more than a token gesture. Although he lost his directorships, he went on managing the developments as before. And while Unilever had bought out his 25% interest in the German companies, he retained an interest in the underlying developments through the deferred purchase arrangement, which meant that he stood to gain from any increase in the value of the properties.

The other striking feature of the rearrangement of the German interests was its apparent generosity to Ronson. When the deal was done in mid-1977, much of the space in the German properties had yet to be let or pre-let. Taking the German and French investments together, less than half the space in properties completed or under development had found tenants. Without the continuing support of the Unilever pension fund, the German companies would almost certainly have been insolvent, for in the course of the 1977–78 financial year, the fund had to write off over £6 million to cover the deficit of rental income against outgoings; the value of the properties, in their condition at the time, was almost certainly less than their cost. The fund managers were sufficiently concerned about this to make a provision in the accounts at the end of that year to cover the whole cost of the investment in the equity capital of the German development companies – the accountant's way of indicating that the investment is potentially worthless. Why, then, did the trustees pay £$\frac{1}{4}$ million to Ronson for his interest in a company that they themselves regarded as having no value?

Part of the answer is that the pension fund managers felt that this was a less expensive course than getting rid of Ronson. Unilever director Ronald Archer, who was put in charge of the pension fund property committee in late 1974 and saw the continental property investment through its period of maximum difficulty, told me that the pension fund had never had any reason to complain about Ronson's management. The problem with the German properties, and to a lesser extent the French properties, was that too high a price had been paid for them in the boom and that good tenants were hard to come by in the recession that followed. Ronson, says Archer, had chosen good sites and he put up his buildings on time and within budget. Without him, it would have been very much harder to complete the letting programme.

As for Chesterfield, the trustees did not think it wise to buy out Chesterfield's interest in the German developments for a nominal sum when the developments were of questionable value. But they did ensure that Chesterfield's stake was reduced from 25% to 12½%. This appears to fall some way short of ruthlessness, but it was no doubt intended to leave Chesterfield with an incentive to help bring the investment to a successful conclusion. Nor would it necessarily have made sense for the Unilever pension fund to alienate Chesterfield when its relationship with the property company had extended beyond this particular venture into Europe.

With the benefit of hindsight, the decision to complete these nine developments in Germany and France was the right one. By 1980 all the buildings were fully let. The two French developments were both valued at well above cost and earning rents in excess of interest charges on the borrowings raised to finance that cost. The German ones were also showing an overall surplus on cost, although they appeared unlikely to show a respectable income for some considerable time. Unilever would not quantify the deficit of income against interest for me and the picture has been further confused because the fund has repaid borrowings with its own money since the abolition of exchange controls late in 1979. But it seems likely that the revenue loss on the German properties was running in millions rather than thousands before the fund put in new capital to pay off the bank borrowings.

The Unilever fund nonetheless remained, even in 1980, involved in an unusually heavy commitment in France and Germany. The extent can be deduced from the pension fund's accounts for 1979. In March of that year, the Unilever fund had borrowed or guaranteed borrowings, most of which arose from the association with Chesterfield and Howard Ronson, to the tune of £113 million – a huge sum in relation to the fund's total investments of £612 million. The fact that these borrowings have now been partly replaced with Unilever pension fund's own money does not affect the relative size of the commitment, as the fund still continued to own the properties. Pension funds rarely borrow significant amounts of money, and when they give guarantees, they are normally kept within tight limits – far tighter than they were in the case of the Unilever trustees' foray into Europe. Few pension fund managers would have been happy to see their own accounts burdened with this degree of borrowing. The question remains: was it right for the then trustees of a pension fund to sanction such a huge speculative investment overseas in a venture managed by a relatively untried entrepreneur? And did the trustees appreciate the full extent of their commitment when the original decision was taken? The 87,000 members and pensioners of the Unilever pension scheme are surely entitled to ask.

Predictably, the Post Office pension fund, with its rapidly accumulating cash flow, was one of the funds that joined the hopeful procession across the channel. And like other institutions it swept into Europe on the coat-tails of an entrepreneur – in this case Jimmy Goldsmith, the Anglo-French financier who ran the Cavenham food group. In the late 1960s and early 1970s Goldsmith had transformed Cavenham from a small food and confectionery concern into a huge multinational food manufacturing and retailing group which was represented in the British high street by several grocery chains, of which Liptons was probably the best known. This transformation had been brought about mainly by astute takeover bids. Goldsmith's most impressive talent was for using the facilities of the stock market for enlarging his empire. When the stock market was at its peak in 1972, he was busy trying to repeat the process in other areas, including banking and property. Among the quoted companies in which he took a controlling interest was Argyle Securities, a property development group whose day-to-day management Goldsmith subsequently entrusted to property entrepreneur Michael Rivkin. It was to Argyle that the Post Office looked with a view to increasing its commitments in property.

This was a bold move on the part of the pension fund trustees. Goldsmith was an immensely powerful personality, capable of great charm, who carried with him an aura of the international jet set. He was also well known, in the City, for the complexity of his business interests and the speed with which he chopped and changed their structure. An investment in one of his companies was prone to instant metamorphosis. The trustees' move was

doubly bold in that certain of the companies controlled by Goldsmith sometimes undertook deals with each other involving
potential conflicts of interest between Goldsmith and other shareholders. And it was not uncommon for investors in one company
to find that the company had advanced money to provide financial
backing to other companies controlled by the same entrepreneur.
At various times while it was both quoted on the stock exchange
and under Goldsmith's effective control, Argyle Securities lent
money to Générale Occidentale, the Paris-based master company
of Goldsmith's international empire, Banque Occidentale pour
l'Industrie et le Commerce, Générale Occidentale's French banking
group, and Anglo-Continental Investment and Finance, a financial
and investment off-shoot of Générale Occidentale that was quoted
in London. Other companies in the loosely-knit empire were involved in similar financing transactions. So anyone who put
money into Goldsmith's companies was demonstrating a conviction that this persuasive entrepreneur would generate profits for
them in circumstances where his own interests sometimes appeared to lie in a conflicting direction.

The Post Office pension fund's trustees, who included representatives of the Post Office's own top management, did have
considerable faith in Goldsmith. So when Argyle Securities
needed finance for a huge redevelopment scheme in the centre of
Paris, the men from the Post Office pension fund gave Goldsmith
a sympathetic hearing. Argyle's plan was to redevelop the Grands
Magasins du Louvre, a well-known building on an island site at
the Place Palais Royal and the rue de Rivoli in the French capital.
The idea was to maintain the façade of this Paris landmark and to
rebuild the interior to provide 420,000 square feet of offices and
shopping space. The purchase price for the Grands Magasins was
expected to be over £11 million – which many regarded as on the
high side even in the boom – and the total cost on completion of
the redevelopment was expected to be just under £30 million.
The Post Office fund enthusiastically agreed to take a half share
in the profits and to guarantee jointly with Argyle the borrowings
raised to finance the project. Later in the year the fund cemented
the relationship by agreeing to acquire over 15% of Argyle's
ordinary share capital.

At first sight the Post Office fund's link-up with Goldsmith's
property concern appears little different from links established by

other institutions with developers elsewhere. But the timing, as in the case of its earlier venture into English and Continental, proved singularly unhappy. The fund acquired its 15% stake soon after Argyle announced a bid for Cornwall Properties late in 1973; by the time the bid had been completed, the property boom had bubbled over and Argyle was confronting 1974 with a balance sheet weighed down with heavy borrowings. The share price plunged.

There was another unusual aspect to the relationship. The terms on which the Grands Magasins deal was financed required both partners to guarantee the borrowings raised to pay for the development. On completion of the development the partners were each to guarantee 50% of a long term mortgage on the property. Yet Argyle enjoyed the right to back out of the guarantee of the long term mortgage if it felt so inclined. In other words the exceptionally persuasive Goldsmith had concluded a deal with the Post Office pension fund trustees which allowed him unilaterally to pull out of the whole project at a crucial point if he wished to. While Argyle stood to receive 50% of the profits if all went well, it could protect itself against losses in the event of trouble.

From the postmen's point of view, the deal was much more onerous. If it went right, the fund would receive 50% of the profit; but if it went wrong, it could be left with 100% of the losses on an open-ended commitment. Whether or not that commitment materialised was entirely out of the fund's control. Few property entrepreneurs enjoyed such favourable treatment at the hands of a long term investment institution, in the course of the 1970s property boom, as Goldsmith did in this instance. And the Post Office fund managers soon found that Goldsmith had not reserved the right to pull out for nothing.

As the Paris property market took a downward turn in 1974 and building costs continued to rise, the financial assumptions on which the Grands Magasins du Louvre development had originally been undertaken looked increasingly shaky. Letting prospects for both the shop and office space were problematical. And Argyle like countless other British property companies, found itself in financial difficulty. In 1975 Argyle announced that it was not prepared to guarantee the long term borrowings on the development and that it wished to withdraw from the investment. The Post Office pension fund ended up taking over Argyle's financial obligations on the Grands Magasins, including guarantees of nearly £22 million in relation to bank borrowings, and paying it £1½ million under the arrangements to unwind the partnership. Argyle's profit, on walking away from this (at the time) potentially very unprofitable and highly risky investment, was £1.1 million. So in a year when other property men were struggling, backs to the wall, with onerous financial commitments, Jimmy Goldsmith stepped lightly out of substantial obligations on the Grands Magasins project and plucked a tidy profit from the Post Office pension fund as he did so. He capped his good fortune in the same year by winning a knighthood in the resignation honours list of Labour Prime Minister Harold Wilson – another impressive feat, given that certain of his companies including Argyle Securities had been by no means ungenerous contributors to Tory party funds.

As sterling declined against the French franc in 1976, the cost of what was now the Post Office's development escalated sharply. It soon threatened to top £60 million, equivalent to nearly 7% of the book value of the Post Office pension fund. Salt was rubbed into the postmen's wound when a subsidiary of Goldsmith's master company, Générale Occidentale, made a takeover bid in July 1976 for Argyle at 50p a share. This was less than half the value at the time Argyle was making its offer for Cornwall Properties and the Post Office fund was about to raise its stake in Argyle to 15% in 1973. The Post Office pension fund managers were doubly unfortunate in that the Grands Magasins du Louvre was one of the few big pension fund investments in Europe of which some details were made public. Because Argyle was a quoted company and the Post Office a public corporation, Goldsmith's decision to back out of the Paris development attracted press publicity. There was some surprise at the way in which the Post Office fund had allowed itself to be burdened with this big commitment.

The fund had little option but to go on with the development. And in the end, after an awkward period in which substantial tenants failed to materialise at the asking rent, the French finance ministry decided to take rather more than half the office space in the building in 1979. The letting problem on the ground floor was overcome by turning it into an antique market, in which more than 200 individual traders took space. But even on optimistic assumptions about the future, it would be surprising if the return on the very considerable cost of this development, which out-stripped the original estimate by a wide margin, had by 1980, matched the return the fund would have received if it had simply put the same sum on deposit at the nearest clearing bank. True, pension funds are long term investors. But there can be little doubt that Jimmy Goldsmith's companies were the more obvious bene-ficiaries in the 1970s of the Post Office fund trustees' flirtation with Argyle Securities over the Grands Magasins du Louvre.

The Post Office pension fund was by no means the only one whose members ended up providing support for Jimmy Gold-smith's financial operations. One of the more surprising backers of the Anglo-French entrepreneur's loosely-knit business empire in the 1970s was the pension scheme of Cavenham, Goldsmith's own British-based food group. In the absence of any requirement to make the pension fund's accounts available to the public, the fact that the Cavenham pension fund's money was helping to finance Goldsmith's wider business interests did not attract attention in financial circles. Yet the circumstances in which the pension fund backed Goldsmith's interests were potentially controversial.

Decisions on the management of pension fund investments should, in theory, be kept entirely independent of decisions on the management of the group in which present and future pensioners were, or are, employed. Part of the reason for this is to ensure that pension payments are not dependent on the financial health of the business empire in which the pensioners have been employed. But this principle was not observed with uniform strictness in the Goldsmith empire. The Cavenham pension fund was no stranger to transactions involving potential conflicts of interest, any more than outside shareholders in the quoted companies that Goldsmith controlled. In the mid-1970s, the investment adviser to the Caven-ham group pension scheme was the London branch of Banque Occidentale pour l'Industrie et le Commerce, the French banking subsidiary of Goldsmith's master company Générale Occidentale. And in addition to providing investment advice, Banque Occi-dentale accepted large deposits from the Cavenham pension fund.

At 31 March 1976, the Cavenham fund had put no less than £1.9 million, out of a total portfolio of £23.1 million, on deposit with Goldsmith's in-house bank. So over 8% of the pension fund's resources were at risk in this single investment in a subsidiary of

Générale Occidentale. Jimmy Goldsmith, a director and substantial shareholder in Générale Occidentale, was the chairman of the Cavenham group pension scheme's committee of management at the time, and the trustees included Jack Greenhalgh, who was a director of Générale Occidentale as well as managing director of Cavenham. Since Banque Occidentale accepted deposits from and lent money to other parts of the Goldsmith empire, the implication is that the 14,600 members and pensioners of the Cavenham group pension scheme were not wholly protected from any financial misfortunes that might have befallen other Goldsmith interests. Surprisingly, there are no direct prohibitions in trust law against pension funds lending money to companies in which their trustees are materially interested.

The Cavenham group pension scheme's behaviour, in this respect, was far from unique. There have been numerous other unpublicised instances of pension fund members' savings being needlessly committed, in part, to the fortunes of the business in which they were employed. One such concerned the pension fund of Solicitors' Law Stationery Society when that company was involved with Slater, Walker Securities.

Slater, Walker Securities, whose chairman Jim Slater was a friend of Jimmy Goldsmith, shared Goldsmith's penchant for promoting deals between loosely related companies in which Slater, Walker Securities – the Slater master company – held shares. His company also made substantial profits by dealing in the shares of its quoted off-shoots, or 'satellites' as they were known, and by charging them fees for banking services. This modus operandi carried the risk, as it did with Goldsmith, that if one part of the empire ran into trouble, other parts could not escape the ill-wind. The point was of some importance for Slater, Walker's investment clients, on whose behalf Slater frequently put money into off-shoots of his empire.

Solicitors' Law Stationery Society was an old-established company that had originally attracted Jim Slater's attention when the value of its head office property in London's Fetter Lane started to soar during the property boom. In 1971 Slater, Walker Securities launched a takeover bid for the company and embarked on a potentially lucrative piece of 'asset stripping'. After plucking the valuable office property out of the company and putting it into Slater, Walker Securities, he spruced up Solicitors' Law's publishing, printing and stationery business and refloated the group on the stock exchange eighteen months later. Slater, Walker retained a 37% stake in Solicitors' Law Stationery Society, while a further 45% was sold to the Thomson Organisation. In the course of this financial operation, Slater, Walker became investment manager of the Solicitors' Law pension fund.

In July 1974 the trustees of the Solicitors' Law pension fund suddenly realised that a huge proportion of the fund's money was being held uninvested by Slater, Walker or its subsidiaries. Some £795,000, equivalent to more than half the total fund of £1.5 million, was effectively on deposit there. While Jim Slater's heavily publicised views about the merits of investing in cash (see chapter two) could no doubt be used to try to justify this unorthodox investment policy, there was no excuse at all for leaving so much cash with a single company or secondary financial concern. The trustees of the pension fund also discovered that the fund's cash deposits were not specifically held in the name of Solicitors' Law Stationery Society pension fund. Over half the money of Solicitors' Law's present and future pensioners was at risk in a business whose banking side later turned out to be particularly vulnerable to the stock market, property and secondary banking crisis.

The response of the trustees of the Solicitors' Law Stationery Society pension scheme trustees in the second half of 1974 to this highly unusual situation was to rearrange their affairs so that half the cash balances were placed on deposit from then on with a clearing bank, while the other half continued to be on deposit with Slater, Walker, but in the Solicitors' Law fund's own name. Yet the members were still fortunate to escape without loss, for in 1975 Slater, Walker Securities was overtaken by acute financial problems and its banking subsidiary had to be rescued by the Bank of England. On Jim Slater's resignation, Jimmy Goldsmith became chairman.

In the public sector, it hardly affects the security of the pension scheme members' pensions if a nationalised industry pension fund lends money to its own parent corporation on commercial terms. Public sector corporations are unlikely to default on their obligations to their own pension funds. But in the private sector, where it is not uncommon for companies to accept deposits from their pension funds, the risks and the potential conflicts of interest can be acute. Nor are these conflicts restricted to companies. In 1979 it emerged that the Natsopa print union's pension fund had been offering financial facilities to union officials. Pension fund money had been used, for example, to purchase a flat for the use of Natsopa's former General Secretary Lord Briginshaw, and to provide mortgage finance for the pension fund's auditors.

Potential conflicts do not only arise where companies and unions borrow from the pension fund. At J. Sainsbury, the food retailing group, for example, the main tenant of the pension fund's properties during the 1970s was the company itself. The potential problem here is that the members of the fund naturally want a high rent, while the shareholders of Sainsbury clearly want as low a rent as possible. If the directors of the company want to close down a store which is owned by the pension fund, their decision may well affect the security of present and future pensioners' benefits. Beneficiaries of the scheme might reasonably ask whether the portfolio was not too heavily weighted towards retail property and towards a particular rent-payer.

Similar potential conflicts of interest arose at J. Lyons, the food group, whose finances were dangerously overstretched in 1975–76. Here the Lyons pension fund, whose trustees included directors with share stakes in Lyons, bought half a dozen of J. Lyons's own properties, helping to relieve the finances of the troubled company. The potential conflict lay in the company's requirement for a high price for its properties, in order to overcome its financial difficulties, while the pension fund's need was for the best properties it could obtain, in the right quantity to suit its portfolio requirements, at the lowest price it could get.

In fact the transactions at both Sainsbury and Lyons were carried out on the basis of independent professional property valuations. But there is nothing in trust law to prevent such deals taking place without independent valuations. And there is no requirement for trustees either to disclose or to consult with members of the pension scheme before embarking on transactions in which they have a personal financial interest.

No doubt most of the transactions between companies or unions and their pension funds are made with the best of intentions. But the prevalence of these incestuous dealings raises serious doubts about how far company managements and pension scheme trustees are allowing the funded pension system to achieve its chief objective: security of pension rights, even if the company goes out of business.

The state-owned Electricity Supply Industry pension fund manages investments on behalf of 180,000 staff, workers and pensioners of Britain's Central Electricity Generating Board and other area electricity boards up and down the country. On the Richter scale of financial misfortune in the 1970s, it rates about nine out of ten – marginally higher, perhaps, than the other pension funds considered in this chapter with the possible exception of ICI. The electricity pension fund's problems date back mainly to the late 1960s when the fund forged links with a number of unquoted entrepreneurial companies promoted by Charles Gordon's Spey Investments. Many of these companies ran into trouble some time after Gordon had ceased to be associated with them. Their difficulties lay behind the suspension of the fund's top two investment managers, Alan Urwin and Bill Lund, in March 1980, in circumstances which the Electricity Council, the holding company of the electricity industry, has only partially explained.

At the centre of the controversy was the electricity fund's stake in Westmoreland Investments, an unquoted property group run by Gordon's one-time partner Boris 'Bobby' Marmor. Marmor's chief backer had originally been Phoenix Assurance, but in the late 1960s when Marmor was in partnership with Gordon in Spey Westmoreland, his ambitions became too big for Britain's eighth largest composite insurance group. He looked around for a more expansive patron and found one in the Electricity Council's deputy financial adviser Sidney Cowtan, who was responsible for managing the pension fund's investment policy.

Cowtan provided Spey Westmoreland with electricity pension fund finance in a number of straightforward property transactions. The idea was that Spey Westmoreland would feed the electricity fund by selling developments to it as they were completed and let. But the fund also offered Spey Westmoreland around £15 million-worth of guarantees for bank borrowings raised to help finance the acquisition of two quoted property groups, Allied Land and Hallmark Securities, in 1969 and 1970. This was an unorthodox step, which the pension fund later had cause to regret.

The unusual feature of this transaction lay in the fact that investment institutions rarely guaranteed bank borrowings, at the stage a transaction was set up, where they were only minority share-holders in the company. Only if all the other shareholders offered comparable guarantees in proportion to their shareholdings was this regarded as an appropriate way to finance a property company. The electricity fund owned a third of Spey Westmoreland's capi-tal. By voluntarily guaranteeing borrowings on this scale – £15 million then was equivalent to over £50 million in 1980 pounds – it was being remarkably generous to the other shareholders in the company, who included Phoenix, ICI pension fund, Gresham Trust and the Direct Spanish Telegraph Investment Trust. These institutions did not offer similar guarantees.

A second unorthodox feature was that guarantees were offered in support of borrowings raised in foreign currencies, even though they were used to finance investment in Britain. And by offering support in this form, the electricity pension fund gave Marmor added flexibility in raising future borrowings. When Marmor's partnership with Gordon came to an end in 1971 and Spey Westmoreland was reorganised under the umbrella of West-moreland Investments, the properties were independently valued at £44 million, borrowings stood at £34 million and the com-pany's net worth amounted to no less than £6½ million.

At this point it would have made obvious sense for Westmore-land to put a brake on expansion in order to digest its two big recent acquisitions and to put its finances onto a sounder footing. Instead it stepped up its activities. And Marmor was given ample encouragement by the electricity pension fund, which was repre-sented on the Westmoreland board from 1972 onwards by George Cumming, the then investment manager. Other directors included Charles Knight, the retired investment manager of Phoenix Assurance, while Bill Lund of the electricity fund acted as an alternative director.

By the time the property boom was at its peak, Westmoreland was putting up a total of 310,000 square feet of offices in Glasgow, Bristol and Worthing. It was developing a new head office for *The Times* in London's Gray's Inn Road. There were hotel deve-lopments at St John's Wood in London and at Gatwick Airport, and two large town centre redevelopment schemes were under way in Middlesborough and Dunbarton. Overseas Westmoreland had a joint venture in the Republic of Ireland, whose develop-ments included a shopping centre on the outskirts of Dublin, which was financed jointly by the pension funds of the electricity industry and ICI. In France, Holland and Germany, Westmoreland had 630,000 square feet of office space either in course of development or fully developed. And there were other investments in Australia and Canada.

In 1972 the electricity pension fund seriously considered the pros and cons of a stock market flotation for Westmoreland. It decided, however, that the company would do better to establish a lengthier track record before inviting the public to subscribe for shares. As long as finance was easy to come by outside the stock market, Marmor was happy to comply. By December 1973 he had put together a property portfolio which was independently valued by Richard Ellis, one of the most reputable firms of chartered surveyors, at £123 million. In the space of two years Westmoreland's borrowings had more than doubled to £78 million. And if borrowings are taken as a more realistic guide to the size of a property company than valuers' figures, Westmoreland was probably just within the ranks of the top dozen or so property groups in the country.

How the trustees of the electricity pension fund, who included some of the top financial and legal management of the nationalised electricity industry, came to support Marmor in such a highly borrowed venture is not easy to understand. True, the property boom was a heady affair. But the industrial managers who sat on the board of trustees were not at the centre of the banking system where the property fever was all-pervasive. And Marmor's enthusiasm for deficit financing was on a scale that might have been expected to worry people who were looking after the interests of pensioners, widows and orphans. In 1973 Westmoreland's bill for interest on its borrowings amounted to £5.9 million, compared with an income from rents of only £2.2 million. It was able to declare a profit only by capitalising interest – that is, by adding interest to the cost of its developments in the balance sheet instead of charging it directly against revenue – and by selling properties at a profit. The assumption was that it could go on meeting the revenue deficit out of property sales made on a rising market.

The frailty of this assumption was soon exposed in 1974 as the financial markets came tumbling down. So, too, were numerous other assumptions on which the electricity pension fund's general investment policy had been based. But George Cumming, the investment manager who had presided over the fund during the boom, did not have to face the consequences: he retired on 31 December 1973. The job of picking up the pieces was left to his successor Alan Urwin.

Urwin, who had previously been an investment manager in the office of the Public Trustee, arrived at the electricity pension fund on 2 February 1974. He was immediately confronted with a mass of urgent financial problems. To start with, the fund had been the biggest backer of Cedar Holdings. As well as owning 10% of the ordinary capital, it had advanced £5.8 million of loans to the company and had already agreed to put in a further £12½ million under the rescue arrangements made at the Bank of England before Christmas. The fund was also the biggest institutional shareholder in First National Finance Corporation, another serious casualty of the banking crisis. There it had 8% of the equity share capital. Other commitments in secondary banking included a 25% investment in a subsidiary of Sir Julian Hodge's Hodge Group called Millbank Finance.

There was a similar tale of woe in property, where the electricity fund was heavily exposed in a string of private entrepreneurial companies. In addition to being the biggest institutional backer of Westmoreland, it was the largest backer of a marina development at Black Rock, Brighton, where it had both a direct 22% stake and a smaller indirect interest through Westmoreland, which also held shares. The first phase of the marina development alone, was expected to cost over £40 million. Yet there were serious doubts, in the recession of the mid-1970s, about the financial viability of the whole scheme. The fund also had another marina investment in a company called Boatex (Holdings) which was developing the London Marina at the Royal Albert Dock Basin. The electricity fund was soon to support Boatex in a more ambitious overseas marina development at Den Helder in Holland. Other unquoted investments where trouble was looming included National Car Parks, Aquatels and Spey Investments (in which it had retained a shareholding after Spey's break with Westmoreland).

Some of these investments did not turn out to be financially troublesome. The secondary banking crisis by-passed Millbank Finance; its parent, the Hodge Group, was taken over by the solidly-based Standard Chartered Bank just before the crisis broke. And the institutional shareholders in NCP eventually extracted themselves from the investment on what they regarded as reasonable terms. But elsewhere, the problems proved more enduring and the electricity pension fund's management resources were spread too thinly over the problem companies. Urwin did what many other fund managers would have done in those circumstances: he concentrated on getting the big figures right. In practice, that meant reorganising the main portfolio of quoted shares. In the year to March 1975 the fund made extensive sales of poorer quality shareholdings at a loss of nearly £30 million and the proceeds were reinvested in less speculative securities. As far as the unquoted companies were concerned, the fund handled them on an *ad hoc* basis. And in the case of the property companies, it relied heavily on Richard Ellis for advice, as it did with the direct property holdings.

The most pressing problem in property was the state of Westmoreland's finances. But in the first half of 1974 a solution appeared to be at hand because Phoenix Assurance was considering a bid for the company. In the event bid discussions did not proceed very far before Phoenix decided that it would prefer to buy Westmoreland's portfolio of British properties instead, which would have left Westmoreland with plenty of cash to pay off borrowings and a portfolio of useful overseas developments still in hand or completed.

As the financial climate worsened, however, Phoenix's enthusiasm waned and its investment manager Brian Oram began to doubt whether Marmor would ever agree to a price for Westmoreland's British properties which realistically reflected the changed conditions in the property market. Eventually it pulled out of negotiations, leaving the property company with no choice but to retrench as best it could.

Westmoreland's bill for interest that year soared to nearly £10 million, while rents brought in only £3 million. Borrowings had risen to nearly £90 million, and part of the rise was due to the fall in the value of sterling against foreign currencies. More than £50 million of Westmoreland's borrowings, many of them guaranteed by the electricity fund, were denominated in US dollars, Deutschemarks, Dutch guilders, Swiss francs and French francs. Where borrowings had been used to finance developments in the country in whose currency they had been raised, the fall in the value of sterling posed no real threat. But at least £22 million of the foreign borrowings had been used to finance commitments in Britain. This mismatch of currencies was to cause considerable financial damage as the British economy sank deeper into crisis.

It soon became clear that Westmoreland could not survive without outside support. And Phoenix, despite its earlier interest, felt that it was not in a position to come to the rescue. It was no giant by the standards of the insurance business and like other insurance companies in 1974 it was worried about the threat of insolvency: it turned nervously to its computer each week for a revaluation of its stock market investments to see how its solvency margin was faring under the strain of the slide in share prices. At 31 December, 1974, it was only able to reveal a solvency margin as high as 27% (around 20% was regarded as the bottom limit of safety) by including a surplus on the revaluation of its own head office in the heart of the City. So while it still owned nearly 15% of Westmoreland, it was reluctant to step into the breach. The smaller shareholders in Westmoreland who remained – Gresham Trust with 4.7% and ICI pension fund with 3.3% – both felt that it was not their job to come to the rescue of a company whose expansion on borrowed money had been underwritten by someone else. So responsibility for Westmoreland fell squarely on the electricity fund, which by this time held 42% of the ordinary capital.

When the picture was looking particularly bleak early in 1975, Urwin and his deputy investment manager Bill Lund presented a paper to the trustees setting out the options that the fund could consider in relation to the investment in Westmoreland. One was to put the company into receivership. But Andrew Huntley, a senior partner of Richard Ellis who acted as property adviser to the electricity fund, assured the trustees that Westmoreland's properties were of relatively high quality; most could be expected to find buyers even when conditions in the market were depressed. So the real choice was between offering just enough support to keep Westmoreland afloat, or launching a full-scale rescue involving some £20 million to £25 million of the fund's money in the hope of repaying bank borrowings on a significant scale and re-establishing Westmoreland on a sounder long term footing. Urwin favoured minimal support. This had the advantage of leaving the fund with more cash to invest in the stock market while share prices were depressed. And it kept Marmor on a tighter rein. The trustees finally decided to go along with Urwin.

In fact the fund had already put a stop to new development and it was agreed that in future no new ventures would be authorised. Marmor was to continue making disposals at the best prices he could obtain in the market, while the pension fund put in small amounts of cash on commercial terms with a view either to floating Westmoreland on the stock market or disposing of the investment by any other means that presented themselves. Richard Ellis, meantime, were to advise on the programme of orderly property disposals.

When a private company runs into trouble of the kind that Westmoreland faced in 1975, the chief rescuer would normally be expected to raise its shareholding to well over 50% in order to obtain control of the company. The simplest way to do this is to invite other shareholders to put up new equity capital in proportion to their shareholdings, in the knowledge that the entrepreneur will probably not have the ready cash to do so and that shareholders other than the principal one will be reluctant to subscribe. The other shareholders' failure to put up fresh capital leads automatically to the dilution of their stake in the company. But the chief rescuer usually allows the entrepreneur to retain just enough capital to have an incentive to stay on and employ his energy and skill to enhance the value of the company.

When the electricity fund arranged to inject £5 million of new capital into Westmoreland in March 1975, however, it did not cut Boris Marmor's stake down to size. The money was advanced in the form of an unsecured loan which was partly convertible into ordinary capital in 1979–80. The terms of conversion were such that Marmor's stake in the company would be reduced only marginally from 24.7% to 23.5%. This was astonishingly generous to him given that Westmoreland was on the brink of insolvency and dependent on the electricity pension fund's guarantees and, quite possibly, further cash support for its survival. Few other companies were able to raise unsecured convertible loan stocks in 1975 and those that did so were in a financial condition that bore no comparison with Westmoreland's sorry state.

Surprisingly neither the managers nor the trustees of the electricity fund felt it was worth taking independent advice from a merchant bank in organising the rescue of this big, and dangerously overborrowed company. Urwin argued that the merchant banks knew very little about property and were expensive to hire, which was true enough; merchant bankers had been slow to recognise the importance of the rapidly growing property market and most of them understood little about the financing of property development. They left a vacuum in this fast-growing part of the financial system which was filled mainly by chartered surveyors, whose knowledge of corporate finance was not necessarily exhaustive. But a merchant bank would not have had to be particularly expert in property to see that Westmoreland was likely to collapse without support and that the terms of the rescue called for a much larger cut in Marmor's share in the company than the electricity fund managers recognised. For their part, the trustees were happy with the terms on which the fund put up its £5 million in March 1975.

By the end of that year Westmoreland's financial position was still parlous. Borrowings stood at £88 million, of which nearly £40 million was due for repayment between 1975 and 1980. And Westmoreland's auditors Lubbock, Fine, in the absence of an independent valuation, felt unable to form an opinion, when they signed their audit report, on the value of their client's properties. Properties remained in the balance sheet at boomtime figures. The grand total looked barely credible at £112 million. Interest continued to outstrip rents. And the guarantees that the electricity fund had originally offered at the start of the decade, had become increasingly onerous for the guarantor as sterling declined. At their worst point, they topped £30 million.

By March 1976 many of the more acute problems among the fringe banking and property investments were beginning to subside a little. But the electricity fund was still heavily overcommitted in these areas. No less than £67 million was invested in equity shares and loans to unquoted companies and there were still some £26 million of guarantees outstanding. In addition, Cedar Holdings was still hanging on to much of the original £12½ million rescue money the fund had advanced at the turn of 1974. So the unquoted investments and commitments in secondary banking and property of the electricity fund totalled more than £100 million – a surprisingly large sum in relation to a fund whose value was then £673 million.

In the summer of 1976 the pension fund decided to rearrange the terms of its support for Westmoreland in order to reduce the burden of interest on the company. At the same time it bought most of Phoenix's shareholding. As a result of this transaction the electricity fund finally took control of Westmoreland. Its stake rose to just over 66% and under new terms for the conversion of unsecured loans into ordinary capital, it stood to raise its stake to nearly 80% in 1982. Part of the *quid pro quo* was that Westmoreland ceased to pay interest on the loan stock until it was due to be converted into ordinary shares in 1982. Once again, no outside merchant bank was asked to advise on the deal.

The final and most controversial transaction between the electricity fund and Westmoreland took place late in 1978, when the fund agreed to buy out all the remaining shareholders. At this point the value of the Westmoreland property portfolio was unusually difficult to assess, because so many of the more saleable properties had already gone. The electricity fund itself had bought some of the larger London office properties, including big blocks in St Martin's Lane and Fetter Lane and it had also bought 70% of the Westmoreland Hotel in St John's Wood. Westmoreland's investments in Europe also presented difficulties in valuation. At the time Urwin and his deputy investment manager Lund started to negotiate the purchase of the remaining shares in Westmoreland, there were still six major investments in Paris and Cergy-Pontoise in France, Dusseldorf, Cologne, Amsterdam and Eindhoven.

On the basis of an up-to-date valuation by Richard Ellis, which put a figure of £75 million on the property portfolio, Westmoreland was insolvent. But Ellis went on to advise the fund that when certain developments were completed and let, and rent reviews had taken place, the value of the portfolio might well come close to the figure that Westmoreland's own directors claimed for the properties. The directors, predictably enough, took a more sanguine view and had valued the portfolio at £92 million. On that basis the share capital of Westmoreland would have been worth nearly £13 million.

Urwin and Lund believed that Richard Ellis's valuations had tended to be on the low side in the past – sometimes materially so. One obvious example had been the sale by Westmoreland of Tolworth Towers, a huge government-occupied office block on the Kingston by-pass in south west London, to the Post Office pension fund, at a premium of several millions over a fairly recent valuation by Richard Ellis. They also believed that the property

market, which had recovered sharply since 1975, would continue
to rise. And it was not unreasonable to pay a premium over net
asset value for Westmoreland's equity capital, where the value of
the company's properties stood to be enhanced considerably by
rent reviews and by the completion of developments. A further
consideration was that Marmor was not keen to sell. As one of the
minority shareholders told me, his attitude was that the shares
would soon be worth £1 apiece, and that the company could only
increase in value. It seemed unlikely that a strong-minded entrepreneur of his ilk could be prized out of Westmoreland without
either a fight or a premium for his shares.

The two investment managers concluded that 40p a share,
against the 48p a share that the company was worth on the directors' valuation, was a realistic figure to aim for in buying out the
remaining 34% of Westmoreland's capital. But they were no
match for Marmor in negotiation. When the deal was finally
struck, the electricity pension fund had agreed to buy out Marmor
and the others at 60p a share. This valued Westmoreland at no less
than £16 million. Marmor, meantime, walked away with more
than £2 million in cash for his personal shareholding. It was an
impressive feat of negotiation on his part, given that one of
Britain's leading firms of valuers had effectively pronounced the
company worthless on the then value of the properties a short
while before. In this, as in earlier negotiations, the other minority
shareholders were happy to leave Marmor to confront the electricity fund alone, in the knowledge that his powers of persuasion
required no additional support from them and that they would
benefit from the terms he managed to extract. An interesting post-
script on the value of the Westmoreland portfolio was added when
Jones, Lang, Wootton were subsequently called in to give an
independent valuation of the properties. On the basis of Jones,
Lang's estimate, which was incorporated in the Westmoreland
balance sheet at 31 December 1979, the property company was
hopelessly insolvent: there was a deficit of net assets of £19.2
million.

Next to Westmoreland, the most troublesome of the electricity
fund's investments was the one in the Brighton Marina Company.
There the fund faced different, but equally daunting, problems.
Construction of the first phase of the marina itself presented a big
technical challenge because its geographical position on the south

coast was exceptionally exposed. And in 1974 part of the building work was damaged while severe gales raged in the channel. By the following year the main construction problems had been overcome. But the cost of the scheme was rising and the rewards looked increasingly remote and uncertain. There were doubts about whether the marina company would attract sufficient people into berths and moorings at economic rents. As one of the participants told me later, it looked to him at that point uncomfortably like 'the sort of investment that comes right after about the third bankruptcy'.

In 1975, when the financial problem of the Brighton Marina Company came to a head, the other big shareholders were National Westminster Bank, which had taken over a shareholding that had originally belonged to its pension fund; EMI, which had come into the scheme with a view to providing leisure facilities; and Royal Insurance. But the burden of deciding whether to go ahead fell more heavily on the electricity fund than the others because it remained the biggest shareholder when Westmoreland's stake in Brighton Marina was taken into the reckoning. At the back of all the shareholders' minds was the thought that if they decided to abandon the development, they were bound to cause a public outcry. No one wanted to be pilloried for leaving a half-built marina as a permanent eyesore on the south coast of England.

In the end the electricity fund decided to take an optimistic view of the marina's future. Boating was at least a fast-growing leisure industry and there was plenty of spending power in the area around Brighton. After comparing the financial arithmetic at Brighton with the figures at a successful marina at Lymington in Hampshire, Urwin and Lund decided, with the support of their trustees, that a case could be put for proceeding with the investment, even though it represented a worryingly big commitment in relation to the size of the electricity fund. The other shareholders agreed to put up money, in proportion to their shareholdings, to complete the first phase of the development.

Over the short term, the decision was undeniably costly. The shareholders' commitment to the marina company, in the form of loans and guarantees, had reached more than £50 million by the end of 1978. At that point, the marina was running at a loss before tax of £2.8 million. But in reality the revenue position was worse because many of the shareholders' loans carried rates of interest as low as 2½%. Had the loans been advanced in the form of standard debentures or bank loans, the shortfall of income against interest charges might have been nearer to £10 million. The marina company directors were forced to concede when the accounts were signed in 1979, that the market value of the marina was less than its £47 million cost. Auditors Peat, Marwick, Mitchell also made it clear in their report that had the shareholders not promised further cash, the company might not have been a going concern.

As a marina, the venture was by no means a failure. It was running reasonably smoothly by the end of the decade. As an investment, it looked sorry, and continues to do so today. Whether the return on the original outlay will, in the forseeable future, match the return that could have been obtained on a more orthodox portfolio investment, depends heavily on the terms on which the company brings in outsiders to undertake residential development on the land created within the marina, together with the development of other leisure and hotel facilities.

There is one respect, however, in which the shareholders in the marina company have been able to make the best of a bad job. In keeping with the spirit of the times, the Brighton Marina Company was made the vehicle, in the late 1970s, for a gigantic tax avoidance scheme. The initial losses were effectively sold to a consortium of leading British companies, which included GEC, Boots, and the Chef and Brewer subsidiary of Grand Metropolitan, together with EMI. These companies technically became the owners of the marina. Whether the beneficiaries of the electricity pension fund enjoy a full commercial return on their investment in the marina project before the twenty-first century may well hinge on the Inland Revenue's attitude towards this arrangement. In the meantime, more improbable proprietors for the most expensive leisure development on the south coast of England than GEC, Britain's biggest heavy electrical engineering and electronics group, or Boots, the pharmaceutical and retail chemist chain concern, would be hard to imagine.

There the whole affair of the electricity pension fund's unquoted investments might have rested, had it not been for an odd combination of circumstances which forced the Electricity Council to take unexpected action against Urwin and Lund. In 1979 interest rates rose sharply. Since over £20 million of Westmoreland's borrowings carried variable rates of interest, this immediately imposed a heavy additional burden on Westmoreland. It also made the timing of the purchase of the outstanding shares in Westmoreland look unfortunate; the two fund managers, in common with most other professional fund managers in 1979, had not anticipated that interest rates would rise so far, so fast.

At the same time there was a change of trustees at the electricity pension fund. Burton Johnson, the then financial adviser to the Electricity Council, was replaced as chairman of the trustees by the deputy chairman of the Electricity Council, Austin Bunch, who became worried about the Westmoreland affair. Soon after, merchant bankers Schroder, Wagg were invited to look at the administrative arrangements at the fund. Sir Kenneth Cork of accountants Cork, Gully was also brought in to report on the unquoted investments. He was asked specifically to look at the quality of the advice given to the trustees by the managers; the extent to which the decisions of the trustees were acted on; the degree of control exercised by the managers over the unquoted companies in which they had investments; and the fund's accounting procedures. Cork found a number of things to criticise at Westmoreland and at Boatex, the smaller of the two marina companies.

When it came to the purchase of the outstanding shares in Westmoreland for £5.4 million, Urwin and Lund had wanted to push the deal through quickly in time for Westmoreland's annual general meeting. Instead of waiting for the next meeting of the trustees, they gave advance warning of the negotiations to the trustees and sent them a paper containing the details of the proposed transaction. The paper was also sent to the Electricity Council's own superannuation committee, on which several of the Electricity Council's top managers were represented.

In this paper Urwin and Lund did not refer specifically to the results of Richard Ellis's valuation, which put a figure of £75 million on the Westmoreland portfolio in its condition at the time. Instead the two men outlined a range of possible values for the portfolio, which ran from a bottom limit of £80 million to an upper limit of £100 million. The trustees were not given a copy of Richard Ellis's letter advising on the deal. Nor were they given a letter from the fund's accountants Peat, Marwick, Mitchell which recommended a full accounting investigation into Westmoreland. These important omissions were criticised in Cork, Gully's report, as were similar omissions in relation to the investment in Boatex. The failure to disclose Richard Ellis's advice on the value of the properties, in particular, was described as reckless by the report. Cork, Gully also argued that Urwin and Lund had overpaid for Westmoreland shares in earlier transactions and alleged that they had not taken adequate professional advice. These omissions and commissions were ultimately to cost the two men their jobs.

Cork, Gully's report was, however, the cause of more immediate embarrassment for the Electricity Council. For one of its unexpected recommendations was that the fraud squad should be asked to look into the fund's relationship with Westmoreland and Boatex. This put the trustees in an awkward position. They could hardly leave Urwin and Lund in charge of £1.3 billion of the beneficiaries' money if the operations they managed were to be at the centre of a fraud squad enquiry. So in March, 1980, the two men were suspended on full pay. The Electricity Council then asked City solicitors Herbert Smith to look at Cork, Gully's report and give their opinion on its findings. The solicitors concluded that Urwin and Lund had shown a lack of judgement and care, in relation to the unquoted investments, and a lack of reliance on outside advisers, though at no point was there any suggestion of fraud. It was however agreed that the two men should retire. A subsequent statement from the Electricity Council declared that while there had been 'some loss of confidence on the part of the Electricity Council about the policies followed in the management of certain unquoted investments', the reasons for the retirement did not include any allegation of impropriety or dishonesty on their part. The Electricity Council also said that it accepted the assurances of Urwin and Lund that they had acted at all times in the interests of the funds which they were employed to manage.

Cork, Gully's criticisms of the managers of the electricity pension fund were doubtless well-founded. Yet Urwin and Lund had arguably performed no worse, in relation to their unquoted investments, than several other managers of major funds. The decisions that led to the mistakes being made in the first place were not Alan Urwin's. Urwin's and Lund's misfortune was that they were almost alone, among pension fund managers, in being subjected to probing outside scrutiny. And there seems little doubt that the two men were the scapegoats in an episode where more senior men, in their capacity as trustees, should have borne a fair measure of responsibility.

Had anyone been asked to look at the role of the trustees in relation to the unquoted investments, their findings would have been less than flattering. Why, for example, did the trustees allow the fund to grant the original guarantees to Westmoreland on terms that were so obviously favourable to the other shareholders? Why did they allow the fund to encourage Westmoreland in its reckless expansion in the first half of the 1970s? Why did they sanction such generous rescue terms for Westmoreland in 1975–76? And why did they fail to insist that the managers took proper outside advice on the rescue of Westmoreland? In the case of the final transaction in which the electricity fund bought out the remaining shareholdings in the company, they could plead that information was withheld from them. But it seems curious that none probed deeper into the advice the fund's own independent advisers had proffered on a £5.4 million transaction. As for the other unquoted investments, many appear to have been injudicious. And the circumstances in which the then trustees sanctioned continuing support for the Brighton Marina Company, despite the question marks over its future viability, are not reassuring.

The chairman of the trustees for much of the period during which these controversial events were taking place was the Electricity Council's own financial adviser Burton Johnson. He was intimately involved in the details of the Westmoreland rescue and was personally responsible for valuing the unquoted investments in the pension fund's accounts. It would be highly surprising if he were unaware that Westmoreland called for particularly close scrutiny. Other management appointees on the board of trustees included the financial controller and the solicitor of the Central Electricity Generating Board, together with chief accountants and secretaries of the area electricity boards. Why did these eminently qualified men, together with the top managers on the Electricity Council's own superannuation committee, which was responsible for keeping an eye on the fund's investments, fail to exercise tighter control over the management of the fund?

The history of the electricity pension fund's unquoted investments in the 1970s surely provides powerful evidence of the need for more formal regulation of pension fund affairs. Fund managers who control billions of pounds-worth of investments enjoy unparalleled power. All the people with whom they do business are inevitably deferential towards them, because the fund managers dispense patronage on a huge scale. Before the collapse of the stock market in 1974, when companies first started to realise the potential cost of poor investment performance, investment managers were often free from criticism within their own companies. Directors were inclined to overlook private dealings by the fund managers (there was no suggestion of this at the electricity pension fund) provided the fund itself performed well. But since the widespread use of performance measurement is a relatively recent development, company directors were often failing to detect what was really a bad performance in relation to a buoyant stock market.

Even today fund managers are largely immune from public scrutiny and press criticism because neither pension fund accounts nor performance figures are necessarily made available to the public. The whole system is designed to cocoon the pension fund manager from uncomfortable realities and to give him an exaggerated view of his own ability. It would be surprising, in these circumstances, if fund managers were not tempted to overreach themselves from time to time.

In the present regulatory vacuum, the only people who have the capacity to keep the fund manager's feet on the ground are the pension fund trustees. In the case of the electricity pension fund they appear to have been, at the very least, ineffective at crucial moments. The performance of the trustees of other pension funds considered in this chapter appears also to have fallen short of what their beneficiaries might have expected – though it is a moot point whether the beneficiaries can expect anything much at all from the supposed trustee safeguard in the present state of trust law. And even if all these pension funds had made their accounts public, it is doubtful whether the members would have derived much benefit from them since the format of the accounts in some cases reflected a bureaucratic preoccupation with secrecy.

At no point, over the past five years, for example, has the ICI pension fund's troublesome investment in Orbisa been adequately explained or even mentioned by name in the pension fund's report and accounts. Nor were the unquoted investments of the electricity pension fund ever named in the accounts in the period when they were a cause of serious concern to the trustees and managers. Still more surprising, no attempt was made by the electricity pension fund managers to consolidate Westmoreland's figures into group accounts, even when the fund owned 100% of the company; it continued to be shown simply as an unquoted investment in the 1979 accounts.[4] As a result, the fund's commitment in property was materially understated. So, too, was its moral, if not legal, responsibility for the £70 million or so of outside borrowings shown in Westmoreland's 1978 accounts. Although the fund had guaranteed only part of these debts, it is inconceivable that the pension fund of a public corporation could allow a wholly-owned subsidiary to default on its obligations. The fund's auditors Peat, Marwick, Mitchell raised no objections to this failure to incorporate Westmoreland's figures in full into group accounts.

Less than stringent standards of accountability, disclosure and financial control might, at a pinch, have been tolerable when occupational pensions represented a very small part of people's overall pension arrangements. Today most workers are dependent for a more significant part of their retirement pensions on occupational pension schemes operating in partnership with the state. After going through this chapter, do you, the reader, feel more or less confident in the ability of the people who manage your pension to provide you with a secure income in retirement?

7
Art for pensioners' sakes

'No profit grows where is no pleasure ta'en.'

William Shakespeare, *The Taming of the Shrew*

IN THEIR INCREASINGLY DESPERATE SEARCH, in the 1970s, for a store of value capable of standing up to inflation, professional money managers scoured the remoter boundaries of the capital market. Prudential stepped up its investment in agricultural land; Commercial Union bought copper both for its policyholders and for the members of its own pension fund; the Post Office pension fund bought hundreds of acres of forest land; Allied Breweries' fund acquired bullion and precious metals; the pension trustees at Ciba-Geigy (the British subsidiary of the big Swiss pharmaceuticals company) dabbled in Krugerrands; and pensioners of food retailer J. Sainsbury saw their fund put money into industrial metals. By far the most controversial of these esoteric investments, however, was one made by the British Rail pension fund. If any single event was responsible for bringing home to the general public that the pension funds were a powerful new force in the land, it was the rail fund's decision to collect works of art.

British Rail pension fund started buying secretly, with advice from fine art auctioneers Sotheby's, late in 1974. In the following five years it accumulated a large and varied collection embracing Tiepolos, Panninis, Renoirs and Picassos, French and Chinese porcelain, antique furniture, silver-gilt cutlery and numerous other kinds of objets d'art. When news of this investment policy first leaked out it prompted an outcry.

In the House of Commons, politicians reacted angrily to the notion that the pension fund of a publicly-owned corporation could speculate freely in the national heritage. Union leaders asked why the money was not going into productive industry. Art dealers, no doubt piqued that Sotheby's had happened on such a money-spinning client, pointed out that there was a conflict of interest between Sotheby's, the adviser, (whose duty was to help its client procure investments as cheaply as possible) and Sotheby's, the auctioneer, (whose job was to sell works of art at the highest possible price). The Comptroller and Auditor General questioned the wisdom and propriety of the venture, only to be told that the government had no legal right to interfere with the rail trustees' investment policy. The press, hitherto unconcerned when million-aire businessmen removed paintings from the public view for their private entertainment and profit, grew hot under the collar at the thought of art contributing to the pensions of porters, ticket collectors and footplate men.

The railmen's decision to go into competition with the likes of Norton Simon, the J. Paul Getty Museum and the National Gallery was effectively taken by the British Rail board, all of whose members act as trustees for the British Rail pension fund. Their motive was no different from that of the trustees of other pension funds that plunged into copper, bullion, forestry and other out of the way investments. The solvency of the main British Rail pension fund (unlike many other nationalised industry funds) was not guaranteed by the government. Unless it could earn a real return on its investments, it was faced with an unpalatable choice: either the board and the rail workers would have to pay more into the fund, or the pensions would have to be reduced. By dipping into the art market it hoped to guarantee a positive return to match its rapidly inflating pension liabilities.

The British Rail fund was not the only institution to show an interest in art, though no other insurance company or pension fund is thought to have become involved on a significant scale. Much earlier in the 1970s, as the rate of inflation accelerated and prices in the art market soared, businessmen, bankers and the ubiquitous property entrepreneurs became increasingly aware of the potential of art works and antiques as a hedge against inflation. A further attraction was that the art market was genuinely international: it provided a hedge against a falling pound, without the investor having to struggle with Britain's complex exchange control regulations (later abolished) in order to buy foreign assets.

Among the first to see the attractions of investment in art in the early 1970s was Rothschild Investment Trust, then closely connected with merchant bankers N. M. Rothschild. The trust bought a big stake in Sotheby's while it was still an unquoted business, and remained the biggest shareholder when the auctioneers were floated on the stock exchange as Sotheby, Parke, Bernet in 1977. Others followed Rothschild Investment Trust's example. An affiliate of J. H. Vavasseur, a fringe banking outfit, built up a stake in Spink & Son, a publicly-quoted coin and fine art dealing firm in St James's in London, which from then on became the subject of constant takeover rumours until it fell to a bid from Andrew Weir, a private Scottish shipping and investment group. Financier Jim Slater decorated the walls of his fringe bank with numerous modern paintings (he had a particular soft spot for the north country artist L. S. Lowry) while Malcolm Horsman, a former colleague of Slater's, became chairman of Lampa Securities, a quoted company whose fine art dealing subsidiary, Hugh Moss, specialised in Chinese porcelain. Property developer Ronald Lyon paid peak prices for impressionist paintings.

Had it been easier to make a real return on investment in industry in the 1970s, it is doubtful whether many of these profit seekers would have sought enrichment in the art market. Works of art do not have particularly good investment characteristics – least of all from the point of view of financial institutions. Their most glaring defect is that they yield no income. This may not be a disadvantage for the rich private individual who pays top marginal rates of income tax. But it is a serious handicap for a pension fund which is not taxed at all on its investments. If the Picasso 'Blue Boy' that the British Rail fund bought for $1m in 1976 is to match the return on a gilt-edged stock yielding a risk-free 13% to redemption in, say, twenty years time, it would not just have to double or treble in value; it would probably have to go up more than tenfold to keep pace.[1] And that is before taking into account the cost of dealing – high these days with a premium on both purchase and sale at Sotheby's and Christie's – as well as insurance, storage, restoration and so on.

Because the value of a painting cannot be assessed by reference to the income it yields, the only satisfactory way of establishing its worth is to put it up for sale. Every work of art is unique, so it is impossible to compile a reliable or generally applicable index of prices, as in the stock market. And values are dictated by taste and fashion. Two paintings by the same artist can fetch widely differing prices at auction for no better reason than that some millionaire takes a fancy to one and not the other. Works of art, then, are highly speculative investments. They have no intrinsic economic worth. Only fund managers or trustees who take an exceptionally gloomy view of prospects for more orthodox investments in industry and commerce would think the speculative risk worth taking.

Moreover, artistic values cannot easily be reconciled with the world of high finance. This holds true even at a purely practical level – a point that was clearly illustrated in the case of a little-publicised investment in the art market made by Commercial Union in partnership with Jacob Rothschild of the Rothschild banking family.

Jacob Rothschild was indirectly involved in art through Rothschild Investment Trust's stake in Sotheby's. But in the early 1970s he also acquired for his own personal account a controlling stake in fine art dealers P & D Colnaghi. Over the years Colnaghi's had maintained a reputation for high scholarship under the guiding hand of art historian and dealer James Byam Shaw. While the firm enjoyed close relationships with top museums and galleries around the world, it was not always inclined to charge them the full market price for the paintings it sold. As inflation accelerated and the financial climate became more difficult, the firm's finances deteriorated. Byam Shaw and his fellow directors decided to look for a buyer who had capital and was willing to preserve the business. They turned to Jacob Rothschild.

Rothschild appeared the ideal man to help. As well as being a keen collector, he was regarded in the City as one of the most talented bankers that the Rothschild family had produced for many years. And he saw in the art dealing firm an opportunity both to make money for himself and colleagues at Rothschilds, and to take pleasure in enhancing its fine art business.

Colnaghi's offered rich pickings. As well as its name, staff and stock of art works, it had a valuable lease at 14, Old Bond Street. On moving in, Jacob Rothschild bought the freehold of number 14, so enhancing the value of the property and creating more security for loans to finance the business. Subsequently he acquired the freehold of the adjacent property at number 13, Old Bond Street.

Yet Rothschild was no crude asset stripper. According to one former director, he brought a wide range of contacts and an unstoppable flow of ideas to the promotion of the art business. Above all he showed exceptional ingenuity in raising capital to rebuild Colnaghi's stock of works of art. As well as introducing fresh bank borrowings into the business, he persuaded Commercial Union to finance the firm's dealings in old masters. A joint venture was set up in 1973, in which Commercial Union took a quarter of the equity capital.

Although this was hardly a significant investment from the big insurance company's point of view, it received top-level attention; Commercial Union's chairman Sir Francis Sandilands, joined the board. Over the next three years Commercial Union put up $£\frac{3}{4}$ million on the security of the firm's property. This was, in fact, one of two investments that the insurance company made in Old Bond Street that year. Commercial Union offered similar financial support to Thos Agnew & Sons, another respected dealer whose valuable property almost opposite Colnaghi's provided collateral for loans.

Prospects for long term investment in art dealing were not entirely auspicious at the time. While it was true that prices of works of art were going up, so creating greater scope for dealing profits, competition was increasing. Auction houses like Sotheby's and Christie's, the wholesalers of the art market, were encroaching on the retail territory of the emporium galleries and offering a highly competitive service to vendors. At the same time inflation was pushing up the cost of keeping works of art in stock and salaries were rising. Rothschild felt, no doubt realistically, that if emporium galleries were to survive, they would have to abandon their leisurely style of business.

When Jacob Rothschild and Commercial Union initially made their investment in Colnaghi's, the firm employed several of Old Bond Street's less worldly fine art dealers. And as one former director candidly admitted to me, it also had its fair share of prima donnas, many of whom found that while Rothschild had taste, it did not coincide with their own.

Diplomatic personnel management was not one of Rothschild's more conspicuous talents. In the middle of the decade several senior staff members and directors left, not all of them on speaking terms with the proprietor. Feelings ran so high that one director started legal proceedings for unfair dismissal.

Unhappiness was not confined to the departing aesthetes. The timing of Commercial Union's investment in art dealing was poor. In its first financial year, the insurance company's joint venture with Jacob Rothschild and his banking colleagues made a £24,000 profit on a turnover of just over £1 million, but thereafter it was overtaken by the downturn in the art market.

In 1974 many of those who had bought in the earlier boom started to sell. Property dealers in particular were forced to dump works of art on the market as their bankers pressed them for payments of principal and interest on speculative property transactions. There was consternation in the art market when the impressionists that property dealer Ronald Lyon had bought at peak prices, reappeared at auction. Not all found buyers. Lampa Securities, the company run by Malcolm Horsman, found itself in trouble when Chinese porcelain prices collapsed.[2] Few parts of the art market emerged wholly unscathed and several fine art dealers were hit by bad debts.

Colnaghi's was not immune from the downturn, which also coincided with its staffing problems. The firm suffered a loss of £154,000 in a year to mid-1975. At the end of its first five years' in business, the company's profits had still not recovered to their level in 1973–74.

So small was the investment in Colnaghi's for an institution the size of Commercial Union that these losses were a mere pin-prick. For Jacob Rothschild, however, the simultaneous downturn in the art and property markets was a more serious affair. Colnaghi's had bought the freehold of 13, Old Bond Street at a boom price on borrowed money. When property prices tumbled and conditions in the art market deteriorated, the holding company of the private Colnaghi's group ran into acute financial difficulties as it faced much-increased interest charges on its heavy borrowings. Had Colnaghi's not been able to fall back on the resources of the Rothschild family, its survival would almost certainly have been in doubt. As it was, Jacob Rothschild burned his fingers: he had to replace outside bank borrowings to the tune of more than £1 million – no small sum for one of the less rich members of the Rothschild family to find.

Colnaghi's has since been reorganising its business and rebuilding its reputation. Jacob Rothschild has bought out Commercial Union's shareholding. And in its latest financial year, the fine art business made profits of £138,000. But this is a far from commercial return on the capital employed, and Rothschild is not convinced that an emporium gallery like Colnaghi's will ever be a fully commercial proposition. He is said to believe that there will always be room for a dealer with a gifted eye; the question is whether the dealer will continue to operate in costly premises in the West End, or whether he will retreat to deal from his own home.

For those who feel no instinctive distaste for art dealing, Commercial Union's flirtation with Old Bond Street will not appear inherently objectionable. Somebody has to finance the art dealers' stocks: few individuals have the money or inclination to do so; and from a purely economic point of view, it hardly matters whether the job is done by a pension fund, an insurance company or a bank. The more direct approach of the British Rail pension fund to investment in art, however, raises wider questions.

British Rail has always emphasised the smallness of its investment in works of art in relation to its overall portfolio. But in relation to the art market itself, the investment is very significant. Moreover, the potential impact of more widespread institutional investment in works of art is daunting. The total value of worldwide sales conducted by Sotheby's and Christie's in 1979 represented less than $3\frac{1}{2}\%$ of the £9 billion that British life assurance companies and pension funds had available for investment that year. Clearly if every institution followed British Rail pension fund in investing 3% or so of its money in works of art, the market would blow its top. As it is, the railmen's decision to put up to £40 million into the art market can hardly have failed to influence prices.

British Rail has made it clear that the pension fund would ultimately like to sell its works of art to British museums. In the meantime, it has sensibly put much of the collection on display by lending works to museums around the country. But if the British Rail pensioner's stake in the national heritage is not to leave the country, how much will the museums, some of whom were underbidders when the pension fund made its original purchases, have to pay? If the price is a good one for the pensioners, it cannot, by definition, be a good one for the museums who were underbidders.

A more fundamental objection to direct institutional investment in works of art is that the economic and social utility of the art market itself is not great. In other financial markets, such as the equity market, the trade in existing investments is justified partly because it facilitates the flow of savings into productive new investment by establishing a price at which fresh capital can be raised. In art, however, the price at which a Monet or a Pisarro changes hands is largely irrelevant to the price that living artists obtain for their work.

It is not entirely coincidental that none of British Rail pension fund's known investment consisted of the work of living artists. For the art market tends to be poor at identifying artists whose work will be prized 50 to 100 years hence. While Monet, Pisarro and their contemporaries were reaching only a limited and unremunerative audience, for example, the public were spending lavishly on the works of such respectable academic painters as Bouguereau and Cabanel, who have been consigned by subsequent generations to oblivion (or the walls and corridors of French provincial officialdom).

A further reason why serious investors devote comparatively limited sums to contemporary art is that the living artist poses a genuine threat to financial values. He can wreck the market in his existing works by expanding the supply beyond the demands of contemporary taste. To anyone whose prime motive is profit, not enjoyment, in art, it could almost be said that the only good artist is a dead artist.

Time alone will tell whether retired railmen draw an adequate dividend from their fund's foray into the art market. There seems no question, though, that the trustees' decision in 1979 to bow to their critics and withdraw from the market was timely in another sense. The announcement that the fund was to put a ceiling of £40 million on its investment in art (and to withdraw from investing in metals at the same time) was made within weeks of the election that brought Mrs Thatcher's Conservative government to power. And the new Minister of Transport to whom the British Rail board was answerable was the former shadow spokesman on transport, Mr Norman Fowler, who had been one of the more vociferous parliamentary critics of the rail fund's artistic speculations. Had the trustees not decided to pull out, a public enquiry into their investment policy might well have ensued.

Future economic historians will probably regard the British Rail pension fund's adventures in the art market, which neatly coincided with the life of the 1974–79 Labour government, as a quirky aberration brought about by the sudden acceleration in the rate of inflation and the near-collapse of financial markets in the mid-1970s. That it happened at all is one more telling indication of how heavily tinged with hysteria the financial climate had become in that exceptionally turbulent year, 1974.

8

The government's paymaster

'One of the greatest pains to human nature is the pain
of a new idea.'

Walter Bagehot, *Physics and Politics*

THE GILT-EDGED MARKET is the main arena in which the
financial institutions confront the government from day to day.
How much power do they wield there?

Certainly enough to make government ministers think twice
before pursuing a monetary policy that they feel might antagonise
professional money managers. This is because governments have,
since 1975, tried to keep a grip on Britain's money supply while
simultaneously running historically high levels of public spending. Reconciling these twin objectives is virtually impossible if
financial institutions are reluctant to help finance that spending by
purchasing government stock. Hence the deferential tone sometimes adopted by ministers in dealing with the institutions.

A classic example of ministerial deference was the speech de-
livered by the Conservative Secretary of State for Industry, Sir
Keith Joseph, to a conference of the National Association of Pension Funds on 14 November, 1979. 'You are,' he told his audience,
in the course of a tactful discourse on the role of the pension funds,
'a great estate of the realm. Ministers are only too well aware of
your importance'. And against the financial background of the
time, it is not difficult to see why tact was in order. The pension
funds and other financial institutions had bought virtually no
government stock since the end of the previous month. Later that
week the Bank of England was to announce an increase in
Minimum Lending Rate (the former Bank Rate) from 14% to a

record 17%, while the Government Broker cut the price of the gilt-edged stock he was offering to the market. The purpose was to coax institutional investors back into the market to allow the government to go on borrowing in an orderly fashion.

This was by no means the last occasion on which Mrs Thatcher's government had reason to worry about its relationship with the institutions. It came perilously close to losing their support after Sir Geoffrey Howe's 1980 budget, which was so heavily leaked in advance to the press that a package of measures otherwise perfectly designed to win City approval failed initially to spark off much buying; the good news had already been discounted by investors. Had American interest rates not shown signs of turning down in the week after the budget, making British interest rates look more attractive to potential buyers of stock, the Conservative government might well have confronted a 'strike' by professional investors.

The previous Labour government had been similarly – and more painfully – cornered in the gilt-edged market by the financial institutions. Eighteen months before Sir Keith Joseph addressed the National Association of Pension Funds, Denis Healey, the Labour Chancellor of the Exchequer, had been forced into a crisis mini-budget and a crisis rate of interest because professional money managers had proved unwilling, for the third time in two years, to buy government stock on the terms that it was offered. These investment strikes led to suspicions on the Labour left that institutional investors were conspiring to subvert government policies.

Yet institutional investors were equally capable, under Labour, of lurching in the other, non-conspiratorial, direction. The most spectacular lurch came early in 1979 and made newspaper headlines because it degenerated into a brawl. On 22 February a queue had developed early at the Bank of England's new issue department in Watling Street beside St Paul's Cathedral in the City. Interest rates had fallen so fast, since the terms of the government's latest issue of stock were announced in the previous week, that successful applicants for stock could hardly fail to make a profit. The profit, moreover, was likely to be large because the issue was in partly-paid form – that is, the investor had to pay only part of the price on application; the rest of the payment became due several months later. If gilt-edged prices rose, the investor enjoyed the gain on the full value of his stock, even though he had paid for only part of it. The astute speculator could then take his profit by selling partly paid stock in the market, leaving the buyer (or any subsequent buyer) to meet the later payments that were due to the government.

So great was the demand for the new issue that the Bank of England decided to treat applications on a first-come-first-served basis. When it dawned on people at the back of the queue that the gate was being closed on them, those least willing to pass up the chance of virtually risk-free profit tried to push past their fellow brokers, messengers and officials, to get at the new issues counter. In the normally dignified surroundings of the Bank, tempers frayed and a scuffle broke out. Those fortunate enough to get at the trough, in what came to be known in the City as the battle of Watling Street, were rewarded with the odd bruise and a profit of more than 50% within the week.

Others were enraged, especially those brokers who felt obliged to fulfil their institutional clients' orders at the original offer price; they had to buy expensively in the stock market when dealings began, and take a loss on handing over the stock to their clients. Also annoyed were the private investors who received more robust treatment than the institutions at the hands of their stock-brokers. And the taxpayer had every right to complain, since he was saddled with a needlessly high bill for interest on the new government stock, which would not be fully redeemed until the year 2003.

The Bank of England's clumsy handling of the affair drew criticism from all sides. Even the City's most cumbersome representative body, the Council for the Securities Industry, roused itself to deliver a public rebuke to the Bank. But it did not criticise the most absurd feature of this buyers' stampede, which was that the Bank of England paid out commissions to stockbrokers who managed to put in applications on behalf of their clients. The Bank's selling methods were still attuned to the twenty-eight-year bear market in gilt-edged stock (dubbed by one City wag as the longest-lasting triumph of hope over experience in British financial history) which ended in 1975. Throughout that period the Bank had had the thankless task of persuading investors to buy an unending stream of government stock when prices were falling steadily. Only in January 1980 did the Bank finally abandon the practice of handing out commissions to people who encouraged clients to take up new issues of stock.

These wild gyrations in the gilt-edged market, which made the conduct of monetary policy peculiarly hazardous for the government in the second half of the 1970s and at the start of the 1980s, were partly a consequence of inflation. Constant changes in the general level of prices create uncertainty about the level of future real returns on investment. The harder it is to quantify uncertainty in arithmetical terms, the less stable financial markets become. This forces investors to take a shorter term view, because today's high return may turn out to be a much lower return in tomorrow's heavily depreciated money. So the Bank of England confronts a naturally jumpy group of investors, in a period of high inflation, when it offers new stock to the market.

The Bank's problems have, however, been compounded by the degree of concentration of savings in the hands of a relatively small number of financial institutions for whom orthodox gilt-edged stocks have only limited appeal. The biggest domestic potential buyers of gilt-edged stock are the insurance companies. They have to meet obligations on life assurance policies and annuities which are fixed in money terms; and they are happy to meet those obligations by investing in government stock on which the income and capital repayment are also fixed in money terms.

A growing proportion of the insurance companies' business, however, is not immutably fixed in today's pounds. Life assurance policyholders are not concerned solely with assuring their lives; they want a bonus on their investment in the life policy. And much of the insurance companies' new business comes from the management of pension funds, which require an investment that is capable of matching the escalating, pay-related cost of pensions. Fixed interest government stock may be able to meet these escalating costs, provided the stock is priced at a level that reflects an accurate or excessive estimate of future inflation. If the stock market underestimates the rate of inflation, however, a fixed interest gilt-edged security will prove to be a poor investment, even though the income from it carries a copper-bottomed government guarantee.

As we have seen in earlier chapters, most money managers, particularly those in pension funds, regard gilt-edged securities as a more speculative investment than ordinary shares or property, both of which hold out more hope of matching unexpected increases in inflation with comparable increases in income and capital value. Since the pension funds have more money to invest than any other domestic group in the stock market, the government is at a considerable disadvantage as long as it offers fixed interest stock instead of a security which affords protection against inflation by, for example, offering a return linked to the movement in the retail price index.

The Bank of England's biggest headache in the gilt-edged market arose, however, from the decision by both Labour and Conservative governments to abandon so-called Keynesian economic policies, which aimed to produce full employment by managing demand within the economy, in favour of monetarism. Among other things, this seachange in the method of economic management gave the investment institutions a new and crucially important role in the economic system.

Monetarism, whose best known advocate is the American economist and Nobel prize winner Milton Friedman, is a more subtle doctrine than its opponents are prepared to admit. But in the crude politicised version in which it has been adopted by successive governments it boils down to an assertion that the rate of increase in the money supply will, very broadly, determine the subsequent rate of domestic inflation. How long it takes for the increase in the money supply to work through to retail prices varies according to the commentator (and, some argue, according to the point in the turbulent monetarist experiment undertaken by Mrs Thatcher's government at which the commentator is commenting). But the time lag is generally put at anything from two to five years.

The political implication of the theory, purists argue, is not that the government can influence the long term level of economic activity by controlling the money supply; the purpose of a monetarist economic policy is simply to influence the future rate of inflation. And the chief tool in bringing about a decline in the rate of inflation is the target that the government sets for the rate of growth in the stock of money.

In practice increases in money supply are brought about mainly by increases in bank lending to industry and commerce or to the government. So one of the principal means by which the government can control the money supply is to reduce its own dependence on the banks in financing public expenditure. The simplest way to do this is to borrow from private investors outside the banking system, including the insurance companies and pension funds, by selling them gilt-edged stock. The co-operation of these institutions, and of the merchant banks and stockbroking firms that manage much of their money, therefore becomes a matter of paramount importance in a monetarist-managed economy. Only if institutional investors retain their confidence in the government's monetary policy can the money supply easily be controlled.

Short term targets for the money supply were first introduced by Denis Healey in 1975. A curious step, one might think, for a Labour chancellor, since he was effectively putting his government's policies to the undemocratic test of institutional approval. But there was little alternative because public expenditure was rising at an unusually rapid rate at the time.

When the Heath government had come to power in 1970 it had inherited a negligible borrowing requirement from its predecessor: Roy Jenkins, the Labour chancellor, had managed to cut public spending to the satisfaction of Britain's international creditors after the 1967 devaluation of sterling. From then on, however, the excess of government spending over revenue increased sharply and the public sector's borrowing requirement soared progressively until it reached a peak of over £10½ billion in the year to April 1976; this was equivalent to nearly 10% of gross domestic product. And in the following year the borrowing requirement was expected to rise to no less than £12 billion – a figure that was bound to frighten the foreign exchange markets, since bankers and businessmen would suspect that the British government might fail to restrain the growth of money supply while borrowing on such a heavy scale. Sterling was therefore vulnerable.

By announcing a short term target for money supply, the British chancellor was doing little more than attaching a veneer of monetarism to an essentially Keynesian reflationary policy for combating the recession induced by OPEC. But by offering this concession to the international money markets, he stood a sporting chance of dispelling pessimistic expectations about sterling. And he was also offering a *quid pro quo* to the financial institutions, whose support he needed in order to finance a high level of government spending.

Signs of a more serious intellectual commitment to monetarism came in 1976, against a background of waning international confidence in sterling. At the Labour Party conference that year James Callaghan, the Prime Minister, bravely declared:

> We used to think that you could just spend your way out of a recession and increase employment by cutting taxes and boosting government spending. I tell you in all candour that that option no longer exists, and that in so far as it ever did exist, it worked by injecting inflation into the economy. And each time that happened the average level of unemployment has risen. Higher inflation, followed by higher unemployment. That is the history of the last twenty years.

With that historic statement (which was made when the International Monetary Fund was already breathing heavily down James Callaghan's neck) the Labour Party's commitment to full employment as the chief aim of economic management appeared at an end.

If Labour came to monetarism by default, the Conservatives embraced it with a more obvious display of fervour. When the Heath government's attempt to tackle inflation through tripartite discussion with management and unions foundered over the miners' strike in 1973–74, the Tories had been left with nothing in their electoral shop window to compete with Labour's 'social contract' with the unions. Under a new leader, Margaret Thatcher, and with a new intellectual guru, Sir Keith Joseph, the Conservatives found in monetarism a philosophy perfectly designed to patch up the holes in Tory policy that most seriously detracted from their credibility as a governing party.

By asserting that the control of the money supply should be at the centre of economic management, monetarism seemed to diminish the importance of harmonious relations with the unions; power politics were reduced to a technical debate about the monetary aggregates conducted in hieratic language full of reference to sterling M3, the PSBR, DCE, eligible liabilities and base drift. Yet the monetarist remedies for Britain's economic ills – cuts in public spending and a progressive reduction in money supply – were beguilingly simple when shorn of the gobbledigook. Better still, they offered a path back to many of the traditional Conservative values from which the Heath government had departed, thereby leaving many of the party faithful in need of reassurance.

Monetarists pointed out that because a high-spending government could borrow as much as it liked, in the short run, without having to worry about the cost, it tended to force interest rates up until private firms were 'crowded out' of the market and unable to borrow because money was too expensive. It followed that the boundaries of the public sector needed to be rolled back to create an economic climate in which non-government enterprise could flourish. This fitted neatly with the traditional Tory distaste for public ownership and the puritanical conviction (rarely adhered to in practice by post-war Tory governments) that public spending is intrinsically undesirable. The emphasis on sound money and old-fashioned financial housekeeping also sat well with the cornershop economics of the less sophisticated members of the party who believed, like Polonius, that borrowing dulls the edge of husbandry.

The assumption that the introduction of short term monetary targets would lead to more stability in the financial markets proved, in the event, to be wholly unfounded.[1] This was partly because the system ran into teething troubles. One obvious problem was that the Bank of England found itself trying to control the indefinable: no single definition of money lent itself well to targetry. Another, which is of greater concern in the present context, was that the structure of the gilt-edged market was not equipped to cope simultaneously with the increasing concentration of money in institutional hands and the introduction of a form of money supply targetry for which it was not designed.

In the days before targets were heard of, the British monetary authorities used to play a unique guessing game with the market. Investors knew that the government had to sell stock, but they had very little idea how much. The Government Broker tried to tailor his tactics to achieve the lowest possible interest cost to the government compatible with maintaining investors' confidence. The system was always difficult to operate because the Government Broker could not sell stock when people expected interest rates to rise (and thus the price of gilt-edged stock to fall); investors could see no point in buying today what could be bought more cheaply tomorrow. But the authorities usually muddled through somehow.

With the introduction in 1975 of monetary targets, however, analysts in stockbrokers' offices started to go through the monetary statistics with a toothcomb and were able to calculate and recalculate components of the money supply, and thus predict the chances of the government meeting (or missing) its target, from day to day. As well as reinforcing institutional investors' preoccupation with the short term prospect, this destroyed the traditional guessing game between investors and the monetary authorities: suddenly the other players in the game were able to see most of the cards in the government's hand. Since the market was dominated by relatively few big decision makers – perhaps as few as 40 or 50 on some stockbrokers' estimates – a consensus about economic prospects tended to emerge far more easily than it would have if buying power had been more widely dispersed. As a result the government's borrowing programme too readily became stuck in a groove whenever investors concluded that the money supply was likely to overshoot its official ceiling and also suspected that their fellow investors had reached the same conclusion.

The hiatus in government borrowing was then followed by one of two possible outcomes. Either some new information – an abstruse monetary statistic, a change in international interest rates, a development in domestic politics – suddenly tipped the balance of expectations and investors plunged headlong into the market all at the same time to absorb hundreds of millions of pounds worth of stock that was previously unsaleable at the Government Broker's ruling price. Or nothing happened and a war of nerves developed between the government and fund managers, in the course of which the fund managers' expectations became self-fulfilling. As their cash mounted up at the bank, the money supply expanded out of control. Sooner or later the government was forced into panic measures. Interest rates invariably had to be raised sharply; other measures forced on the government included cuts in public expenditure and higher taxes. Having won their point the fund managers returned to the market to buy the government's stock and the whole rigmarole began all over again.

The 1974–79 Labour government was a victim of the second and more disruptive outcome most notably in the early summer of 1976, when the institutions lost all confidence in both the government's monetary policy and its wider economic strategy. Their reluctance to finance the government's spending was a contributory factor in precipitating the crisis that led to intervention by the

International Monetary Fund in November of that year. Economic ministers rightly concluded that power to impose financial discipline on the government had passed in part from the foreign exchange market to the gilt-edged market as a consequence of the introduction of monetary targets. Instead of excoriating 'the gnomes of Zurich' as Sir Harold Wilson had done in the 1960s, Denis Healey was later to pronounce anathemas on 'the young men who write brokers' circulars' in the City. Other Labour politicians claimed on this and other occasions that the brokers' analysts were dictating policy to the government through the institutions. For their part, the institutions argued that they were acting solely in the financial interest of their beneficiaries without wider political considerations in mind. Yet their actions were helping impose a disruptive regime of monetary fits and starts on the whole economy. It was at least arguable that such disruption was not, in every instance, in the wider interest of the beneficiaries. When the institutions forced the Labour government into higher interest rates and a mini-budget that imposed increased national insurance contributions on British industry, for example, they were effectively undermining the value of their equity investment in British industry, which was much larger than their total investment in government stock.

The suggestion that the institutions might be keen to play a more important part in framing economic policy was given further credibility in 1978, when the then chief investment manager of the Prudential, Peter Moody, said in his capacity as president of the Institute of Actuaries:

> We need more formal consultation between long term investors and government to add to what already exists with the banks, building societies and others. In the discussion of future policy there is the traditional tripartite discussion between government, CBI and TUC. Finance is obviously regarded as having a relatively passive role to play and I am inclined to believe that this is correct. But some aspects of policy, acting on the financial system do produce far reaching effects and the lack of adequate consultation with long term investors is an obvious gap.[2]

This sounded a modest enough demand at first sight. But since the aspect of policy that most concerned long term investors was the overall level of government income and expenditure, the institutions would inevitably have wanted to talk to the government about whether they could, or would, finance a given level of public sector borrowing. So Moody's words appeared to carry a hint that institutional investors were grooming themselves for a new disciplinary role as a kind of domestic equivalent of the International Monetary Fund.

The Left's natural suspicion of the institutions' motives was further heightened when the Conservatives returned to power. For while Mrs Thatcher's government did not initially have an easy time in the financial markets, it was not subject to an institutional investment 'strike' in its first two and a half years of office. Not surprisingly, some Labour supporters argued that if fund managers' political prejudices led them to smooth the path of the Tories, then they should be compelled under Labour to put an officially agreed proportion of their money into government stock.

Those who called for government direction of institutional money into government stock were, however, attacking the wrong target. For as Joel Barnett pointed out while he was Chief Secretary to the Treasury in James Callaghan's Labour government,

> experience during the past few years shows that it is hardly necessary to introduce direction of funds in order to induce a significant shift in the pattern of investment by long term institutions. The funding of the public sector borrowing requirement . . . has been achieved by the institutions virtually doubling the proportion of their new funds invested in gilts, compared with the proportion in the first half of the decade. . . . It seems to me very doubtful whether any government would have dared to direct a significant shift in the investment pattern of funds.

The near-doubling of institutional investment in gilt-edged during the 1970s, to which Joel Barnett referred, hardly suggests that the institutions were exercising stern financial discipline over the government. And in reality, the insurance companies and pension funds had far too little control over their single, exceptionally blunt, weapon – the ability to refrain from buying – to make the government toe a financially orthodox line. Under Denis Healey, for example, monetarism went overboard from the moment a

general election hove into sight: the chief, though unacknow-
ledged, objective of economic policy in 1978 was to ensure not
that money supply targets were met, but that pay rose faster than
prices in the run up to the election.

As for the institutions' relationship with the Tories, those fund
managers who would have liked to exercise some financial discipline (and there were plenty of them, despite the pro-Tory
allegiance of many of the individuals concerned) were nonetheless
unable to do so when Mrs Thatcher's government refused to confront the political implications of monetarist economics in mid-
1979. Despite the sharp increase in Minimum Lending Rate after
the budget, money market interest rates continued to rise. Yet the
government could not bring itself to let home owners and buyers
be exposed to market rates of interest. And when money market
rates rose again after the November jump in Minimum Lending
Rate to 17%, the government risked jeopardising its monetary
policy even more seriously because it feared a hostile response
from home owners. Ironically, one result of trying to insulate
home owners and buyers from the effects of the general rise in
interest rates was that the building societies themselves ran down
their holdings of government stock in order to meet the huge
demand for home loans at below-market rates of interest while
they were unable to generate enough new deposits. This made the
government's financial position yet more difficult.

For good measure, Sir Geoffrey Howe demonstrated in his
government's first two years of office that there were circumstances in which the institutions co-operation could not be brought
into play to keep monetary policy on course. In explaining the
mechanism whereby excess growth in money supply leads to an
increase in the rate of inflation, monetarists lay heavy emphasis on
the expectations of unions and management, whose bargaining
posture is supposed to be influenced by the government's money
supply target and its medium term financial strategy. If they
recognise that the target implies a financial squeeze, they will be
less keen, so the argument runs, to price themselves out of jobs
and to bankrupt their companies with excessive pay settlements.

Inflationary pay settlements were not, however, to be wished
away so easily. Trade unions were more impressed by the increase
in retail prices that followed the 1979 budget increase in value
added tax, which helped push the retail price index up by more

than 20% in 1980, than the monetary target. A wage explosion followed. And since the exchange rate had been soaring in 1980 to reflect the rising value of Britain's North Sea oil wealth – thus making British goods less competitive in international markets – industrialists found it hard to recoup these increased wage costs by charging higher prices for their goods. They were forced, instead, to cut costs by laying off workers on a devastating scale. They also borrowed heavily from the banks to finance stocks that they could not run down as rapidly as they wished in the deepening recession. The outcome was that the money supply ran wildly out of control in 1980 not just because the public sector borrowing requirement was rising as a result of high public sector pay settlements, but because bank lending to the private sector of industry and commerce was rocketing as a result of this phenomenon of 'distress borrowing'.

Had inflation not been running at such a high level, companies would have borrowed long term money from the institutions to refinance their bank borrowings. Excess money supply would thereby have been mopped up. But few companies dared to commit themselves to rates of interest of 14%, 15% or more, into the twenty-first century since the cost would have been prohibitive if inflation (and thus long term interest rates) had subsequently come down.

For its part, the government had no other means of controlling bank lending in the short term because it had abolished the 'corset' controls on bank lending shortly after taking office. This led to a paradoxical situation in which the Chancellor came under attack from his own supporters, who complained that monetarist economics had gone by the board, while many members of the public were simultaneously convinced that 2½ million had been thrown out of work for the sake of proving the monetarist theory.

By 1981 fund managers in the City were worrying again about a rapidly rising public sector borrowing requirement. The huge increase in the cost of unemployment and other welfare benefits was partly responsible for the upsurge. But if the Tories had less difficulty until then in financing the borrowing requirement than Labour had had earlier on, this was due more to the advent of North Sea oil than to more active support from the institutions. Sterling had become a petrocurrency and the gilt-edged market had turned into a convenient parking lot for OPEC's surplus funds. So the government was less dependent on the institutions in financing its spending because foreigners were busily snapping up gilt-edged stock.

All this suggests that while the institutions' power in the gilt-edged market is real enough, it is not as great as it appears at first sight. For fund managers are not always in a position to help a Conservative government implement the 'sound money' policies that many of them consider to be in the interest of their beneficiaries; nor can they prevent the government from shrinking from the task. Under Labour, moreover, the strange courtship ritual that takes place between the government and the institutions always comes to the same conclusion: the government wins over the institutions by increasing the dowry. The argument between the two sides is not so much about the overall level of government borrowing as about the price the government should pay to raise the finance it requires.

It is true that this courtship process resembles collective wage bargaining in its disruptive effects, but there are obvious differences in kind and scale. Fund managers, unlike shop stewards, cannot bring manufacturing industry to a halt. And the sums involved in conceding an extra 2% interest to the institutions on a new issue of gilt-edged stock are far less than those involved in conceding an extra 2% on public sector pay. This suggests that the institutions' power is too limited ever to win them a say in a Labour government's deliberations on economic policy – the more so since the act of giving way to the institutions is relatively painless for the politicians themselves.

The pension funds could not have been induced to increase their holdings of gilt-edged securities from 12.7% of their total investments at the start of 1970 to more than 21% at the end of 1979 without compensation in the form of a high rate of interest. The cost of this falls partly on the taxpayer, who has been saddled with a bill for high nominal rates of interest running well into the twenty-first century. It also falls on British industry, which has had to carry an additional financial burden in the shape of higher and more volatile interest rates and increased national insurance contributions as a result of recurring monetary crises and mini-budgets. Only to the extent that the bargaining process between institutions and the government in the gilt-edged market affects building society mortgage rates or leads to public expenditure cuts does it become politically embarrassing for the politicians. The cost of inducing financial institutions to buy a form of security for which they had only a limited appetite might have been reduced if they had been offered an inflation-proofed bond. Yet for years officials in the Bank of England and the Treasury argued in private against the introduction of index-linked government bonds on the grounds that it would lead to a loss of financial discipline. They were reluctant to give politicians the opportunity to embark on 'irresponsible' public spending.

In reality the existence of a large and growing pool of savings concentrated in the hands of a small number of investment institutions is more of a boon than a hindrance to any government bent on pursuing a high level of public spending, no matter what kind of stock it offers to the institutions. And while many fund managers regard an extensive public sector borrowing requirement as inflationary and thus inimical to the interests of their beneficiaries, they are unable, individually, to resist the lure of a gilt-edged 'bargain' offer for long.

In the gilt-edged market, then, the insurance companies and pension funds have, despite appearances to the contrary, behaved more like willing collaborators than saboteurs. What little financial discipline they have been able to exercise over the government has in consequence been mainly short term in its effect. To put it more crudely, the institutions have been bought – and by the standards of the more financially orthodox among them, they have been cheaply bought at that.

9
The paradox of pensions

'Those who have been once intoxicated with power
and have derived any kind of emolument from it . . .
can never willingly abandon it.'
Edmund Burke, Letter to a Member of the National
Assembly

BENEFICIAL OWNERSHIP of the means of production in Britain
is more widely spread over the adult population in the 1980s than
ever before, even if control remains narrowly concentrated in
institutional hands. And never before has such a large pool of
immensely stable private sector capital been available for long
term investment in British industry. In both these developments
there ought to be cause for optimism. Yet many of the economic
and social benefits that might have been expected to flow from
encouraging a wider spread of ownership have somehow failed to
materialise. Nor have the capital markets been noticeably more
stable since they came to be dominated by insurance companies,
pension funds and other professionally managed institutions; if
anything they have been more volatile. Two fundamental questions therefore arise. Is the money that the institutions control
being properly administered? And is it necessary to have such
huge institutionally administered sums swilling around the capital
markets in the first place?

As far as the administration of the institutions' money is concerned, it would be wrong to assume that fund managers are
exclusively to blame for lost opportunities and investment mishaps. Politicians, both Conservative and Labour, contributed
heavily to such events as the collapse in the equity market in the
mid-1970s. And it was primarily inflation that undermined the
structure of the gilt-edged market. The flight of money into art,

commodities and other tangible assets was not, perhaps, a product of the fund managers' finest hour. But before condemning the institutions it is as well to remember that it was unusually difficult to make money in equities and gilt-edged securities – the two most orthodox investment outlets for the savings handled by insurance companies and pension funds – in the 1970s. The Government Actuary's Department estimates that equities showed a real return before tax between January 1970 and December 1979 of minus 2.1% while the real return on government stock over the same period was minus 4.5%. The choice of dates is obviously arbitrary and some institutional investors will have done better than this. But the Government Actuary's figures are probably not unrepresentative of the stock market performance of pension funds in the 1970s. For life assurance funds, which (unlike pension funds) pay tax, returns may well have been still more depressed. Trustees and fund managers would not have been doing their job properly if they had failed to give some consideration to alternative forms of investment in this decade of exceptional economic turbulence.

Moreover, the Wilson Committee did not find that investment institutions had necessarily been failing either British industry or the nation. Its report emphasised that there was a lack of demand for finance, rather than a shortage of it, and it argued that the chief financial constraint on industrial investment in plant and machinery was that the real cost of capital was higher than the real profitability of industrial and commercial companies.

There are other respects, however, in which the growing power of billionaire institutions does give rise to serious problems. The Wilson Committee report also concluded that the financial community had been slow to come to terms with the implications of the trend towards institutionalised saving. And the evidence unearthed in this book suggests that in the absence of proper accountability some very haphazard investment judgements have been made at some of Britain's larger pension funds; also that the power of financial institutions is not being exercised in uniformly productive ways.

In some cases, particularly where their actions have attracted public attention, the institutions have undoubtedly learned from their mistakes. In the past three years, for example, many insurance companies and pension funds have tried to remedy their earlier neglect of small business. It is possible, too, that equity prices might have tumbled much further in 1980, as a result of the intense squeeze imposed on British industry by a high exchange rate, had the institutions not lived through the dark days of 1974.

Yet dangers remain. Savings are now so heavily concentrated in the hands of the few that an inherent bias towards instability has been built into financial markets. A new and unexpected set of economic and political circumstances may yet cause institutional money to respond in unforeseen and possibly disruptive ways. A more serious worry arises from the fact that low standards of pension fund disclosure have prevented spectacularly ill-judged investments from attracting widespread attention. Had there been more press publicity, the lesson that investment in unquoted entrepreneurial companies calls for a different range of skills from those needed in the less demanding business of stock market investment, might have been usefully reinforced. As it is, a new generation of pension fund managers has not had sufficient opportunity to learn from the mistakes of the old, while those fund managers and trustees who sailed close to the wind in the past have presumably drawn a far from salutary lesson from their experience – to wit, that as long as they tell the world as little as possible about their investments, time and a growing cash flow will heal any number of investment wounds.

Investors in life assurance, who are more interested nowadays in the savings element of their policy than in the (often relatively low) life cover it provides, can no doubt decide for themselves whether standards of regulation in the insurance business are adequate and tailor their investment policy accordingly. With pensions, however, it is a rather different matter. A large proportion of the workforce is compelled to save through occupational pension schemes whether it likes it or not. And in the absence of a degree of accountability and regulation commensurate with the huge sums now handled by the pension funds, it seems inevitable that financial scandals will arise in this area in the 1980s.

Despite some uncanny parallels, the pension funds' problems will not be quite like those that overtook the secondary banks or the Crown Agents in 1974. Prospective pensioners, unlike those who deposit cash with a bank, cannot withdraw their money, so forcing the fund to sell its investments. Trouble could arise, however, where pension funds become lenders of last resort to their own or to their directors' private businesses. And if fund money is lost, beneficiaries and members of pension schemes will not find it easy to obtain redress, for the law, as a learned judge once remarked, is open to all, like the doors of the Ritz Hotel. When it comes to the management of pension funds the law is, in addition, more than usually uncertain.

The National Association of Pension Funds has recently made commendable efforts to encourage its members to disclose more about their affairs.[1] But the association has few obvious sanctions to bring to bear against those of its members who are not disposed to listen to exhortation – and none at all against non-members. Even today the accounts of some of Britain's biggest pension funds vary from relatively full and open (as at Unilever) to the singularly uninformative (as at ICI). Steps have also been taken, under the aegis of the Council for the Securities Industry through which various City institutions seek to co-ordinate the regulation of their own affairs, to tighten up the rules on share dealing by pension fund and other investment managers on their own account. But it remains to be seen how effective the rules would be in restricting the activity of any fund manager who chose to make use of nominee names or deliberately to conceal personal account investments that involved a potential conflict with the interests of the present and future beneficiaries of the funds he managed.

It is questionable, however, whether self-regulation is really an appropriate way to protect the interests of employees and pensioners who are forced to put their money into pension funds as a condition of employment. If their legitimate pension expectations are frustrated and their savings squandered as a result of poor or wayward management, they cannot be expected to respond sympathetically on being told that only a small minority of trustees are abusing an otherwise satisfactory system of non-statutory regulation.

A more frequent cause of concern will be an unnecessarily high incidence of troublesome investments which, while failing actually to bankrupt anyone, will depress investment performance so that companies have to pump huge sums into their pension funds to keep them solvent, so diverting money from more productive use elsewhere. The danger will be particularly acute in overseas investment, where the lack of more widespread publicity for the pension funds' earlier foreign adventures looks doubly unfortunate in the light of the recent rapid increase in insurance companies' and pension funds' foreign investments.

At the start of 1980 overseas securities represented only 2.9% of life assurance funds while the comparable figure for pension funds was 6.0%. But as fund managers started to exploit the new opportunities that followed the lifting of exchange controls in October, 1979, institutional investment overseas accelerated sharply. In the first nine months of 1980, life assurance companies and pension funds invested more than £1.1 billion – equivalent to over £4 million each working day – in overseas securities. This represented nearly 15% of the new money flowing into their coffers.

This, in fact, understates the magnitude of the exodus, for British institutional investments in overseas property are not included in the above figures, and are not separately identified in official statistics.[2] Those of the pension funds are by no means insignificant. The Post Office fund, undeterred by the initial difficulties over its investment in the Grands Magasins du Louvre in Paris, has continued to buy properties in Holland, the Irish Republic and North America, where it has purchased numerous buildings in such cities as Chicago, Philadelphia, Houston and Montreal. All told, the postmen had spent over £150 million on foreign property, equivalent to more than $7\frac{1}{2}$% of the total fund, even before exchange controls were abolished. For its part, the National Coal Board pension fund made headlines in the United States in 1979 by purchasing the Watergate complex, scene of the pre-election break-in that led to President Nixon's downfall, in Washington; it did so via the $144 million takeover of a real estate investment trust, Continental Illinois Properties. Others that have been buying busily in North America include the pension funds of British Rail, the Electricity Supply Industry, British Airways, British Gas, Imperial Group and Boots.

Some have bought properties directly; others have bought through pooled funds in which they share the ownership joinly with other institutional investors. At least one major pension fund has followed the Post Office, ICI and Unilever funds into financing overseas development: in 1979 the National Westminster Bank pension fund, with assets then valued at around £600 million, had nearly £28 million of property development financing commitments in Europe.

I estimate that the gross book value of overseas properties, together with development financing commitments, owned by British pension funds amounted to between £$\frac{1}{2}$ billion and £$\frac{3}{4}$ billion even before the lifting of exchange controls. Moreover, the elephantine pension fund march across the international exchanges seems certain to continue for, as we saw in chapter one, there is a dearth of domestic investments at prices that compare favourably with those in North America, the Far East and elsewhere. And in theory foreign investment need not be altogether objectionable in a period when Britain's exchange rate is buoyed up by huge reserves of North Sea oil. Increased investment overseas puts a brake on sterling's appreciation against other currencies, thereby helping to prevent British manufacturing companies being priced out of foreign markets. At the same same it builds up an overseas nest-egg which provides a future source of foreign currency earnings when North Sea oil runs out and sterling ceases to be a petro-currency capable of attracting the surplus funds of oil-producing countries.

In practice, however, the huge increase in portfolio investment overseas in 1980 and early 1981 was not enough to prevent sterling reaching peak levels against the dollar and other currencies that had not been seen for seven years or more. And what of the quality of the nest-egg? Insurance companies and pension funds may well prove to be effective investors in overseas quoted securities; the City of London's long experience of international securities management will probably ensure that they do not come unstuck here. In overseas property, however, past experiences of both property companies and pension funds point to expensive mishaps.

One lesson to be drawn from the experiences of the pension funds of ICI, Unilever and the Post Office described in chapter six is that the risks in overseas property markets are all too easy to underestimate. In a business where so much depends on a judgement about the exact location of a building, foreigners are unusually dependent on their local advisers. How many will turn out to be fair-weather friends to the British?

There are signs, moreover, that some pension funds feel instinctively happier taking big risks overseas than small risks at home. In its 1979 annual report, the pension fund of British Airways revealed that it had bought a large office complex in Palm Beach in Florida, while simultaneously declaring:

The scheme has not made any significant purchases in unquoted investments during the year. Although attractive in terms of possible growth, the trustees have viewed this area of investment as one that should only be undertaken where there is an established 'track record' of proven management and financial performance.

A curious feature here is that owning an office block in the United States is, if anything, more akin to investing in a small private business than to making a more normal portfolio investment. This is because landlords in North America, unlike their opposite numbers in Britain, have traditionally been responsible for managing and maintaining buildings. And in a country where land is plentiful and businesses are highly mobile, a failure to keep to high standards of management (which is not easy to monitor, incidentally, from outside the country) may easily cause the tenant to move elsewhere. The much greater leasing risks in American real estate, together with lower historic rates of inflation, explain why pension funds in the United States have only between 1% and 2% of their total assets in commercial properties, compared with the 17% that pension funds in Britain have in British property.

The greatest worry in the wake of the abolition of exchange controls, however, is that fund managers have been given an open invitation to indulge the same profound pessimism about British economic prospects that afflicts so many in the upper echelons of government and industry. This pessimism is exemplified, symbolically perhaps, in the investment policy of the pension fund of the Bank of England. Early in 1979 before exchange controls had even been lifted, the Bank of England fund had invested no less than 15% of its £140 million-worth of assets in overseas securities – about three times the then average level for all the pension funds in Britain.

This high percentage in overseas investment, so the Bank told me, simply represented the preference of the fund's investment manager. Though an employee of the Bank of England, he was apparently regarded as being 'detached from the official side of the Bank'. Overall responsibility for the management of the fund's investment does, nonetheless, fall on the Court of Directors of the Bank, where executive directors including the Governor and Deputy Governor sit side by side with outsiders recruited from the ranks of the great and good in industry and banking. In practice they delegate responsibility for supervising the pension fund's investments to a group known as 'The Committee to Consider the Securities of Certain Funds'. The members of this quaintly named gathering were, at the time in question, Leopold David de Rothschild, of the Rothschild banking family, John Fforde, an executive director of the Bank of England whose signature used to appear on British bank notes, Sir Alastair Pilkington, chairman of the Pilkington Brothers glass-manufacturing concern and Sir Robert Clark, chairman of merchant bankers Hill Samuel. Is it fanciful to suggest that the readiness of this quartet of notables to sanction such a high level of overseas investment for the pension fund of Britain's publicly-owned central bank tells us something about the way modern Britain is run? And at what point does this apparent pessimism about British economic prospects become self-fulfilling?

Ironically, the one powerful group that does not appear to have lost faith in the future of capitalism in Britain consists of the leaders of the trade union movement. They, together with the more left-inclined politicians in the Labour party, have an instinctive dislike of overseas investment – whether by portfolio investors or companies – and argue that pension fund money would be better employed in restoring Britain's industrial base. Sceptics will ask, reasonably enough, whether union leaders are not more anxious to preserve their members' jobs in declining industries, than to create jobs in newer, less heavily unionised industries that appear to hold out more promise for the future. But the sceptics could well be wasting their breath if Labour returns to power sooner rather than later. So great has been the recent erosion of the industrial base, and the consequent loss of jobs, that a Labour government would find it difficult to resist union demands for a return to the financial protectionism of exchange controls. It would find it equally difficult to resist the TUC's demand, which was taken up by a minority group on the Wilson committee, for £1 billion of the institutions' annual inflow of cash to be directed into a new National Investment Bank which would advance loan and equity capital to industry under the supervision of a tripartite steering committee.

This is not the place for a detailed examination of the TUC's proposal. But in the present limited context it is worth noting that the compulsory channelling of institutional investment into productive industry is a more complex issue than some of its opponents admit. Pension fund money is already being directed by a set of entrenched attitudes about where the interests of pensioners really lie. Money is also directed by specific legislation: local authority pension funds, for example, are restricted by law in the amount they invest in property and overseas securities. Nor are examples of direction by 'persuasion' unknown. Insurance company, pension fund and bank money was directed by the Bank of England into secondary banking and property in the 1970s in its bid to rescue the banking system and, when the City was under attack from the left, into Equity Capital for Industry. Some stockbrokers and bankers also suspect that in their anxiety to preserve their independence from government interference the pension funds will pump money into any given area of industry following a nod or a wink from a government minister who feels that institutional money would ease one of his department's problems.

And as far as the direction of investment by government is concerned, the end result would be little different from the present system in which the government attracts institutional money via the gilt-edged market. Selling government stock to insurance companies and pension funds is, in effect, a way of extending state control over institutional money. It transfers the decision about what should be done with a significant part of the nation's savings, from private sector fund managers to politicians and bureaucrats in the public sector. What can be said with reasonable certainty is that whether it is the private sector, the state, or a tripartite committee, that ends up administering the institutions' cash, there is unlikely to be more than rudimentary consultation, at best, with those whose money is to be invested.

This brings us to the crucial question of what purpose the institutions serve and where capitalism in Britain is going. Allowing the mass of the population to have a direct stake in ownership of the means of production has always been regarded by capitalism's apologists as the ultimate guarantee of its survival. It seems unlikely, however, that the type of popular capitalism embodied in occupational pension schemes will help contribute to this end. While several million employees in the private and public sectors enjoy a form of property right by virtue of their pension scheme membership, the right amounts to little more than an impersonal claim on the revenue generated by industry and commerce, and it entails few responsibilities or obligations – and virtually no power.

Attempts to introduce worker participation into pension fund investment decision-making have not noticeably changed the way in which pension funds invest their money. Not surprisingly, many worker trustees feel intense frustration at their inability to wield real influence or to offer alternative policies to the investment committees on which they sit. Control of the pension funds' £40 billion nest-egg remains in the hands either of management or of a powerful and largely centralised bureaucracy of pension and investment experts who tend to share similar values and attitudes. The same is true of the even more attenuated form of property right attached to life assurance.

Perhaps this sanitised and neutered form of capital ownership, in which profits accrue discreetly to anonymous institutions, is more acceptable in the present social and political climate than the more individualistic brand of capitalism that preceded it. But members of occupational pension schemes have, ironically, seen their ownership of industrial assets build up just when profits in Britain and other advanced industrialised nations have gone into decline, partly as a result of the increased share of output taken by labour. The most that private sector pension scheme members can do to improve the value of their claim on these declining profits is to resort to collective bargaining, which leads to a trap: the present pensioners' share of the payroll cannot easily be increased except at the expense of the current workforce, whose bargaining position is much stronger. This fundamental conflict between the interests of present and future beneficiaries also makes it difficult for pension fund managers to get away from slavish adherence to narrowly financial investment criteria. In the average pension fund where the number of wage-earners far exceeds pensioners, it would be inequitable to put a 'socially conscious' investment policy to the vote when the short term cost of that policy would fall more heavily on the pensioner-minority, or on unrepresented taxpayers and ratepayers who had guaranteed to keep the fund solvent.

Another problem, from the point of view of employees, is that there are fundamental weaknesses in the structure of the funded pension system. These scarcely affect workers in the public sector, most of whom enjoy fully index-linked pensions on retirement, even in cases where inflation-proofing is not formally guaranteed. But they lead private sector pension schemes to offer benefits that lack some of the most basic requirements of any conventional sound investment.

For most pension scheme members, a stake in the pension fund is the biggest investment they will ever make except in their own home. But while the return on this investment depends heavily on the investment manager's performance, pension scheme members have no real say in the manager's appointment, little opportunity to assess his abilities and no right to ask for their pension contributions to be invested in an alternative fund of their own choosing.

Equally important, private sector pension schemes have been built around the palpable fiction that the general price level is broadly stable. In reality stable prices are the exception, not the rule and at no time over the past 100 years has it been possible for anyone whose career ran from the age of 18 to 65 to escape at least one heavy inflation or deflation. Broadly, the state pension scheme offers inflation-proofed benefits up to a certain (relatively low) level of pay and private pension schemes that have contracted out of the state scheme are obliged to match this inflation-proofed, earnings-related part of the state pension. But the remaining benefits that private pension schemes provide over and above the guaranteed minimum are not inflation-proofed.

Most private pension schemes offer their members some protection from inflation up to the date of retirement because the overall level of pension is calculated by reference to final pay. But from then on few private pension schemes formally guarantee to protect the retired employee against future inflation, even though a handful do in practice stump up. Others guarantee to mitigate the effects of inflation by raising the pension entitlement to the extent of 3% or so each year. This is not much help. At 13% inflation, for example, it takes roughly six years for the non-inflation proofed part of a pension to halve in value; with the 3% bonus, it takes seven years for it to halve. So for private sector employees, longevity carries the threat of progressive penury. The inflation-proofed guaranteed minimum pension does, it is true, provide an ultimate safety net. But the part of the pension which makes the difference between enjoyable living and mere existence will dwindle in real terms until the pensioner dies. (Similar problems confront the self-employed, who have traditionally provided for their retirement by purchasing fixed interest annuities or by investing in 'money purchase' pension schemes which pay out a level of benefit that reflects the return earned by the insurance company on their money.)

Another, equally palpable, fiction underlying the typical occupational pension scheme is that employees remain with the same employer for the whole of their working lives. So for the large number who no longer live in a Victorian twilight of lifetime employment or who involuntarily lose their jobs through redundancy there is a heavy financial penalty on changing jobs. If the pension entitlement of the employee who leaves early is 'frozen' in the fund of the old employer, the employee forfeits the protection from inflation he would otherwise have enjoyed as a result of the pension being related to his final salary on retirement. The part of the early leaver's pension that is paid by the old employer will instead be based on the employee's salary level when he was still working for that employer. So anyone who left a job in 1970 would have seen his 'frozen' pension lose two-thirds of its value by 1980 unless his 1970 employer felt disposed (most do not, except to a minor extent) to mitigate the damage. And his pension from the new employer, though related to final salary, would only reflect benefits earned over the ten years to 1980.

Nor can those who change jobs escape this penal forfeit by transferring into the new employer's pension scheme, for the quirks of actuarial practice make pension rights shrink in transit. An employee who constantly transfers from pension fund to pension fund as he changes jobs will find that his past contributions buy him fewer and fewer years service in the new pension scheme at every change. And those lost years of service can never be made up.

No estimates are available of how these shortcomings affect the average private sector worker's pension. But a rough indication can be seen in the British Institute of Management's assertion that on present patterns of mobility between jobs, two-thirds of all managers will receive pensions of little over half the full entitlement – at best – of those who spend a lifetime with the same employer. Certainly it is true that a majority of pension scheme members in the private sector are subsidising the much smaller number of employees who stay *in situ*.

Private occupational pension schemes are based, then, on the principal of robbing job-changing Peter to pay time-serving Paul, which undermines the whole concept of trust on which the legal foundation of occupational pension schemes rests. And to suggest, as many pension experts do, that the problem would resolve itself if inflation were brought down, is to oversimplify the issue. If inflation came down sharply, it would precipitate another kind of crisis because the extent of the subsidy from early leavers to time servers would be sharply reduced. Unless the returns on portfolio investment increased dramatically to compensate, companies would be confronted with an awkward choice between going back on earlier pension promises which they assumed would only have to be honoured in full for a small minority, or making expensive additional contributions into the pension fund.

Some people may be tempted to look for a conspiracy in an arrangement which forces so many people to throw away part of their pay on an investment that not only offers a progressively declining real income to the aged, but which also imposes near-servitude on employees by extracting heavy financial penalties from those who have the temerity to leave an employer before retirement age, or who have the misfortune to be made redundant. Yet no conspiracy exists. All that has happened is that successive governments, by failing to offer adequate state pension benefits, have created a vacuum which the private sector naturally moved to fill with the best that it could offer. Since the two main methods of meeting the cost of retirement pensions – the pay-as-you-go system and the funded system – are fundamentally flawed when operated by the private sector, the best fell a long way short of the ideal.

Under the pay-as-you-go system it is relatively easy to cope with inflation because working sons and grandsons ostensibly pay in today's money for the current pensions of retired fathers and grandfathers. But if the employer goes bankrupt or operates in a declining industry where a waning population of sons and grandsons pays for a growing population of greybeards, pensions are jeopardised unless they are insured or guaranteed. Under the funded system the present generation pays for its own pension by saving up in advance and the pension remains secure even if the company goes bankrupt because the fund's assets are widely spread over a number of investments. But if, as we have seen, the investments into which those savings go prove to be unprofitable, in real terms, pensioners suffer a declining income.

Looked at from a broader economic point of view, however, both systems are trying to meet the same basic cost, which consists of the economic resources used up (in the form of goods and services) by the retired population. This cost cannot be passed from one generation to another and at any given moment a question arises about how much consumption the existing workforce is willing to forego in order to look after the aged. Funding and pay-as-you-go are simply different ways of financing this cost. But under the funded system a higher level of pension contributions is needed in the early years when the fund is building up than under pay-as-you-go; and a lower level is required later on as pensions are paid increasingly from investment income.

It was no doubt inevitable in Britain, where the financial sector is stronger and more influential than in, say, Germany or France, that a funded occupational pension system should have been adopted despite the long British experience of both inflation and deflation. And the whole frail structure that the private sector tried to create has since been heavily subsidised with tax reliefs, brought into partnership with the state and loaded with a burden that was far beyond its natural capacity to support. Since the subject of pensions is wrapped in mystique, bedevilled by jargon and rendered yet more confusing by inflation, few non-experts have noticed that the structure is creaking at its foundations. Or that a private pension system which started as an expression of proprietorial benevolence, has turned into an unwitting abuse of labour comparable in other respects with the trucking practices of the nineteenth century whereby workers were forced to spend their pay on goods provided by their employers.

One respect in which the funded system of pension provision does offer genuine advantages over pay-as-you-go is that it is reckoned to produce a higher level of savings in the economy, and thus to pave the way for higher investment. The final irony in this whole muddled chain of events, however, is that while Britain is indeed awash with a huge reservoir of tax-sheltered pension and life assurance money, the cash has yet to find its way into increased productive investment. For the growth of institutional saving has, as the Wilson Committee pointed out, been matched by a reduction in saving (which in practice means increased borrowing) by the government and by companies. The compulsory savings boom has, on the other hand, created enormous economic and social problems.

One obvious concern is that employees now have an overwhelming incentive to make a beeline for the index-linked pensions and greater job security that only the public sector can provide. Alternatively, private sector employees have an incentive, to borrow a phrase from the poet Louis Macneice, to sit on their arse for fifty years and hang their hat on a pension. The result is that occupational pensions are second only to the British rented housing system in discouraging labour mobility. The economic arteries of the nation are thereby hardened. At the same time a new social division, which gives considerable cause for envy, has opened up between the public sector fortunates and the underprivileged of the private sector.

A second difficulty arises because the value of tax subsidies for different kinds of savings has been so greatly enhanced by inflation. The subsidies are now so large that they bring about a material reduction in the total income on which the government can levy tax. So it has to charge higher tax on what remains. This makes it difficult for governments to manage their financial deficits unless they are willing to raise tax rates to politically unacceptable levels. It also causes a disproportionate share of the tax burden to fall on those who have no cash to save.

Meanwhile a time bomb is ticking away beneath the pension system. For when workers in Britain's private sector come to a wider understanding of the terms on which they have been allowed to share in the ownership of the means of production they may not be inclined to put up with them for long. There will be bitterness, too, when many of those who were made redundant in the 1980–81 recession discover the extent of the forfeit they have suffered on being removed from full membership of their pension schemes. They will not find it easy, however, to improve their lot.

The most oppressive aspect of the present private pension system lies not in its financing, but in the fact that employees' pensions are so tightly linked to their occupations. This opens up the whole question of whether pensions should be provided by the private sector or by the state. Most people accept that an element of compulsion in pensions is a necessary evil to ensure that improvident youth does not build up trouble for itself by failing to look to its old age. Given that there has to be compulsion, it remains strange that employees are not given more choice in deciding whether their savings go into alternative pension arrangements elsewhere. It is surprising, too, that trade unions have not made greater efforts to obtain such a right for those of their members who have no wish to swear fealty for life to the same employer.

Unless the state intervenes, there is no solution (except for those who believe in a fairyland world of stable prices) to the second serious problem in the present system which concerns the inability of private employers to guarantee pensions that do not decline in value. To many private sector employers further state involvement would, however, sound like anathema, to judge by the enthusiasm with which an unexpectedly large number of them took on onerous pension liabilities by contracting out of the new state pension scheme. And economic liberals will object that a greater role for the state invariably means a loss of freedom for the individual and a loss of efficiency.

Yet in this, as in other respects, occupational pensions defy conventional political labels. If the state pays the employee's pension, there is no reason why pension benefits should be affected if he changes jobs. So the individual not only enjoys more freedom but is able to make a more effective contribution to the economic effort of the nation.

It is inevitable that any suggestion of reducing the present reliance on the private sector in providing pensions would be greeted by vociferous resistance from pension consultants, insurance companies, merchant bankers and stockbrokers whose businesses have grown on the back of institutional money – and particularly from the small handful of fund managers for whom the taste of power has been a heady experience. One objection would be that a move from private sector funded pensions to a state or state-guaranteed scheme might lead to a lower level of savings in the economy. But this hardly looks a problem when all the signs point to a glut of savings.

A more powerful objection to further state involvement is that it would cost more to provide for everybody the level of benefits that private sector schemes claim to offer, but in practice grant only to the few who spend their whole working life at the same company. Lacking the benefit of the subsidy that private pension schemes enjoy from early leavers, the government would have to turn to the taxpayer to match such a level of benefits, though the increased cost could be mitigated in part by phasing out some of the more arbitrary existing tax reliefs of which the relief on life assurance is perhaps the most obvious candidate.

On this ground alone any attempt to raise state pension benefits to levels comparable with those found in many other European countries can probably be ruled out in the immediate future. And similar cost considerations make it unlikely that the decision announced in the March 1981 budget to introduce index-linked government stock for pension funds will lead to uniform improvement in the level of private sector pension benefits – despite the enthusiasm shown for the idea by a committee of enquiry into the cost of public sector pensions headed by Sir Bernard Scott, the former head of Lucas Industries.[3]

In its report, published in February 1981, the Scott committee argued that the benefits of inflation-proofed pensions should be extended to the private sector, possibly by offering index-linked government stock to pension funds. And at first sight the recommendation appears to have considerable appeal. For if pension funds can earn a guaranteed real, inflation-proofed return on government stock, they ought in theory to find it easier to promise to maintain the real value of retired employees' pensions together with the real value of early leavers' pension rights; this would help remove the inequity between the position of pensioners in the public and private sectors, while simultaneously rolling back one of the most troublesome barriers to labour mobility in the private sector.

The Scott committee did not, however, examine in detail the true cost of providing index-linked pensions in the private sector and for many – probably most – pension funds, the cost of maintaining the real value of pensions will continue to appear prohibitive. When the government came to make its first issue of £1 billion of 15-year index-linked gilt-edged stock, to which only pension funds were allowed to subscribe, at the end of March 1981, the initial rate of return amounted to only 2%. This figure was lower than the real rate of return that many actuaries had assumed that pension funds would earn on their investments when deciding how much individual companies and their employees should contribute towards future pensions. So pension funds that had worked on the assumption that they would earn a real return of more than 2% would have found it difficult to go on paying pensions equivalent to the generally accepted level of two-thirds of employees' final salaries, while simultaneously promising to protect their real value, unless the company and employees were willing to pump additional cash into the pension fund.

Much the same problem arises over the pension rights of early leavers. The existence of index-linked government stock may indeed imply that the early leavers' pension rights could henceforth enjoy guaranteed protection against the ravages of inflation. But few pension fund trustees will be willing to offer that protection because it would undermine a benefit structure that is based on the principle of robbing early-leaving Peter to subsidise time-serving Paul. A better index-linked deal for Peter would mean a reduction in the subsidy. So it would become more costly to pay for Paul's pension. The introduction of index-linked pensions may have done more, in the event, to underline the weaknesses of the private occupational pension system than to ensure better benefits for pensioners. The goal of index-linked pensions for all remains as elusive as ever.

That is not to say that the move towards index-linking will have no wider benefits. In the area of monetary policy the government now has more weapons in its armoury when it comes to controlling the money supply. Instead of being restricted to peddling a form of security that is fundamentally unattractive to the biggest group of long term investors in the gilt-edged market, the Bank of England would, assuming that the number of issues of index-linked stock is allowed to multiply, enjoy far greater flexibility in implementing the government's monetary policy. Moreover, the real cost of public sector borrowing might fall sharply over the longer run if the rate of inflation comes down, since the government (and thus the taxpayer) would not be saddled with a huge burden of interest running at 15% or more into the twenty-first century.

But no private sector pensioner would be wise to stake his shirt on any of these wider economic benefits filtering down to him and his fellow pensioners under a Conservative government that is overwhelmingly preoccupied with the need to curb public expenditure. Nor does Labour appear to be a more promising ally for pensioners since many politicians on the left seem less concerned to remedy the inequities of the pension system than to dispose of part of the mountainous cash hoard that they allowed to grow by default. For the more radical among them the concentration of ownership in institutional hands opens up a convenient short cut to winning control of Britain's industrial heartland with someone else's money – which would be an ironic outcome, indeed, of the shift from private share ownership to the type of popular capitalism that Britain's occupational pension system offers to working people.

The phenomenon of institutionalised thrift appears to be here to stay. Yet from almost any standpoint it looks suspiciously as though Britain's part-compulsory savings boom has done more to raise awkward questions than to provide uniform satisfaction to savers. And since the Wilson Committee's plea for improved accountability, regulation and disclosure among financial institutions has so far fallen largely on deaf ears, those savers do not enjoy the degree of security and protection under the law which they are surely entitled to expect.

To what end have the British people handed £100 billion of their money to this powerful new financial estate?

NOTES

CHAPTER I

1. Most of the statistics in the present chapter have been gleaned either from *Financial Statistics,* published monthly by the Central Statistical Office, the *Report of the Royal Commission on the Distribution of Income and Wealth* (The Diamond Commission) or the *Report of the Committee to Review the Functioning of Financial Institutions* (HMSO 1980, Cmnd 7937) – the Wilson Committee. The estimate of pre-war ordinary share ownership is my own; it is based on data in the 1959 Radcliffe Committee Report on the monetary system.

2. *The Economist:* Survey of Property and the Financial Institutions (10 June 1978).

3. These figures, taken at the nearest date to 31 March 1979, are not intended to be more than a rough guide. With insurance companies I have, in the main, taken total investments as disclosed in the annual accounts; in most cases they are at market value. In the case of the National Coal Board, where staff and workers have separate funds with different year ends, I have simply amalgamated the two sets of figures. The figures should not be taken as an indication of the insurance companies' potential influence in the domestic capital markets because many of them are genuinely multinational and their investments are spread over the world's main stock markets.

4. The institutions that rebuffed S. Pearson's bid for the outstanding shares in Pearson Longman were Atlas Electrical and General Trust, Clerical Medical & General Life Assurance, Equity & Law Life and the British Petroleum pension fund. Between them they owned around 10% of Pearson Longman, 36% of whose capital was not already owned by S. Pearson at that time.

5. Since writing this chapter I have seen the extensive research into pension fund share ownership and control carried out by Richard Minns in *Pension Funds and British Capitalism* (Heinemann, 1980). He estimates that 67% of pension fund assets are controlled by financial institutions other than the pension funds themselves (such as merchant banks and stockbrokers); and that out of £17¼ billion of pension fund

money managed externally in 1978–79, over £13 billion was managed by twenty institutions alone.

6. Richard M. Titmuss, *The Irresponsible Society* (George Allen & Unwin, 1958).

7. Estimate contained in '1980 Prospects for Financial Markets' produced by Salomon Brothers of New York.

8. See *The Economist*'s survey of life assurance in the issue of 26 July 1980.

CHAPTER 2

1. The figures on the flow of investment funds in this chapter are taken mainly from *Financial Statistics*.

2. A detailed comparison of the investment holdings of insurance companies in Britain and other countries, is contained in the Insurance Company Associations' second stage evidence to the Wilson Committee (HMSO, February 1979).

3. For a blow-by-blow account of what happened in the financial markets in 1974, see the excellent coverage of that year's events in the *Investors Chronicle*.

4. The vulnerability of British industry, while it was unable to deduct stock appreciation in calculating taxable profits, can be gauged from figures in *Financial Statistics*. In the first quarter of 1974 more than 70% of British companies' gross trading profits came from stock appreciation, while for 1974 as a whole, stock appreciation accounted for over half gross trading profits.

5. A highly readable account of the Crown Agents' headlong plunge into speculative investments in banking and property is contained in the *Report by the Committee of Inquiry appointed by the Minister of Overseas Development into the circumstances which led to the Crown Agents requesting assistance from the government in 1974*, The Fay Report (HMSO, 1977).

6. It is not always appreciated that the corporate sector enjoyed an unprecedented tax holiday under the 1974–79 Labour government. Largely thanks to Denis Healey's decision to introduce stock appreciation relief, the share of corporation tax in the Inland Revenue's tax receipts fell from 27.8% in 1974–75 (which mainly reflected profits earned in 1973–74) to only 11% in the following year. The proportion remained well below 20% for the rest of the decade.

7. Denis Healey's image as a scourge of the rich is at odds with several facts and figures. During his period as Chancellor the 1974 Labour manifesto commitments to introduce a wealth tax were not honoured. Taxes on capital (capital gains tax, development land tax, estate duty and capital transfer tax) provided less of the Inland Revenue's total tax

yield in each consecutive year of the Labour government's term of office, even though capital markets recovered sharply from their depressed levels in 1974; from 6.9% in 1974–75 the percentage more than halved to 3.1% in 1978–79. In 1978 the Chancellor implicitly endorsed the principle of heredity by granting relief against capital transfer tax for parents who wished to pass on their business to their children. He also made a conciliatory gesture to the landed interest (whose representatives in the cabinet included Wilson's successor as prime minister, James Callaghan) by giving them specific reliefs against capital gains tax. The distaste felt by newspaper editors and by the British upper middle class for Denis Healey probably owes more to his aggressive personality and to the enduring power of his rhetoric than to anything he did while in office.

8. The article (*Investors Chronicle*, 3 January 1975) named the four insurance companies concerned, but also erroneously included Equity and Law among the rescuers.

9. Net sales of United Kingdom ordinary shares in the last quarter of 1974 were as follows: life insurance companies (£60 million), investment trusts (£33 million), private sector pension funds (£8 million) and unit trusts (£8 million).

10. The overseas sector's purchases of company securities were higher in 1974 than in any other year in the 1970s. Quarter by quarter their respective outlay was £192 million, £119 million, £222 million and £504 million. The final quarter figure may well have been swollen by the £107 million purchase of St Martins Property Corporation by the Kuwait Investment Office.

CHAPTER 3

1. Here, by way of illustration, are the directorships of the sixteen outside directors of Sun Alliance at 1 January 1980:

Lord Aldington (Chairman)	GEC
	Lloyds Bank
	Westland Aircraft
	Citicorp
	National Nuclear Corporation
Lord Aberconway (Deputy chairman)	John Brown
	English China Clays
	National Westminster Bank
	Sheepbridge Engineering
	Westland Aircraft

Earl of Crawford and Balcarres	National Westminster Bank
	Scottish American Investment Co
H. V. A. Lambert	Barclays Bank
H. N. Sporborg	Bishopsgate Property
	Thorn Electrical
	Gomme Holdings
A. R. C. Arbuthnot	Arbuthnot Latham
Sir Charles Ball Bt.	Peachey Properties
	Rockware Group
	Telephone Rentals
	Tunnel Holdings
Viscount Bearsted	Hill Samuel
	Lloyds Bank
	Samuel Properties
Sir Hugh Fraser	A. I. Welders
Sir Alan Dalton	English China Clays
Sir Derrick Holden-Brown	Allied Breweries
Henry Keswick	Jardine Matheson
	Robert Fleming
	Hong Kong Land
	The Spectator
Lord Kindersley	Lazard Brothers
	Witan Investment
J. Martin Ritchie	British Enkalon
	Vickers
Sir Peter Matthews	Vickers
	BET
	Lloyds Bank
	Pegler-Hattersley
Edmund L. de Rothschild	N. M. Rothschild
	Alfred Dunhill
	Carreras Rothmans

These directorships covered over 8% of the stock market capitalisation of just over 2,000 British registered companies at the end of January 1980. They also took in some of Britain's leading merchant banks – Hill Samuel, Lazard Brothers, N. M. Rothschild, Robert Fleming and less directly, Hambros, where H. N. Sporborg was no longer a director but retained close links. If the stock market value of the company clients of these banks is added to that of the companies on whose boards Sun Alliance directors sit, more than 30% of the market capitalisation of all British listed companies is covered by these board-room connections.

This does not, of course, mean that the fund managers at Sun Alliance never intervene in the 30% of the stock market in which their board is directly or indirectly involved. But it does indicate how they, and fund managers with similar connections at other insurance companies, cannot stir up British industry without causing a stir in their own boardrooms.

2. These figures are taken from *Financial Statistics* and from the accounts of individual funds at the nearest date to 31 March 1979. They are intended only as a rough guide. Where there are separate funds for staff and workers with different year ends, I have simply combined the two sets of figures and in those cases where the figures differ from those in published pension fund year books, it is usually because I have included the funds' investments at market value.

3. Active share dealing by institutions is, in fact, what game theorists call a 'negative sum game'. In the stock market one man's profit is another man's loss, so the sum of the two men's buying and selling activity is zero. But the cut taken by jobbers, brokers and the government reduces the sum to a minus figure. It follows that the fund manager who feels obliged not merely to invest new money but also to sell shares he already owns is involved in an activity that resembles a game of roulette in which the wheel has been biased towards the house: a majority of those playing for any length of time can only come out at a loss. If there is some wider justification for playing the game (such as ensuring a steadier flow of fresh capital to industry via the primary market) there may nonetheless be some reason to participate. The question that then arises is, what level of share sales is needed to achieve that wider end?

4. The result of this performance survey is referred to in a paper by David Hager entitled 'Measurement of Pension Fund Investment Performance' (Paper to the Institute of Actuaries Student Society, January 1980).

5. See table 7.3 (page 699) in the appendices to the Wilson committee report.

6. *Committee to Review the Functioning of Financial Institutions,* First Stage Evidence on the Financing of Industry and Trade, volume 3 (HMSO 1978).

7. Shortly after *The Economist* drew attention to Britannic's audit arrangements in an article on 25 August 1979, the insurance company announced that Flint & Thompson, who had been the company's auditors since 1894, had advised the directors that their audit position

should be strengthened by the appointment of joint auditors. Another small firm, Clement Keys, which has few quoted company clients, was appointed joint auditor.

8. Two recent exceptions to this rule are, however, worth recording. Alfred Singer, a non-executive director of the international trading group Dalgety, resigned in disagreement over this company's takeover bid for the Spillers food group in 1980, thus alerting Dalgety's own shareholders to the problems inherent in the bid. And Angus Murray, a non-executive director of Newman Industries, criticised transactions undertaken by Newman in 1975 which involved a potential conflict of interest between the public and private interests of certain directors of the company. This action caused one of Newman's biggest institutional shareholders, the Prudential, to bring legal proceedings which coincidentally contributed to the evolution of company law in Britain.

CHAPTER 4

1. *The Financing of Small Firms* – Interim Report of the Committee to Review the Functioning of Financial Institutions, March 1979 (Cmnd 7503). The Wilson Committee's terms of reference were 'To enquire into the role and functioning, at home and abroad, of financial institutions in the United Kingdom and their value to the economy; to review in particular the provision of funds for industry and trade; to consider what changes are required in the existing arrangements for the supervision of these institutions, including the possible extension of the public sector, and to make recommendations.'

2. When the reform of the financial system and the clearing banks is at issue, Sir Anthony Tuke seems to be a natural *arrièriste*: it was he who told the Radcliffe Committee, 'we do not want the public to discuss our affairs. We would much rather they did not. The more information we give them the more they will discuss our affairs, and that is what we do not want.'

CHAPTER 5

1. The figures in this chapter for the level of insurance company and pension fund investment in property have been taken from *Financial Statistics*. I have estimated the value of properties held by quoted companies in 1970 on the basis of figures contained in the *Investors Chronicle* property survey (26 March 1971). For the comparable figure in 1980 I am indebted to Peter Hardy of stockbrokers Rowe & Pitman, whose estimate is based on that firm's extensive records of property company accounts.

2. For an account of the first post-war property boom, and of the way property development was financed in the 1950s and 1960s, see *The Property Boom* by Oliver Marriott (Hamish Hamilton, 1967). This remains the most useful reference book on post-war property development. For changes in development financing that occurred in the second half of the 1970s, see *The Economist*'s survey of property and the financial institutions (10 June 1978).

3. 'How the Crown Agents manage their £1,000 million' by Charles Raw and Lindsey Vincent (5 August 1971). There is a brief resumé of this impressive investigation in the Fay Report.

4. 'Keyser-Dalton's earnings make-up' – *The Times* (23 August 1972).

5. 'Town & City: gearing with a vengeance' – *The Times* (7 July 1973).

6. 'Town & City's £100 million deal – we buy, you pay' – *Investors Chronicle* (13 July 1973).

7. Among the foreign banks that had lent to the Stern group directly or through subsidiaries, were Banco Totta y Acores, Bank of America, Bank Leumi (UK), Bank of Nova Scotia, Banque Belge, Banque Nationale de Paris, Chemical Bank, Continental Illinois, Continental Trade Bank, Dow Banking Corporation, First Chicago, First International Bancshares, First National City Bank, International Credit Bank of Geneva, Marine Midland Bank, Royal Trust Company of Canada and Trade Development Bank.

8. An account of this unusual episode is contained in an investigation entitled 'The Trouble with Freshwater' (*The Economist*, 29 October 1977) and a subsequent article in the same paper on 5 November 1977.

CHAPTER 6

1. This investment was first publicised in an article in the *Daily Mail* (20 April 1977). The enterprising reporter was Christopher Hird.

2. Other Department of Trade Reports in which Binstock featured heavily included those on Peachey Property and Darjeeling Holdings, together with a related report on Central Provinces Manganese Ore Company.

Sir Eric Miller was also to appear on the Dobman register, but it is not clear whether the company was still under the control of Dobbie and Freeman at the time; the relevant annual returns at Companies House are not complete. In this, as in other business dealings of the late Sir Eric Miller, there appears to have been confusion over what belonged to him personally and what belonged to Peachey Property Corporation. While Miller was originally registered as a shareholder in Dobman (which had been renamed Coote Property and Investment) the shares were subsequently re-registered in the name of Peachey.

3. Rodo Investment Trust's losses resulted partly from the fall in the value of its holding in Dufay Bitumastic. Dufay had run into heavy losses, having forecast a £½ million profit shortly before in the course of a contested takeover bid for International Paint.

4. This omission was largely remedied in the pension fund's 1980 accounts, which included a summary of Westmoreland's latest audited balance sheet.

CHAPTER 7

1. The exact amount that the Picasso would have to rise in value would depend on the rates of interest at which the future income on the gilt-edged security was reinvested over its twenty-year life.

2. The history of Lampa's involvement in porcelain well illustrates the speculative nature of the art market. During 1973–74 Hugh Moss, the dealer who ran Lampa's Hugh Moss Ltd subsidiary, was one of the two heavy buyers of certain types of Chinese porcelain. The other was a Portuguese buyer represented by a London dealer called Mrs Glatz. After the Portuguese coup in 1974 the other buyer withdrew from the market and the value of Hugh Moss's £2.9 million stock promptly plunged by an estimated £1 million.

CHAPTER 8

1. See Gordon Richardson's 1978 Mais Lecture, in which short term money supply targetry is justified not in terms of controlling inflation, but of introducing stability into the monetary system.

2. Peter Moody, Presidential Address to the Institute of Actuaries (23 October 1978).

CHAPTER 9

1. The National Association of Pension Funds has recently issued a voluntary code of practice to its members on disclosure entitled Code of Practice: Information to Members of Pension Schemes.

2. At the time of writing, life assurance and pension fund investments in overseas property are, in theory, respectively included under the headings of 'other assets' and 'other investments' in *Financial Statistics'* analysis of insurance company and pension fund assets. A spokesman at the Central Statistical Office warns, however, that where investments do not fall neatly into one of the existing categories, pension funds do not necessarily put them under the heading 'other' when making their returns.

3. *Inquiry into the value of pensions*, 1981 (Cmnd 8147).

INDEX